Somalia at the Crossroads: Challenges and Perspectives in Reconstituting a Failed State

Published by
Adonis & Abbey Publishers Ltd
P.O. Box 43418
London
SE11 4XZ
http://www.adonis-abbey.com
Email: editor@adonis-abbey.com

First Edition, August 2007

British Library Cataloguing-in-Publication Data
A catalogue record for this book is available from the British Library

ISBN: 9781905068593 (HB), 9781905068975 (PB)

Printed and bound in Great Britain

Somalia at the Crossroads: Challenges and Perspectives in Reconstituting A Failed State

Edited by

Abdulahi A. Osman & Issaka K. Souaré

Contents

v

ACKNOWLEDGMENTS

This volume is an outgrowth of a 2006 special issue of the journal *African Renaissance*. That issue of the journal focused on Somalia and how to reconstruct it after nearly two decades of armed conflict and life without a central government. This makes us indebted first and foremost to Dr. Jideofor Adibe, the editor and publisher of *African Renaissance*, who suggested that we create this volume from that issue and allowed us to use articles published in the journal. We are also indebted to him for publishing this volume and for helping us throughout the publication process.

Secondly, we thank all the contributors to this volume for their hard work and, especially, their patience with us and punctuality in meeting deadlines. We also indirectly extend our thanks to all those that might have assisted them, in any way, in the process of writing their chapters.

We thank our families for their patience, understanding, and for providing us with intellectual environments conducive to working on this volume.

Last but not least, we would like to thank Kathryn Johnson for her assistance in editing this volume and compiling the index. Sincere thanks also go to Murat Bayar, at the University of Georgia, for assisting in the compilation of the acronyms and bibliography and for doing this in record time.

We dedicate this volume to all the victims, dead or alive, of this fratricidal conflict, which has unfortunately made Somalia a textbook example of a "failed state."

Abdulahi A. Osman & Issaka K. Souaré
The Editors
June 2007

Chapter 1

INTRODUCTION

Abdulahi A. Osman & Issaka K. Souaré

Once again, Mogadishu is burning with bigger guns, tanks, and helicopters. Thousands, like their predecessors in the early 1990s, die while others are being made refugees and are internally displaced. This war is a continuation of the wars that began in 1991 when the late dictator Siad Barre's regime was brought to end. At the center of this unfortunate and deadly conflict are misused tribalism and clanism coupled with abundantly available fresh weaponry. Although this war might seem to some as a mindless conflict between the "Somalis," there is a method to the madness. For the past 16 years young armed tribal militias, with the support and legitimation of some of their clan leaders, continue to murder, rob, rape and pillage the unarmed civilians locally known as the *looma ooyayaasha* or *looma aareyaasha* (those that no body cries for or cares to defend). Since 1991, much of the economy and infrastructure, including roads and electric wires, of the country has been destroyed or looted in order to finance the war efforts. What are the bases of the war? What are the main factors prolonging it? And what, if any, solutions can be instituted in order to end this deadly conflict?

This volume intends to address these questions by examining the causes of the Somali conflict and all of the opportunities that were missed to resolve it. The volume intends to contribute to the ongoing debate on the intractable Somali conflict, which continues to baffle many Somali and non-Somali scholars and policy makers. This introduction will be divided into three sections. First, we will briefly examine the main of causes of the conflict. The second section examines the factors that are prolonging the conflict, while the third section examines the factors behind the failure of the resolution efforts.

Genesis of the Somali Conflict

The Somali conflict has both unique and shared patterns with other conflicts in the developing world. The beginning of the conflict coincided with the end of the Cold War (1945-1990) and the recrudescence of armed conflicts around the globe, mainly in the developing world and more specifically in Sub Saharan Africa. For example, in 1998 there were a total of 13 conflicts in the world (an increase of 7 from the previous year), of which nine were fought in Africa. These wars caused thousands of casualties[1] and thousands of refugees and internally displaced persons.[2] Similarly, Adedeji (1999) observed that the number of countries in Sub Saharan Africa with severe conflict jumped from 12 in 1996 to 18 in 1998. Many of these countries including Rwanda, Sierra Leone and Liberia have had some success in resolving their conflicts, while, despite 14 publicized attempts for resolution, Somalia remains the ultimate *failed state* as its conflict continues with no end in sight. This section attempts to examine what some of the causes of this conflict are and why is it being prolonged. Literature groups the causes of internal wars into three categories: ethnicity/identity, economics and politics. Despite attempts to separate these factors, they overlap and interact in political systems. Ethnicity has been at the forefront of conflict analyses in Sub Saharan Africa.

---

[1] An estimated 2.5 million or 5% of the Congolese (formerly Zaire) population since August 1998; see
http://news.bbc.co.uk/hi/english/world/africa/newsid1308000/13089   63.stm.
Also, nearly one million people were slaughtered in the Rwandan one hundred days genocide. See Gourevitchp (1998).

[2] The United States Committee for Refugees reports that there were 4.5 million internally displaced people in Sudan, Somalia, Ethiopia and Eritrea alone. In 1997, Sub Saharan Africa produced nearly 24% of all the world's refugees, the highest in the world. See United States Committee for Refugees at *www.refugees.org*.

Ethnicity/ identity, Economics and Politics and the Somali Conflict

An ethnic group is defined as a "...large or small group of people, in either backward or advanced societies, who are united by common inherited culture (including language, music, food, dress, and customs and practices), racial similarity, common religion, and belief in common history and ancestry and who exhibit a strong psychological sentiment of belonging to the group" (Ganguly and Taras, 1998, p.9). Proponents of the ethnic thesis argue that many internal conflicts stem from ethnicity and ethnic group mobilization to achieve goals such as political power, security and economic wealth. There are three approaches in which the relationship between ethnicity and conflict is analyzed. First is *primordialism,* which views ethnicity as a given; a person belongs to a group automatically at birth (Kaplan, 1993; Connor, 1994). Group membership is a given, whether based on clan/tribal lines (i.e. Zulu or Serbs,[1]) or common history. However, this approach does not fully explain other sources of conflict. Political, social, economic and environmental factors also contribute to many conflicts.

The second approach, *instrumentalism,* looks at ethnicity as an instrument used by individuals, groups or elite in order to gain more power, mainly material power (Steinberg, 1981; Brass, 1985). In this approach, ethnicity is only one of many tools available to the organizers, most of the time elite, to reach their target. In Somalia, for example, warlords have been using ethnicity, the most accessible tool, to mobilize their tribesmen for the past 17 years. Yet most of the time the combatants, organized along clan lines, do not even know what they are fighting for. In this approach, ethnic violence should not be differentiated from other conflicts.

Finally, *constructivism* attempts to bridge the former two approaches and argues that ethnicity is neither given as primordialists argue, nor used as an instrument by the elite as instrumentalists argue, but that it stems from social interactions (Brubaker, 1995; Kuran, 1998). Constructivism argues that individuals belong to a multitude of groups including merchants, intellectuals and, during the absence of fear and economic and political insecurity, to the nation. Between 1960 and

---

[1] In the Somali culture one is obligated to participate in tribal activities, including monetary contribution or opinions.

1990, for example, although the Somalis belonged to their particular clans, members of the different clans intermingled and worked side by side. In fact, it was politically incorrect for someone to ask another to which clan he belonged, especially in the urban areas. The inquiring person was then known as *reer baadiye*, or country folk. After the collapse of the central government in early 1991, however, all people, including urban dwellers, were forced to seek security and protection from their particular clan (Kuran, 1998). Therefore, ethnic conflict in this approach results from "…pathological social system, which individuals do not control…it is the social system that breeds violent social conflict, not individuals, and it is the socially constructed nature of ethnicity that can cause conflict, once begun, to spin rapidly out of control" (Lake and Rothchild, 1998:6).

The second factor that causes conflicts is economic decline, which most of the developing world faced during the 1980s. The global recession of the 1980s was most damaging in the Sub Saharan African region. The majority of the economies in the region experienced decline and experienced little growth or modernization since regaining their independence. For example, the African per capita growth between 1965 and 1980 was 1.5, while that of South Asia was 1.4. In contrast, however, this figure declined to -1.7 for Africa between 1980 and 1989, while South Asia's grew to 2.9 (World Bank, 1989). Somalia's economic decline was more severe; between 1960 and 1990 the real per capita GDP declined by 25 per cent (Mubarak, 2006). This economic decline was further worsened by an unequal economic distribution based on tribalism and clanism, which disproportionately benefited the clan of the rulers. In fact, the Somalis often identified their governments with the ruler's clan. The interim government from 1956 to 1960, for example, was often called *governo Saad* because its leader, the late Prime Minister Abdulahi Isse, was from Saad, a sub-clan of Habargidir. Similarly, during the Siad Barre regime (1969-1991), the government was named after Barre's sub-clan of Mareehaan. The unequal distribution and disproportionate benefits for the members of the clan in office made Somalia's politics a *zero-sum* game and certainly explains why the conflict began and continues with no end in sight.

Both ethnicity and economic decline, however, have to play in the political arena where, as argued, the state has been the sole arbiter for *who gets what*. David (1994) advances two major causes of internal conflicts: *bad leadership* and *neo-realism*. He argues that the quality of leadership, if bad, tends to exacerbate conflict within the borders of the state. He writes:

> Internal wars happen not because one people hate another, but rather because of the rational and deliberate decision of 'bad' leaders. Heads of state make decisions that lead to war because they are primarily more interested in staying in power than preserving the peace for their citizens (David, 1997:563).

The bad leader theories argue that leadership is what makes or breaks a state. This type of leadership is abundant in Africa, where many of the rulers become leaders for life and impoverish their societies, e.g. Mobutu Sese Seko, the late president of Zaire (now Democratic Republic of Congo) who ruled the country for 32 years and deposited billions of dollars outside the country.

Since its independence, the Somali state certainly experienced more than its share of bad leadership, especially during the dictatorship of the Barre regime (1969-1991). During this period, Somalia suffered from bad policies that caused severe economic decline and social strife. This was most visible in policies concerning agriculture, food production, and military expenditure. Immediately following his coming to power in 1969, General Barre began to control food production and distribution. The residents of the major cities such as Mogadishu began to line up for their daily food supply. More importantly, the Barre regime began to target and take away farmlands from the inter-river people of Southern Somalia, which further exacerbated the food shortage. Barre's regime instituted policies that reduced food production to the benefit of his clansmen.

The first policy was the establishment of the Agricultural Development Corporation (ADC) in 1970. The agency was designed to exercise price controls over agricultural commodities. Policy prohibited private sale, purchase and distribution of commodities, particularly corn, maize and sorghum. The price for these commodities was fixed by the government and all selling activities were taken over by the ADC. The individual farmer and his family were permitted to keep enough food to last until the next harvest, while the rest had to be sold to the ADC. This policy was enforced by the country's police and a militia that Barre named *Guulwade* (victory bearers). These prices were usually lower than the production cost, which in turn forced many

11

farmers to cultivate perishable vegetables, such as tomatoes and watermelons. Exacerbating the situation, the Barre regime opened large grain silos and grind mills in the central and north-eastern regions to benefit his nomadic clans. This caused a 20 percent decrease in grain production between 1969 and 1980, and forced the country to import grain from abroad.[1]

In addition to the ADC, the Barre regime instituted another policy that further reduced food production. In 1974, there was a drought known as the *Dabadher* (the long tailed) in the central regions of the country. The government resettled over 140 nomads into the inter-river regions (Kurtuwarrey and Sablaale) and gave them farmlands confiscated from the farmers. The regime could have alternatively helped alleviate the draught condition by creating water and grazing facilities for the nomadic clans.

The most devastating policy, however, was the passing of the 1975 Land Reform Act. This law was intended to intensify the confiscation of fertile land from its owners. The law declared all land resources government property. The ministry of the agriculture was given full authority to give leases on land to any individual, state farm, cooperative, or company. Any sale or lease of land had to be registered with the government. Most of the farmers, who did not understand the land reform law, continued the custom of inheriting land from generation to generation. This tenure system had been part of their cultural fabric since the beginning of farming history. The government then levied heavy monetary fines on these farmers. Many of them could not afford to pay the fines and had to give up their generations-old land. The regime, in turn, redistributed these confiscated farmlands mainly to the members of Barre's clan, especially the Mareehaan sub-clan. Additionally, the government gave a vast amount of money, in the form of loans and grants from the Somali Development Bank, to the new tenants, who had no idea how to farm. Money was provided for the purchase of agricultural machinery and equipment, but most of it went to other luxury items – big villas and luxury cars like the Toyota Land Cruiser (known locally as the Camel of the Mareehaan).

In the 1970s, the Barre government established the Ministry of the Jubba Valley to administer large scale mechanized farms. Among its largest projects were the Jubba Sugar Project (JSP) and the Mugambo

---

[1] Somalia Country Profile. The Economist Intelligence Unit. 1992-93:44.

12

Irrigation Project (MIP). These projects were financed with foreign aid and loans from the Western and Arab countries. The JSP had a funding of U.S $210 million, and the MIP got U.S $71 million. The government's justification for these projects was that they would allow the country to be self-sufficient in food production, but the projects backfired. In fact, the reverse occurred; the project's funds were misused and abused. The projects left many farmers landless and destitute, and, worse yet, damaged the ecology of the area.

Another devastating policy was the refugee resettlement program of 1977-1978, during and after the Ogaden War. In 1977, there was a flood of refugees from the war areas of eastern Ethiopia. Most of these refugees were from the Ogaden clan (a subgroup of Barre's Darood tribe). According to the UNHCR, the total number of refugees was estimated at one million. Not surprisingly, the majority of these refugees were settled in the inter-river region (i.e. Qoryooley).

Military Expenditure

The second indication of the Barre regime's bad leadership was its investment in the military and military-related activities. Since its independence, Somalia has received great attention from the antagonists of the Cold War, the U.S. and former USSR, who showered the country with huge supply of weapons. Somalia always had a great appetite for weapons, an appetite matched by the willingness of superpowers, and regional powers such as Egypt, during the Cold War. Since its independence in 1960, different Somali governments have engaged in hyper-militarization policies. Between 1960 and 1990, Somalia spent an average of 20.45% of its budget on the military and had an average of 8 soldiers per 1000 population, well above the regional average of less than 4 per 1000 population (Osman, 2003, pp. 175-7). Somalia's military grew steadily, despite being one of the poorest states in the world. The military expanded from 5,000 troops at independence in 1960 to to 65,000 in 1990 (Lefebvre, 1991).

Somalia's hyper-militarization was greatly enhanced by its location, which is of great geo-political and strategic interest to the regional and superpowers. First, it is proximate to the all-important oil production centers of the Middle East. Secondly, it lies on the important trade routes through the Suez Canal and the Red Sea. In the early 1970s, the Soviets were allowed to establish a naval base on the

13

Berbera port on the Red Sea. This base was built by the former Soviet Union in order to establish a presence on this strategic strip, where there was already a large-scale American military presence. During the Ethiopia-Somali war in 1977-78, after a Marxist regime had come to power in Ethiopia in 1974, superpowers switched their allegiances. The Soviets became allies of of Colonel Mingistu Haile Mariam of Ethiopia's Marxist regime (1974-1991), while the U.S. became Somalia's ally. Between 1979 and 1990, the U.S. sent hundreds of millions of dollars worth of arms to Siad Barre's regime in return for the use of military facilities at Berbera (Ayittey, 1994, Lefebver, 1991). In addition to the superpowers, the country received military support from Arab countries, China, West Germany, Italy and Apartheid South Africa (Ottaway, 1982; Lefebvre, 1991).

In January of 1991, Siad Barre's regime (1969-1991) came to an end and Somalia descended into full scale internal war. This internal war had been in the making for several years. It resulted from a combination of several factors – local and international – and involved many different actors. At the national level, several years of continued frustration over basic human needs caused social unrest. Additionally, the government's ineffective policies created economic stagnation and brought extreme poverty. This decline made the government unstable, as evidenced by the constant cabinet reshuffles, defections and loss of state authority. Worst of all, it politicized the armed forces. The difficult living conditions, in turn, created an incentive for young men to join clan-based militia that opposed the government of Siad Barre.

Neo-realism and Internal War

The majority of scholars today are from the Cold War era, when neo-realism was the leading paradigm. One of the assumptions of neo-realism is that the state is a unitary actor that protects the interests of its citizens. The exception, however, is when the state is weak and can no longer protect the interests of its citizens. Thus, neo-realists contend that once groups inside the state disintegrate, they behave just like states in interstate conflicts. Moreover, once the state ceases to exist, the groups within the state, which fear for their security, try to protect their interests in the same way that states do. Neo-realists also explain wars from the *security dilemma* perspective. The core of the security dilemma is that other groups may interpret the enhancement of one group's security as a threat to theirs. Thus, once the state fails to exist, the groups inside its borders will see each other as threat.

To apply this theory to Somalia, we may argue that as the Somali state structures weakened, the transfer of weapons to the public became apparent, in part due to the states' inability to pay the salaries of the armed forces, who in turn sold their weapons in order to maintain their livelihood. As a result, power struggles between and among politicians and new warlords intensified. Some ethnic groups became more capable of asserting themselves politically, seeking more administrative autonomy or even forming their own states. The ethnic groups that were protected or had exercised authority through the weakened state became more vulnerable. Criminal organizations became more powerful, as in Sierra Leone and Liberia. Additionally, the control of state borders became less effective, thus attracting illegal smuggling of weapons and other valuable commodities such as diamonds, coltan, gold, drugs and, finally, refugees and migrants.

Second, as the states grew weaker or in some cases ceased to exist, individual groups within the state felt compelled to provide for their own defense (Bayart et al., 1999; Adedji, 1995). Many groups began seeking alternative forms of governance and security, especially in the anti-state movements that promised better government, security and living standards (Migdal, 1988; Holsti, 1996; Duffield, 1988, Keen, 1998). As they provided for their own needs, however, groups become a threat to others in the state. This led neighboring groups to take steps to diminish the security of the first group, hence the security dilemma (Posen 1993; Jervis 1978). This is so because the same weapons – primarily light arms – claimed to be defensive can easily be used for offensive purposes, inevitably intensifying the security concerns of neighboring groups (Posen, 1993; Esman, 1994). The collapse of the Barre regime in 1991 gave way to the current phenomenon of warlordism in Somalia.

Factors that Prolonged the War: Warlordism

Barre's regime came to an end in 1991 as a result of a weakened state and the clan-based armed factions gaining the upper hand. A new political era was set in motion in Somalia, in which a number of warlords, each ruling its own enclave, divided the country into fiefdoms. Over the years, these warlords became the *de facto* rulers of these areas with the voluntary or involuntary support of their clansmen. They recruited young unsuspecting militia from their clans and profited from their efforts while they themselves crisscrossed the globe, gaining wealth, notoriety and, more importantly, sending their families abroad for safety. In order to finance the war efforts, the warlords and their clan militia resorted to *bililiqo* (or robbery) and *is baaro* (road blocks). The overwhelming majority of those affected by these illegal activities were the residents of Southern Somalia in cities such as Mogadishu, Merka and Baidoa.

As time progressed, the number and power of the warlords continued to increase, owing mainly to two factors. First, the UNITAF and UNOSOM I & II mandates, intended to bring stability in Somalia, were instituted at the end of 1992. Indeed, these operations saved millions of lives, mainly in Southern Somalia. However, the operations also created a lucrative business and in turn glorified warlordism in Somalia. The warlords acquired their power through all means necessary (except political legitimacy), i.e. arms, intimidation, harassment, intrigue, etc. The UN put a lot of effort into the distribution of food and medication. They tried to feed the hungry, who were concentrated mainly in the areas south of Mogadishu, especially in the Baay, Bakool, Gedo, Lower Shabelle, and the Upper and Middle Jubba areas. One of the major difficulties that the UN faced was the delivery of food to these regions. Food convoys were robbed and sold at markets like Bakaaraha in Mogadishu in order to finance the war machinery. General Aideed, for example, claimed that he fed all the regions south of Mogadishu. Ironically, these regions were where most of the deaths occurred. The UN allowed the General to take 60 percent of the donated food, while his rival Ali Mahdi received the remaining 40 percent. The humanitarian effort completely failed because of unsafe roads, and the death toll continued to rise. Not surprisingly, General Aideed refused the deployment of international forces to secure food delivery several times, and instead insisted that he should provide forces to secure food delivery.

The second factor was the UN's failure to enforce its own mandate vis-à-vis the warlords, which may partly explain the unwarranted death of 25 Pakistani soldiers, the capture of 10 peacekeepers as prisoners, and the maiming of 54 in June 1993 (Makinda, 1993:12). UNOSOM II concluded that Aideed and his USC/SNA faction were responsible for these actions. They issued warrants for their arrest and put a lot of effort into the operation. On October 3, 1993, Aideed's faction killed 18 U.S. soldiers, wounded 75, and captured one, who was later released. Unfortunately, Aideed, who was responsible not only for the death of the UN soldiers but also the death of thousands of Somalis, was never punished for his crimes. In fact, a U.S. military plane transported him yet to another important meeting for the Somali people, the Humanitarian conference in Addis Ababa held from November 29 to December 1, 1993. This sent the signal to other warlords that they could do whatever they wanted without fear of consequences. As a result, their numbers continued to increase from about 4 to over 70, and those of them that remained at the completion of this book continue to rob the country's human and natural resources.

Attempts to Resolve the Conflict

The international community attempted to end the Somali conflict through 14 multilateral conferences. It seemed as though the international community gave the warlords a blank page on which to draw Somalia's future. They met in Egypt, Djibouti, Ethiopia and Kenya, each time staying at luxurious hotels and living lavishly. Each conference presented a compromised deal in some kind of governmental format, but, unfortunately, each one of these compromises has ended in failure and the devastation continues. On October 15, 2002, the 14th multilateral conference, spearheaded by the Inter-governmental Authority on Development (IGAD), convened in Eldoret, Kenya. This conference adopted a provisional federal constitution that lacked any viable institutional mechanism for checks and balances, offered complete immunity to the warlords from past and future violations, and concentrated the power of the state into the hands of the president.

This meeting also produced and selected a parliament of 275 members, elected on the basis of a 4.5[1] tribal breakdown. The parliament elected Sharif Hassan Sheikh Adan as the speaker on September 15, 2004. Finally, on October 15, 2004, the parliament elected

---

[1] Each of the four large tribes Darood, Dighil and Mirilfe, Hawiye, Isaaq and Dir each receiving 61 members and a cluster of minority tribes receiving 31 members.

a warlord, Mr. Abdulahi Yusuf Ahmed, as president. On November 3, 2004 the President in turn appointed Mohamed Ali Gedi, a 51 year-old veteran, as Prime Minister, and Gedi in turn appointed a cabinet consisting mainly of warlords.

The new president, Mr. Ahmed, is a former colonel in the army and the ruler of the self-styled region of Puntland in the Northeast. He is the third president selected outside of Somalia since January 1991. The preceding two presidents, Ali Mahdi Mohamed (1991-2000) and Abdiqasim Salaad Hassan (2000-2004) were not successful in curbing the violence and stabilizing the nation. Several factors contributed to their failure, including tribal chauvinism, abundance of weapons, lack of authority, lack of international support, and more importantly, lack of trust.

Initially, it appeared that the selection of Mr. Ahmed constituted a greater opportunity than that experienced by his predecessors. There seemed to be a significant amount of fatigue among the Somali people, leaving them with the view that "a bad government is better than no government." Second, neighboring countries and the regional organization IGAD also showed signs of fatigue and seemed to support Ahmed's government. Third, there was also sign of fatigue at the international level, which wanted to see a functioning government in Somalia. These three factors gave the government of Mr. Ahmed the opportunity to rebuild the country from the ashes of a 14-year internal war.

The potential for resolution and reconciliation in Somalia is not, however, without its challenges. Mr. Ahmed is a controversial figure both in Puntland and other regions of the country. He is known more for his *Machiavellian* qualities than for his charisma. Many accuse him of having assembled the first anti-Siad Barre movement and having led the first military *coup d'état* against Barre's regime. Others accuse him of being hand picked by external forces, specifically Ethiopia. Mr. Ahmed has also been accused of plotting several murders and of having dictatorial tendencies, demonstrated in his Puntland regional state. More importantly, since his election, the controversy surrounding his leadership style has continued to grow. In this age of the Internet and instant polling, a popular Somali webpage (Hiiraan.com) conducted a survey, which asked whether Mr. Ahmed was the appropriate person to rule Somalia and bring peace and stability into the country. There were a total of 6,403 respondents, of which 3, 053 (or

48%) replied in the affirmative, and 3,350 (or 52%) responded negatively. Although this poll is unscientific, the results seem to reveal uncertainty on the part of the Somali people (at least those that have access to the Internet – mainly in the diaspora). More importantly, the results of the poll demonstrated the difficulty of the President's task to rebuild Somalia.

Yet since his election, President Ahmed has failed to address the Somali people directly, including through broadcasting facilities such as radio and TV. Addressing the public would give his government much needed grassroots support and legitimacy. Worse yet, on the few occasions that he has used the airwaves, President Ahmed used combative rather than conciliatory words, which could bring Somalia's warring factions together on a peaceful course. Moreover, the President is pushing the international community, the African Union in particular, to support his government with troops to help seize weapons from the remaining warlords and guarantee the existence of his state. Recently, in early 2007, the African Union authorized the deployment of 1,500 Ugandan peacekeepers in Mogadishu. Prior to this, in late 2006, the President unilaterally invited Ethiopian forces into to the country to help his embattled government fight the militants of the Union of Islamic Courts (UIC), but the Ethiopian forces were already engaged in bitter armed struggles with the revived forces of the UIC and militias of some of the clans of Mogadishu.

Overall, as argued, the Somali conflict has been prolonged due to the combination of the several aforementioned reasons. Nevertheless, it could be argued that the most persistent factor accounting for the prolongation of the conflict is the war between two diametrically opposed clans: the Hawiye and the Darood. These two tribes have conflicting goals that create a *zero-sum*. Their leaders stress winning the war at any cost, as losing would be deadly for the clan. This state of affairs has created a political situation where all other options, specifically peaceful negotiations, are completely neglected. On the one hand, the Daroods have occupied the political throne since the independence of the country in 1960, for which they earned the nickname of "Dowlad ku nool" (those living on the government property). Over the years, they have gained economic power, accumulating great wealth and occuping almost all aspects of the political system. More importantly, they have developed a dynastic

19

view of politics, in which only they can effectively rule the Somali state, often citing their 30 years of experience (1960-1991) as proof.

On the other hand, the Hawiye, who in reality have not been absent from political power since 1960, have mobilized themselves as the victims of the Darood-dominated politics. After 1991, unfortunately, the Hawiye experienced a split between actual victims who genuinely wanted change and those who had benefited from the *ancien regime*, had political clout, and wanted to use the victims' cries and grievances to increase their political power. As the war continued, however, some of the young fighters, or Mooryans, who were recruited from remote villages in the name of the clan, gained wealth and sophistication as a result of the lawlessness. They became merchants who paid no taxes, formed their own militias, obeyed no rules, and gained power over the political mentors who had recruited them. Today these new powerful players have the weapons and, more importantly, the illicitly gained wealth. Their biggest fear is the establishment of any semblance of government that will tax and regulate their commerce and enforce the rule of law. We can thus fear that the conflict will continue in the foreseeable future, because the war is between the *Dowlad ku-nool* (those that live on the government property) and the *Dowlad diid* (those that do not want government).

* * *

The idea for this volume came from the publication of a special issue of the journal *African Renaissance* titled, "Somalia: Reconstituting a Failed State" (vol. 3, no. 5, 2006). Many of the chapters are revised versions of articles that appeared in that issue. Additionally, we solicited chapters from other notables in the field. The volume consists of eleven chapters and is divided into three parts. The first part is a historical overview of both the Somali state and conflict that puts the conflict in its social context. This section has three chapters; the first, provided by Brock Tessman, gives an overview of the Somali state in the context of the African states, especially in comparison with some of its IGAD neighbors. The last two chapters, written by Mohamed A. Eno and Abdirahman Baadiyow, examine respectively the role of social factors of the state collapse and the issue of inequality.

The second part of the volume examines the factors that led to the conflict; in other words, the root causes of the conflict. This part has two chapters; one by Abdulahi A. Osman and the other by Geri

Stewart, which examine respectively the role of inequality in the Somali politics and the continuous failure of the Somali state.

The third section addresses the continuous attempts to resolve the conflict and how and why they have so far failed. Five chapters examine these attempts, analyzing them from different perspectives. Mohamed H. Mukhtar addresses the factors behind the consistent failure of the reconciliation efforts. Omar A. Eno addresses the genesis of the failure, stemming from unrealistic tribal and clan ambitions. Issaka Souaré revisits the United Nations intervention in Somalia between 1993 and 1995 and wonders what lessons can be learned from the failure of this intervention for future Africa-UN partnerships in peacekeeping on the continent. And whilst Franco Henwood puts forward the case for the international recognition of Somaliland, Akinloye Ojo's chapter addresses the potential role the Somali Diaspora can play in rebuilding the country. The volume concludes with some humble suggestions and recommendations for the way forward.

Part I

Historical and Social Contexts

Chapter 2

A QUANTITATIVE DEPICTION OF SOMALIA AT THE CROSSROADS: ASSESSING NATIONAL CAPABILITY AND HUMANITARIAN DEVELOPMENT

Brock F. Tessman

In a recent study by *The Fund for Peace* and the *Carnegie Endowment for International Peace*, Somalia ranked alongside Sudan, Iraq, Côte d'Ivoire (also known as Ivory Coast), Chad, Democratic Republic of the Congo and Zimbabwe as one of the most failed states in the world.[1] This characterization should come as no surprise to those with even a passing knowledge of African politics; other states classified as in a "critical" or "dangerous" state of failure include Somalia's neighbors Ethiopia and Kenya. States such as Sudan, Uganda and Eritrea were also classified this way. Thus, the term "failed state" is not an uncommon one when referring to countries in the region. Indeed, Somalia is surrounded by states that – due to a multitude of factors, including colonialism, religious differences, and environmental disasters – are all struggling to prosper. Effectively gauging the situation in Somalia requires that its challenges be placed in context.

In this paper, I compare Somalia to its IGAD (Intergovernmental Authority on Development) partners, both in terms of traditional measures of national capability and in terms of performance on a human development scale that I build from a recent World Bank dataset. I find that – even in the IGAD context – Somalia has virtually no national military or industrial capability to speak of, and is also well below the IGAD average when it comes to human development as measured by social, economic and technological indicators. And existing trends do not bode well for Somalia. National capability and human development scores are slipping as internal turmoil prevents

---

[1] Data are reproduced in the following article: "The Failed States Index." *Foreign Policy* (May/June 2006):50-58.

23

Somalia from getting back on its feet. The purpose of this study is simply to lay the empirical groundwork for the more substantive analyses that follow. This analysis seeks primarily to quantitatively assess the weakness of the Somali state. I do not attempt to speculate about the causal factors that have generated this reality; my aim is simply to produce quantifiable evidence of Somalia's decline and then analyze this evidence from my perspective as an international relations scholar who is trained in the assessment of capability trends among a set of actors in a given system. This seems like an appropriate precursor to the detailed and persuasive pieces that comprise the heart and soul of this volume.

As such, I refrain from extensive commentary and instead focus on outlining Somalia's current position vis-à-vis politically relevant countries in its near vicinity. Such commentaries and a more in-depth analysis of the Somali crisis are provided by Osman (Ch. 5) and Swart (Ch. 6). This notwithstanding, it is still impossible to refrain from noting the vicious cycle within which Somalia finds itself. Its lack of national capability relative to outside actors leaves Somalia open to foreign intervention, which further destabilizes the country and reduces the chance that any unity government can emerge and restore *de facto* sovereignty. Until this happens, Somalia will remain lodged at a chaotic crossroad where it is the innocent that suffer most.

The rest of this paper is structured around two quantitative analyses of Somalia and five IGAD countries that are Uganda, Kenya, Djibouti, Sudan and Ethiopia.[1] I address traditional measures of national capability first, using the Correlates of War Project's *CINC* (Composite Indicator of National Capability) data from 1963 to 2001.[2] After that, I use the World Bank's *World Development Indicators* to construct a multi-faceted scale of human development.[3] These data are more recent, covering the five-year period between 2000 and 2004. Both sections contain detailed explanations about the data and methodology used, along with graphical and tabular presentations of the results. A short concluding section includes some more commentary about the

---

[1] Eritrea is not included because its recent independence (1993) precludes an analysis of long term trends.

[2] The Composite Indicators of National Capability data can be found at the Correlates of War Project homepage: http://cow2.la.psu.edu.

[3] Data selected for this paper can be found online at the World Bank's website: http://www.worldbank.org.

relationship between state weakness, foreign intervention and the lack of human development.

Somalia's Relative National Capability: The Traditional Perspective

Traditionally, international relations scholars have defined a state's "power" as the ability to influence outcomes in its favor (Claude, 1962; Morgenthau, 1967; Deutsch, 1968). Ideally, power would thus be measured by comparing the actual outcomes of events involving generic state alpha ("α") with the outcomes desired by α. From an analyst's perspective, however it is impossible to systematically assess power this way because variables such as the desired outcomes of α are often unobservable. As a result, most scholars measure state power indirectly by assessing a state's *capability* to influence outcomes rather than trying to directly measure what a state wants and how effective it is at getting what it wants.

A number of different strategies have been used to assess national capability in the past. Abstract concepts like national prestige, legitimacy or resolve are important to consider as part of a country's capability, but – again – there are problems associated with observing these phenomena. In order to get around the "observation" problem, most scholars define national capability in a material sense. Single indicators such as national Gross Domestic Product (GDP) capture the raw size of a state's economy, while per capita GDP is a measure that emphasizes individual prosperity instead of raw size. When national capability is defined with multiple variables, there is typically an effort to incorporate indicators of military, economic and demographic strength.

The *material* capabilities a state possesses are not a perfect indicator of its *actual* capability (Liska, 1990). Quality leadership, national cohesiveness, geographical location and even climate can affect the power of any state. But basic material capabilities do give us a good idea of – broadly – the ability of a state to get what it wants. Entire research programs in international relations are based on assessing the distribution of material capabilities in the international system (Waltz,

1979; Mearsheimer, 2001).[1] Scholars apply findings from analyses of material capabilities to everything from studies on the balance of power to predictions about the formulation of grand strategy.[2] For these scholars, material capabilities are a basic way to determine state strength. One objective of this paper is to use capability data to determine Somalia's basic strength vis-à-vis key states in its vicinity.

Because statistics tend to tell a richer story when placed in some context, material capabilities are often approached from the perspective of relativity (e.g. "What is the material capability of state α compared to that of state β?). While it is not particularly helpful to consider Somalia's material capabilities in comparison to the capability of distant states like Norway or Mongolia, there is some value in addressing Somali state strength in the context of politically relevant states in the immediate East African region, such as members of the Intergovernmental Authority on Development (IGAD).

In the remainder of this section, I present a summary of material capabilities in the IGAD countries for the time period between 1963 and 2001.[3] By looking at state strength in very rough terms over a wide range of time, it is possible to look at long term trends in the distribution of material capabilities of the IGAD states relative to one another. As mentioned, I use data from the Correlates of War Project

---

[1] The Correlates of War Project (COW), developed at the University of Michigan but currently run by Penn State University, is perhaps the best example of one such research program.

[2] The theoretical framework of realism is based on power as measure by material capabilities. Classical realists like Thucydides stressed power considerations when he claimed that Sparta launched a preventive war against Athens before it grew too strong to contain. Hans Morgenthau claimed that power (both material power and prestige) was the only enduring truth in international relations. Neorealists such as Kenneth Waltz and John Mearsheimer have gone so far as to claim that almost all general patterns in the global system can be explained by the distribution of material capabilities between states.

[3] Because Eritrea in only included in the database from 1993 onward, it is excluded from the analysis here. Djibouti is included, even though data are only available for it as of 1977. All other IGAD countries are included for the entire temporal domain of 1963-2001.

26

National Material Capabilities dataset.[1] This dataset measures state power by including six variables:

- Total population (in thousands);
- Urbanization (population living in cities with more than 100,000 inhabitants);
- Energy consumption (thousands of coal-ton equivalents);
- Iron and steel production (thousands of tons);
- Military personnel (in thousands);
- Military expenditure (calculated in U.S dollars).

The CINC dataset is the most widely used way of defining state power (Singer and Small, 1972; Small and Singer, 1982; Singer and Diehl, 1990).[2] Data exist for most countries, with annual scores for long-established states like France dating back to the year 1816. There is significant debate about the validity of the CINC data. For example, "iron and steel production" in State α might not tell analysts much at all about State α's ability to influence international outcomes in the twenty-first century. This critique may be particularly relevant when talking about countries like Somalia and the other IGAD members. Still, the CINC measurements provide a consistent, basic picture of the economic, demographic and military clout that countries possess. Because it is consistent across all countries, and measurements occur annually over extended periods of time, this dataset is an appropriate place to start when one is attempting to highlight the long-term erosion of Somalia's state strength vis-à-vis other states in its immediate vicinity. Measurements are made annually, with countries receiving a raw score that is compared to the scores of other countries during that same year. For each indicator during every year, a country possesses a "share" of the total score for the six IGAD countries. A country's average share across all six indicators is its overall CINC score for that year. Mathematically, this process is defined in the following equation:

$$CINC\alpha_t = (T\alpha_t + U\alpha_t + E\alpha_t + I\alpha_t + M\alpha_t + X\alpha_t) / 6,$$

---

[1] These data, along with documentation of data sources, coding and missing values can be found at: http://cow2.la.psu.edu/.
[2] The most comprehensive studies based on the COW data are authored or edited by J. David Singer.

In this equation, $CINC\alpha_t$ is the CINC score of α at time t, and $T\alpha_t$, $U\alpha_t$, $E\alpha_t$, $I\alpha_t$, $M\alpha_t$, and $X\alpha_t$ are, respectively: the total population, urban population, energy consumption, iron and steel production, military personnel and military expenditure, of α at time t.

Admittedly, there are some limitations to this approach. The COW material capabilities data are among the most comprehensive available, but there are occasionally problems with missing data, particularly when dealing with states like Somalia that have a significant amount of internal turmoil. Missing values are generally computed by linear regression; observations from surrounding time points are used to estimate any missing values. This strategy is well established in other analyses of large datasets similar to CINC. Critics might also argue that a "hard power" approach to measuring capability does not tell the whole story when it comes to measuring state strength in Somalia. I agree that, for a state like Somalia, "soft power" measures in areas like nutrition, health care, and education are more appropriate than measures of military personnel as a litmus test for any governing force in Somalia. I deal with this critique in two ways: First, I complement this analysis of national capabilities with a second one focusing on humanitarian development. Second, I think it is important to account for the impact that Somalia's capability inferiority has on its vulnerability to foreign intervention. This intervention prevents a stable central authority from emerging in Somalia, and ultimately hinders progress in the "soft power" areas mentioned above. In summary, I do believe that it is important to evaluate just how weak the Somali "state" is if we are to understand the ease with which other (stronger) states are able to intervene in Somali affairs. Most often, this intervention is structured to further the interests of the intervening states at the expense of the Somali state as a whole.

Appendix 1 contains the annual CINC scores for Ethiopia, Djibouti, Kenya, Somalia, Sudan and Uganda. Numbers represent each country's share of capability in the system. At each time point, system capability equals 1.0. Upon initial inspection, two realities become quickly apparent. First, Somalia's CINC share has traditionally been inferior to all of the other states included in this study, with the exception of relative newcomer Djibouti. During the first year covered in this analysis, Somalia could claim 7.9 percent of the system capability, compared to 44 percent for Ethiopia and 15.6 percent for Uganda. Somalia enjoyed its peak of relative capability in 1979 (9.5 percent of system capability), but since that time the country has seen its relative national capability decline. After an era of growth during the 1970s and early 1980s, Somalia was back to its original 7.9 percent relative capability share by 1988. This number fell all the way to 4.9 percent ten years later, after the chaos of the 1990s left the country in total disarray. To underscore Somalia's inferiority by this point in time, one need only notice that in 1979, Somalia's capability share was roughly on par with that of Uganda (9.5 percent and 10.1 percent, respectively) and a little less than half that of Sudan (9.5 percent and 22.2 percent, respectively). By 1998, Uganda and Sudan had capability levels that were, respectively, 2.53 and 5.27 times larger than that of Somalia. After a brief increase during 1999 and 2000, Somalia's relative share of national capability within the IGAD context reached its all time low of 4.7 percent during the last year covered in this study (2001). Given the erosion of central authority in the ensuing five years, one would expect that Somalia's military, industrial and demographic clout is even lower today. Data from Appendix 1 are presented in graphical form in Figure 1.

Figure 1: National Capability of IGAD Countries: 1963-2001

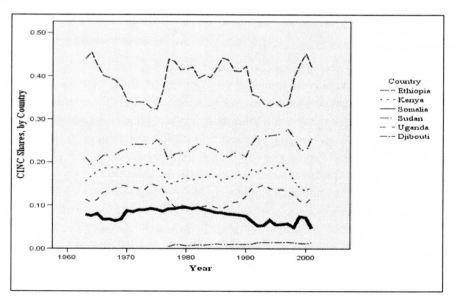

In terms of traditional military, economic and demographic strength, Somalia ranks behind almost all of its regional counterparts. Furthermore, Somalia's relative position seems to be deteriorating over time. A lack of traditional state strength has made it easier for external actors to interfere in Somali affairs. As one would expect, external interventions often prioritize the interests of the intervening actors at the expense of the local government and people. A downward spiral emerges as a lack of traditional state strength makes Somalia vulnerable to interventions that, in turn, further weaken the state. By placing Somalia's CINC scores in the context of neighboring states (several of which have extensive interest in Somalia and even an armed presence inside its borders), one can understand how it is difficult for any central authority – be it the transitional government of Abdullahi Yusuf or the Union of Islamic Courts in Mogadishu before their withdrawal in early 2007– to secure Somalia's borders and produce the kind of internal stability that is a prerequisite for *de facto* sovereignty. At some point then, a stable Somalia will have to be a Somalia that makes some improvement in the kind of nuts-and-bolts areas that are covered by the CINC index.

A Different View: Human Development in the IGAD Countries (2000-2004)

In a country that is devastated by internal turmoil and plagued by foreign interventions, material capabilities of the state are of less immediate concern than factors affecting everyday life for ordinary Somalis. Factors like immunization rates, foreign investment and internet availability are not included in traditional measure of national capability, yet they are extremely important barometers of the quality of everyday life in a country. In assessing the relative progress of Somalia within the IGAD context, it is important to look beyond traditional measures of hard power and address human development. In this second analytical section, I develop a scale of "Human Development" for the IGAD states. The scale includes six variables, divided into three categories: social development, economic development and technological development. Data are taken from the *2006 World Development Indicators* dataset, which is produced by the World Bank. Data availability is an issue, as accurate measurements from Somalia are even more infrequent than in other IGAD countries.

Recent data are more readily available, so the numbers used in this study are restricted to the time period from 2000 to 2004. Based on the objective of measuring human development broadly, the following variables are included:

Social Development
a)   Measles immunization (percent of children ages 12-23 months);
b)   Life expectancy at birth, total (in years).
Economic Development
a)   Foreign direct investment, net inflows (Balance of Payments, U.S dollars as of early 2007);
b)   Long-term debt (U.S dollars as of early 2007)
Technological Development
a)   Fixed line and mobile phone subscribers (per 1,000 people);
b)   Internet users (per 1,000 people).

Annual measurements of each variable are taken for the same list of IGAD countries included in the earlier section of this paper.[1] Due to the particular data used in this analysis, the scale of measurement differs greatly from one variable to another. For example, literacy rate is measured on a scale from zero percent to 100 percent, while foreign direct investment ranges from zero to numbers in the billions. The nature of these variables also precludes one from thinking in terms of each country's "share" of strength in any given area as was done when dealing with the CINC data. As an alternative way of assessing human development, I translate raw scores for each variable into Z scores, which indicate to what extent an observed value is above or below the mean for that variable during the year in question. Positive Z scores represent values that are greater than the mean, while negative Z scores represent values that are below the mean. The Z score itself is measured in standard deviations from the mean. If we assume a normal distribution, Z scores greater than negative one and less than one include roughly 68 percent of the observations in any given sample; scores greater than negative two and less than two include 95 percent of the observations in any given sample. Thus, a Z score below negative two or above two indicates that – in theory – only five percent

---

[1] Eritrea is again excluded from the analysis. This decision is made in the interest of consistency, as data are not available for Eritrea given the narrower (and more recent) time period under consideration.

of the remaining observations in the sample will be equal to or greater than the observation in question.

For the six countries addressed in this study, Z scores are computed for each variable, and then grouped into the three categories of interest to produce an average Z score for social development, economic development and technological development. The average Z scores for all six variables are used to compute the total human development score. Table 1 presents Z scores by category and in the form of a "Total Human Development" score. Figure 3 presents the same information in a series of three-dimensional graphs. Z scores are aggregated into a five-year average for each category of development. The Y, Z, and X axes represent social, economic and technological development, respectively. Scores on each axis are plotted and then connected with one another to form a "Development Triangle." Larger triangles are formed when a country's aggregate Z scores indicate observed values well above the mean. Equilateral triangles suggest even development in all three categories of development, while skewed triangles occur when a country is more developed in one or two areas than in other(s). As a matter of reference, an 'average' development triangle (defined by 'average' Z scores of zero on each axis and connected by a dotted line) serves as a template to which a country's actual triangle is compared.

Somalia's human development scores, like its CINC scores, are well below the IGAD average. For every year between 2000 and 2004, Somalia's total human development Z score is negative. The only other country with this dubious distinction is Ethiopia, but that country's poor record on human development is somewhat mitigated by its relative clout in areas of hard power (recall that – depending on the year – Ethiopia alone accounts for between 39 and 45 percent of the military, industrial and demographic power in the IGAD system). Because many of the indicators I use to measure human development are measured in per capita terms, countries with larger population (like Ethiopia) are required to have higher raw scores than their smaller counterparts. Conversely, one would expect countries with a low score on CINC measures that value absolute size to score higher on the human development measures that are based on per capita variables. Djibouti is a good example. That country is the only one that rates below Somalia in terms of national capability. This is partially due to Djibouti's small absolute size. When it comes to the human

32

development, however, Djibouti's total score is above the IGAD average for four of five years. Uganda, which ranked just above Somalia in the analysis of CINC scores, also scores above average on the human development scale for all years save 2001.

Table 1: Human Development Scores in the IGAD Countries: 2000-2004

Country	Year	Economic Development	Social Development	Technological Development	Total Human Development
Uganda	2000	0.50	-0.01	-0.13	0.12
Uganda	2001	0.27	0.00	-0.33	-0.02
Uganda	2002	0.34	0.52	-0.63	0.07
Uganda	2003	0.08	0.57	-0.55	0.03
Uganda	2004	-0.09	0.71	-0.63	0.00
Kenya	2000	-0.16	0.83	1.04	0.57
Kenya	2001	-0.36	0.52	0.92	0.36
Kenya	2002	-0.28	0.32	1.30	0.45
Kenya	2003	-0.25	0.22	1.35	0.44
Kenya	2004	-0.36	0.09	1.24	0.32
Somalia	2000	-0.88	-0.91	0.21	-0.53
Somalia	2001	-0.73	-1.06	1.04	-0.25
Somalia	2002	-0.67	-0.86	0.30	-0.41
Somalia	2003	-0.63	-0.99	-0.02	-0.55
Somalia	2004	-0.60	-0.98	0.69	-0.30
Djibouti	2000	-0.44	0.24	0.57	0.12
Djibouti	2001	-0.50	0.11	-0.62	-0.34
Djibouti	2002	-0.61	0.51	0.18	0.03
Djibouti	2003	-0.43	0.52	-0.07	0.01
Djibouti	2004	0.13	0.19	-0.32	0.00
Sudan	2000	0.44	0.51	-0.14	0.27
Sudan	2001	0.49	1.13	0.02	0.54
Sudan	2002	0.55	0.29	0.20	0.35
Sudan	2003	0.56	0.52	0.68	0.59
Sudan	2004	0.27	0.55	0.38	0.40
Ethiopia	2000	0.53	-0.65	-1.55	-0.56
Ethiopia	2001	0.84	-0.69	-1.03	-0.29
Ethiopia	2002	0.67	-0.77	-1.35	-0.49
Ethiopia	2003	0.66	-0.84	-1.39	-0.52
Ethiopia	2004	0.65	-0.55	-1.37	-0.42

Figure 2 groups IGAD countries by their relative performance in both areas of analysis. As a basic pattern within IGAD, then, countries typically score well *either* on the national capability *or* the human development measures. Kenya, to its credit, is the only country that scores above average on both. On the other end of the spectrum, Somalia is the only country that scores below average on CINC scores and human development.

Figure 2: Relative Performance on CINC and Human Development Scales

	Above IGAD Average: Human Development	Below IGAD Average: Human Development
Above IGAD Average: CINC	Kenya Sudan	Ethiopia
Below IGAD Average: CINC	Uganda Djibouti	**Somalia**

Somalia's poor performance on the human development scale is due to extraordinary under-development in the social and economic areas. Particularly remarkable were very low levels of foreign direct investment, immunization and literacy. Internal stability is of paramount importance when it comes to attracting foreign capital, allowing non-governmental organizations to function and building educational success. With this in mind, it is not surprising that the breakdown of order in Somalia has hindered progress in these areas. Interestingly, the country actually scored well on technological indicators. With the exception of one year (2003), there were above average per capita levels of internet and phone connections in Somalia. This could be explained by the need for mobile phones and wireless internet in a country that – outside of major urban areas – has very little traditional infrastructure. On the other hand, it hints at a relatively high level of technological competence among the Somali population. This could be a promising sign when it comes to the country's long term potential for development.

Also promising is the stability in Somalia's relative performance in the area of human development. In contrast, the most recent measurements indicate that Somalia's share of national capability is disappearing very quickly. Although increased tension at the time of this writing (early 2007) may destroy recent progress in areas of human development, it is encouraging to see this study does not identify a sizeable connection between Somalia's plummeting national capability and the human development indicators that are available for analysis. Two caveats are important to introduce at this point. First, the data used in this analysis can only capture a small sliver of what is reality in

Figure 3: Development Triangles for IGAD Countries: 2000-2004

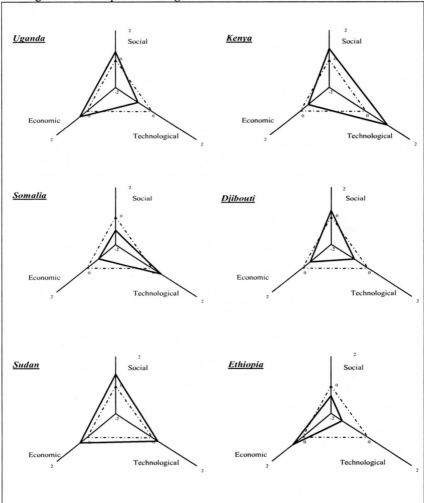

Somalia. Even a casual observer realizes that the situation on the ground cannot be captured by a narrow set of numbers that are at least a few years old. Second, it is vital to remember that all of the numbers presented here are relative to the IGAD context. Even if one is encouraged by growth in comparison to countries like Sudan and Uganda, it is sobering to reflect upon the difficulty that countries like Somalia have had in erasing the enormous capability and development gap that separates them from the "developed" world.

Conclusion: Linking National Capability, Foreign Intervention and Human Development

The analyses included in this study offer evidence of Somalia's lack of traditional national capability and overall low levels of human development. Somalia's CINC scores have historically been below those of other IGAD states. In recent years, Somalia has fallen even further behind countries like Uganda and Kenya. When it comes to human development, Somalia scores fairly well on indicators of technology, but is well below the IGAD average in remaining areas. On their own, each analysis offers an incomplete picture of state failure in Somalia, but together they depict a state that is very much in crisis and on the brink of disintegration. Of the six countries addressed here, Somalia is the only one with very poor performance in both national capability and human development. Even more alarming is that these results are presented within a context of other countries that are anything but models of stability. If Somalia's CINC scores and human development were compared to that of countries in just about any other part of the world, its relative performance would be significantly worse. Even in a region of troubled states, Somalia is plagued by intervention from state and non-state actors. Today, Somalia functions as a battlefield for rival states such as Eritrea and Ethiopia, as well as non-state organizations such as the Union of Islamic Courts and other armed groups. Intervention is made possible because there is no central authority that can maintain border security and internal order in Somalia. One need only glance at events during the autumn months of 2006 to understand the extent of foreign involvement in Somalia.

An 80-page report submitted to the United Nations Security Council in November of 2006 listed a total of ten countries allegedly ignoring the 1992 ban on arms imports and acting as arms suppliers to the different parties to the conflict in Somalia (Reuters, 2006). The list of countries supplying UIC forces included: Egypt, Libya, Djibouti, Yemen, Saudi Arabia, Syria and Iran. Supplies from these countries are most often funneled into Somalia through Eritrea, which is also supporting the Islamic forces. Hezbollah has acknowledged that it has helped train UIC elements who, in exchange for such training, sent a force of 700 to fight with Hezbollah forces in their war against Israel in the summer of 2006 (Worth, 2006). For their part, Ethiopia and Uganda are accused of supplying the transitional government forces based in Baidoa.

Ethiopian and Eritrean involvement has gone beyond acting as arms suppliers; Somalia serves as a theater of combat in what many see as a proxy war between the two rivals. Ethiopia has recently acknowledged the presence of several hundred "military advisors" in Baidoa, but international observers put the actual number of Ethiopian military personnel well into the thousands. Ethiopian Prime Minister Meles Zanawi has said that Ethiopia is "technically" at war against what he called jihadists in Somalia that are, in his words, "spoiling for a fight" (World Briefing, 2006). All this changed when Ethiopian troops publicly supported the transitional government in the latter's armed confrontation with the UIC forces in early 2007 that led to the forced withdrawal of the latter from Mogadishu and surroundings.

International intervention in Somalia may stretch well beyond neighboring states or even regional powers. Because Ethiopia is a strong ally of the United States and Islamic forces in Somalia are allegedly tied to Al Qaeda, there has been speculation that Ethiopia's struggle against the "Islamic forces" is also fueled by an overarching American interest to confront Al Qaeda wherever possible (Gettleman, 2006). Eventually, the United States intervened militarily in Somalia through two bombing raids in January 2007, supposedly aimed at Al Qaeda suspects.

For its part, before their overthrow, the Union of Islamic Courts had taken on the role of the state in much of the country. In many cases, security matters typically addressed by national governments were now dealt with by the UIC in Mogadishu. Thus, when a Somali ship was hijacked by pirates off the coast in early November of 2006, it was they that engaged the pirates in the intense gunfight that ultimately freed the captive ship. Chairman of the Union Sheik Sharif Ahmed indicated that the multinational group of pirates would be tried according to Shariah law and may be sentenced to death (AFP 2006).

Importantly, the effects of the current situation are not contained within Somalia's existing territorial boundaries. Internal instability (particularly the weakness of the transitional government and the new insurgent fighting that triggered the overthrow of the UIC) is a matter of grave concern for neighboring countries with large Somali populations like Ethiopia, Djibouti and Kenya. As I completed this paper, IGAD neighbors were also troubled by a refugee crisis that was already blossoming in border areas; tens of thousands of Somalis had fled across the border with Kenya in order to escape the violence. The Kenyan government reported that a Somali refugee staying at a United Nations refugee camp had been diagnosed with the first case of polio seen in Kenya in almost 20 years. Within three weeks, two additional polio cases had been reported in the same camp (World Report, 2006). Countries such as Kenya were already wary of the potential for a chaotic Somalia to be used as a staging base for terrorist attacks like the embassy bombings of 1998. Those attacks were allegedly planned in, and supported by supplies from, Somalia (Murunga, 2006).

The general situation inside and around Somalia will continue to worsen until some semblance of central authority is established. In February 2007, both the African Union and the United Nations committed to place peacekeepers in the country. This might restore some order, but these forces are historically much more adept at keeping a peace rather than making one, which is presently necessary in Somalia. In this paper, I argue that progress in the important areas of human development is extremely unlikely if Somalia is unable to prevent external political and military intervention. The only way to do this is for a single governing body to emerge, and for that governing body to develop the "hard power" capabilities that are necessary to establish territorial integrity and internal order. In this way, national capability is very much tied to human development. Until the former is improved, the latter will continue to lag. I am confident that the remaining chapters in this volume will contribute to a greater understanding of how Somalia has arrived at this difficult crossroads and what is necessary for the country to move down the best path possible.

Appendix 1: CINC Scores for IGAD Countries: 1963-2001

Year	Uganda	Kenya	Somalia	Djibouti	Sudan	Ethiopia
1963	0.114	0.156	0.079		0.211	0.440
1964	0.107	0.168	0.076		0.194	0.455
1965	0.113	0.179	0.080		0.203	0.424
1966	0.130	0.186	0.067		0.216	0.400
1967	0.133	0.186	0.068		0.217	0.396
1968	0.139	0.191	0.064		0.217	0.390
1969	0.146	0.185	0.068		0.227	0.374
1970	0.144	0.195	0.087		0.230	0.343
1971	0.142	0.193	0.085		0.242	0.339
1972	0.139	0.190	0.089		0.241	0.340
1973	0.137	0.195	0.089		0.241	0.338
1974	0.150	0.194	0.092		0.238	0.326
1975	0.146	0.189	0.090		0.252	0.323
1976	0.137	0.174	0.086		0.238	0.365
1977	0.113	0.150	0.092	0.004	0.203	0.439
1978	0.096	0.151	0.092	0.009	0.219	0.434
1979	0.101	0.160	0.095	0.009	0.222	0.414
1980	0.098	0.165	0.095	0.007	0.220	0.416
1981	0.089	0.159	0.092	0.007	0.233	0.421
1982	0.095	0.165	0.095	0.009	0.241	0.395
1983	0.097	0.163	0.090	0.008	0.239	0.402
1984	0.100	0.173	0.087	0.009	0.234	0.396
1985	0.095	0.167	0.083	0.011	0.228	0.416
1986	0.092	0.158	0.083	0.010	0.215	0.442
1987	0.098	0.163	0.080	0.010	0.212	0.437
1988	0.108	0.169	0.079	0.010	0.222	0.412
1989	0.109	0.171	0.077	0.010	0.221	0.411
1990	0.121	0.158	0.075	0.010	0.212	0.423
1991	0.140	0.185	0.063	0.011	0.244	0.358
1992	0.143	0.176	0.053	0.014	0.262	0.352
1993	0.149	0.188	0.054	0.015	0.260	0.335
1994	0.140	0.186	0.066	0.014	0.262	0.332
1995	0.135	0.191	0.055	0.014	0.264	0.341
1996	0.137	0.196	0.056	0.015	0.267	0.330
1997	0.133	0.182	0.058	0.015	0.277	0.335
1998	0.124	0.159	0.049	0.014	0.258	0.396
1999	0.111	0.141	0.074	0.012	0.232	0.430
2000	0.106	0.134	0.072	0.012	0.225	0.452
2001	0.119	0.146	0.047	0.014	0.257	0.417

Chapter 3

PERSPECTIVES ON THE STATE COLLAPSE IN SOMALIA

Abdurahman M. Abdullahi (Baadiyow)

*If we are to annihilate any community, We let the leaders commit
vast corruption therein. Once they deserve retribution,
We annihilate it completely.*
– Holy Qur'an (17:16)

*Expatriates in Somalia misunderstood Somalis, Somalis
misunderstood one another, the West misperceived the "state"
of Somalia, the regime in Somalia misunderstood its exact place
in the world, and all sides mistook the extent to which they could
or could not influence events and each other.
And the compounded result of all of this
misunderstanding has been singular disaster.*
– Anna Simons, *Network of Dissolution: Somalia Undone*

The Somali state collapse has brought renewed academic interest to
Somali studies, yet many enquiries have concentrated on topics of
practical relevance, such as options for international intervention,
issues of terrorism and security, or the human consequences of the
state collapse. Meanwhile, the more general study of state collapse has
exposed Somalia as emblematic of the phenomenon.[1] Again, most of
these works have been in the form of articles and occasional academic
papers (such as Lyons and Samatar, 1995; Samatar, 1994; Adam, 2000;

---

[1] Examples include Harvard University's "Failed State Project" under the
auspices of the World Peace Foundation and the "Failed State Project" at
Perdue University. These two projects have produced considerable literature
and research papers on this topic.

Clarke, 2000; Brons, 1991; Luling, 1997) which, though focused on Somalia, remain insufficient to paint a comprehensive picture of the causes of the collapse.

This paper intends to investigate and organise the perspectives on the Somali state collapse into major themes. To do so, it will firstly provide background information on the Somali encounter with colonialism and the rise and fall of the Somali state. Following this, the theory of state capabilities will be outlined. Thirdly, the major perspectives on the Somali state collapse will be classified into sub-groups. The fourth section will provide a critical review followed by a conclusion that will contain some policy recommendations.

Somali Encounters with Colonialism

Towards the end of the 19th century, Somalia was colonised by four countries: Italy, Great Britain, France and Ethiopia, and divided into five parts. Two of these were united to form the Somali Republic in 1960, while two remained under Ethiopian and Kenyan rule. The fifth part gained independence as the Republic of Djibouti (Somali Government, 1962; Drysdale, 1964).

The Somali reaction to colonial rule was initially led by religious leaders. Sayid Mohamed Abdullah Hassan led a Dervish Movement between 1900 and 1921 against British, Italian and Ethiopian forces. Other anti-colonial movements were observed in many parts of Somalia. Examples include the Lafole massacre (1896), the Biimal revolt (1896-1908) and revolts led by Sheikh Hassan Barsane (d.1926) and Sheikh Bashir (d.1945). Most of these movements were suppressed by 1925, and their leaders eliminated or neutralised.

To create new elite, the colonial powers employed Somalis in the lower echelons of the colonial administrative and military hierarchy and opened limited schools for the children of the traditional elite (Pankhurast, 1951:212, 214). Meanwhile, the traditional elite were contained through various forms of persuasion and intimidation. Thus Somalia was gradually incorporated into the colonial economic and political system. Importantly, the anti-colonial sentiment of the early years did not die out entirely, but was transformed into a modern, peaceful struggle for independence (Touval, 1963).

Modern state formation began in Somalia with the establishment of social and political organisations different in form and function from

41

the traditional religious and clan structures. These new social organisations began with the Somali Islamic Association (1925), Khayriyah (1930), Officials Union (1935), and Somali Youth Club (SYC) (1943). Following the Second World War, Somalis began to form more overt political parties: in April 1947, SYC was transformed into the Somali Youth League (SYL), the first national political party in the Italian colony. Meanwhile, in British Somaliland, the Somali National Society (SNS) (established in Berbera in 1945), was transformed into a full-fledged political party in 1948, taking the name of the Somali National League (SNL) (Abdullahi, 2004a:57-87). Many other small political parties also formed in this period; these mostly represented clan politics.

During the Second World War, most of the Somali territory fell under British military administration. At the four powers' conference at the close of the war it was proposed that all Somali territory be placed under British administration.[1] Though hailed by the people of Somalia this plan was rejected by the other great powers, perhaps most importantly thanks to Ethiopian lobbying of the U.S. administration.[2] As a result, the former Italian colony was returned to Italy under UN trusteeship in 1949. Under this arrangement, Italy had to manage the colony and bring it to independence in 1960. During this period, the United States, obsessed with Nasser in Egypt and the march of communism, provided financial support to Somalia's economic development to keep Somalia within its sphere of influence. After ten years, in a haphazard fashion, the Somali Republic gained independence on the 1st July 1960.[3]

The Rise and Fall of the Somali State

Following independence, the Somali state faced a number of profound challenges: poorly trained human resources, a politicised clan system, huge rural migrations, low economic performance,

---

[1] This project was known as the Bevin Plan, named after the then Foreign Minister of Britain.
[2] Ethiopia, according to this plan, would have lost Somali territory it had captured in the 19th century.
[3] 1st July 1960 is the independence day of the Italian colony of Somalia, and the date of its unification with the former British Somaliland that had gained independence on June 26, 1960.

pressure from hostile neighbours, and problems with the integration of different colonial systems. Nevertheless, Somalia had embraced a democratic system of governance, whereby freedom of association and political participation was granted. Two parliamentary and presidential elections were held and embryonic social organisations emerged, strikes and demonstrations were tolerated, and political prisoners were not known. However, this hasty application of democracy in a tradition-bound society ushered in clan conflict, political anarchy and immeasurable political turmoil. The experience of this period could be characterised, to quote Abdulla Mansur, as "democracy gone mad" (1995:114). Somali masses, dismayed with the prevalent corruption and economic stagnation, looked to the army as the only route out of the impasse. Meanwhile, Somalia established closer relations with the USSR in 1963 and received substantial military and economic aid. The superpower rivalry played out in the region with the build-up of both Somalia's and Ethiopia's military forces.

The year 1969 can be considered the first milestone on the road to the collapse of the Somali state. The earlier years of multiparty democratic rule were faltering, and elections had been overtly rigged. In the election of 1969, more than 60 sub-clan based parties took part; yet the ruling SYL party rigged the election and won a majority of the seats (Lewis, 1980:204). Further, SYL absorbed all members of the parliament from the opposition parties to establish one party rule.[1] In sum, the nationalist SYL of the early struggle for independence, domesticated by the colonial powers between 1950 and 1960, had drifted towards one party dictatorial rule in 1969. The grievances against the overt election rigging, rampant bureaucratic corruption, widespread unemployment and a lukewarm Igal government policy of pan-Somalism culminated in further political turmoil and the assassination of President Sharmarke. During this period, the national army was the only organisation qualified to take the lead in saving the collapsing Somali state.

The Somali National Army launched a coup d'état on 21 October 1969, winning support from the majority of the Somali people. Initially, the regime gained support due to improved economic performance, expanding social services and a better culture of governance. Yet after a

---

[1] The former Prime Minister, Mr. Abdirizak Hagi Hussein, alone stayed in the opposition; quipping; Allah is one and I am the one."

short time, the new regime curtailed freedoms and banned all social and political organisations, exercised heavy-handedness on the opposition and practiced extrajudicial detentions and persecutions. Moreover, proclaiming rigorous socialist and nationalist goals, the military regime developed closer relations with the Soviets and launched clan-loaded socialist programs, recruiting members of specific clans for the sensitive departments of security, presidential guard and foreign services. After the first few years of dictatorial regime, resistance began to mount. The first political challenge emerged from within the revolutionary council: some prominent leaders of the regime organised an unsuccessful counter coup in 1971 and its leaders were publicly executed. The second challenge came from the Islamic scholars, who railed against the regime's interference with the Islamic family law. The regime's reaction to the peacefully protesting scholars was imprudent and barbarous. On 23 January 1975, ten leading Islamic scholars were executed and hundreds more prosecuted. Executed officers belonged to Isaq, Majertain and Abgal clans. From then on, their close relatives and sub-lineages were targeted and dealt with as anti-revolutionaries (Abukar, 1992:109-137 and 181-185).

The high profile executions were catalytic to the collapsing of the Somali state. Because the executed officers belonged to three of the major clans, clannish sentiments took on a new dimension, infiltrating the regime, bureaucracy and population at large. Under the pretext of promoting revolutionaries and eliminating anti-revolutionary elements, the regime adopted a covert policy of targeting particular clans and privileging others. Those targeted launched armed rebel factions. Meanwhile, the execution of the Islamic scholars gave new momentum to dormant Islamic movements. Underground organisations proliferated in every region in defence of the faith against the "Godless socialists". At this point, the Islamic movements formulated an ideological foundation and launched reformist social programs. Gradually, the two forces of clanism and Islamism came to unite in favour of regime change, yet they were unable to agree on the means of achieving this goal. The clash between the military regime and these two rival forces opened a crack in the fabric of the Somali society. The regime had toyed with the two strong and inviolable bases of "Somaliness" which are, according to Somali wisdom: "the clan and Islam" (Abdullahi, 2004b; 2001).

The military regime's socialist policies and the 1977-78 war with Ethiopia constitute the second milestone on the road to the collapse. The political situation in 1978 was very similar to that of 1969, when the one party regime was established and political grievances were not addressed but exacerbated. The army had become fragmented, and its command structure had lost its independence and professionalism, becoming an inseparable part of the party and the regime. That is why the attempted coup d'état of 9 April 1978 was easily foiled, resulting in the execution of 18 army officers and the detention of hundreds. The coup plotters who fled began to form armed oppositions, receiving assistance from hostile neighbours, particularly Ethiopia. The regime adopted a policy of extreme security measures, pitting "friendly" clans against others labelled as the enemies of the Somali nation.

In 1978, the first armed faction was established. Throughout the 1980s, a succession of such clannish armed factions – like the Somali Salvation Democratic Front (SSDF) (1978), the Somali National Movement (SNM) (1981), the United Somali Congress (USC) (1989), and the Somali Patriotic Movement (SPM) (1988) – began to establish bases in Ethiopia. These clannish factions lacked both organisational capacity and national vision, and failed to formulate a common strategy to seize control of the state. Thus without any coordination, USC forces overran the presidential residence in Mogadishu on 26 January 1991, bringing the military regime to its disgraceful conclusion. Meanwhile, the SNM gained control of the northern cities, and the SPM established a similar presence in the south. Thus on that 26th of January, the Somali State ceased to operate and a brutal civil war broke out. The centrifugal forces of Somali clannish particularism overwhelmed the centripetal forces of nationalism and Islam. Since that date, Somalia has been the only country in the world without a functioning central government.

Theory of State Capability

As amply noted by Tessman (Ch. 2), state capability is measured by the capacity of a state to 'penetrate society, regulate social relationships, extract resources, and appropriate or use resources in determined ways' (Migdal, 1988:4). Strong states normally perform these tasks effectively, while weak states perform poorly in each of these four categories. With this classification, comparative state

45

capacities can be calculated relative to their governance capabilities. The measurable indicator is the state's performance in delivering the most fundamental "political good," that is, effectively supplying security to citizens and inhabitants within the state's borders. Thus it is the prime responsibility of the state to thwart external threats and to check and diminish domestic threats. Second in the hierarchy of "political goods" is establishing effective systems for arbitrating disputes and maintaining law and order. Third in the hierarchy of "political goods" is delivering essential infrastructure like roads and railways and social services such as health care, education and protection of the environment. Fourth in the hierarchy of "political goods" is supplying and protecting the arteries of commerce and providing a space for civil society (Rotberg, 2003a:2-4). According to the literature on state capability and performance in developmental and security studies, states can be placed on a developmental continuum, classifying them as "strong," "weak," "failed" or "collapsed".

Strong states are those that effectively 'control their territories and deliver a full range and a high quality of political goods to their citizens' (Rotberg, 2003b:3-5). Their high performance can be detected through recognised indicators, like 'per capita GDP, the UNDP Human Development Index, Transparency International's Corruption Perceptions Index, and Freedom House's Freedom of the World Report' (Rotberg, 2003b:2). Strong states also tend to show higher marks on the eight major characteristics of good governance: they are participatory, consensus oriented, accountable, transparent, responsive, effective and efficient, equitable and inclusive and following of the rule of law. Moreover, corruption is minimised, the views of minorities are taken into account and the voices of the society's most vulnerable are heard in decision making. Strong states are also responsive to the present and future needs of the society.

Weak states include both those developing in a positive direction towards being a strong state, and those moving in a negative direction towards being a failing state. Those moving towards failure include states that may be weak for a variety of geographical, physical and economic reasons, or due to problems with internal cohesion or an adequate political system. Weak states in general fail to solve ethnic, religious, linguistic, or other grievances that might culminate in tension and conflict. The capability of the state to provide satisfactory "political goods" is low; the physical infrastructure often shows signs of erosion. Most of the indicators (such as per capita GDP) are falling, corruption is escalating, the rule of law is diminished, civil society is harassed and despots rule (Rotberg, 2004:1-45). Some weak states, ruled by an autocracy, show high levels of security, though they provide few other political goods. Examples of such states are Somalia under Siad Barre, Cambodia under Pol Pot, Iraq under Saddam Hussein, and Belarus, Turkmenistan, Libya, and North Korea of 2006.

Failed States include two extremes. One is when a state is no longer capable of functioning; the other is when a state becomes "too effective," too intrusive into the private realms of its citizens. The first form of state failure is visible in a state's limited ability to provide essential political goods. Most of the institutions in a failed state are defective; legislatures are often merely rubber stamps for a strong executive, and the judiciary has little credibility in the eyes of the citizens. The bureaucracy is unaccountable, unprofessional, and unresponsive to the public. The infrastructure of a failed state is damaged; utilities like telecommunications, water and power supply are in disarray. Social service facilities (schools and hospitals) are crumbling. National literacy rates fall and infant mortality rates rise. Most of the industrial projects no longer function and unemployment becomes rampant. All of this causes the population to become dissatisfied with state performance and lose hope. International investors shy away, inflation skyrockets and local currency loses its value. Security forces cooperate with criminals and collect illegal taxations. The middle class shrinks and migrates. Loyalty to the state diminishes and patriotism/nationalism fades away in favour of more parochial loyalties. Finally, failed states offer enormous economic opportunity for a privileged few who use the prevailing scarcity to enrich themselves through corruption and patronage.

A *Collapsed State* is the extreme form of a failed state. States collapse when their structure and political authority fall apart and law and order collapse. Meanwhile, an extensive breakdown in social coherence occurs as civil society can no longer create, aggregate and articulate the support and demands upon which a state relies. States do not collapse overnight; rather, they do so as a result of an incremental process of decay. They pass through stages of weakness and failure before collapse. The process of decay usually begins when the government loses the ability to exert legitimate authority over the entire territory of its jurisdiction. Following this, communities often realign along ethnic, kinship and cultural lines. Security becomes the rule of the strong. Sub-state actors such as business groups, religious leaders, and clan elders may take over and attempt to restore some form of functionality to the parts of the collapsed state, yet recovering the capability of the original state requires strong external support. Collapsed states can recover partially by returning to the status of a failed state if sufficient security is restored to rebuild the institutions and strengthen the legitimacy of the resuscitated state. Lebanon did so thanks to Syrian security, Tajikistan because of Russia, Afghanistan because of the U.S. led invasion and Sierra Leone thanks to the intervention of the Economic Community of West African States (ECOWAS) and the help of the wider international community spearheaded by Britain (Rotberg, 2003b).

States do not collapse without conflict. The causes of conflict can be divided into "original causes," "operational causes," and "proximate efficient causes." The "original causes" are those deeply rooted conditions that date to the very formation of the society or state. "Operational causes" nurture a possible conflict and deepen its probabilities, depending on the magnitude and pervasiveness of the original causes. "Proximate and efficient causes" serve as trigger mechanisms for the outbreak of the conflict. Theories consider "primordial," "class," and "eclectic" bases as the prime causes for conflicts.

The Primordial Theory is based on the premise that group identities – clan, sub-clan or racial groups – are things people are either born with or that emerge through deep psychological processes. The implication is that these identities cannot be changed, and that individual choices are permanently defined by these identities. Accordingly, in a nation of clans like Somalia, when conflicts occur, people are organised by their primordial attachments. In this theory, a hegemonic pattern of relations can exist in which one group controls the others. George Kaly Kieth and Ida Rousseau Mukenge (2002:10) explain how hegemonic patterns function within postcolonial states. The Somali example in particular shows how specific clans have dominated political power structures to gain economic privileges. Consequently, civil and military elites belonging to marginalised clans have formed armed insurgencies.

48

The Class Theory, which may be identified also as the Marxist theory, is based on the argument that every society has its mode of production, and that each member of a society falls in this mode of production into either the owning or the subaltern class. The owning class controls the means of production and determines the allocation and distribution of resources. This leads to the exploitation of one class by the other and, subsequently, class conflict. Importantly, however, the actual eruption of conflict requires further conditions, including consciousness of the exploitation and the organisation necessary to wage class struggle.

The Eclectic Theory holds that conflict is the product of a confluence of cultural, economic, historical, political, social, and other factors. This theory suggests that any one variable is insufficient to explain the complexity of war. Thus individual and regional disparities, political repression, the abuse of human rights, the concentration of power at the political centre, and the willingness of neighbouring states to interfere in domestic political conflicts can all contribute to conflict.

The remaining pages of the chapter explore the plethora of perspectives on the collapse of the Somali state produced by Somalist scholars. These will be classified according to their focus before a comprehensive model is constructed to link all the causes together.

Perspectives on the Collapse of the Somali State

Academics have looked at the collapse of the Somali state from a variety of perspectives. These include Cold War and foreign aid, Somali irredentism and the war with Ethiopia, primordialism, resource overextension, moral degradation and eclectic explanations.

The Cold War and Foreign Aid Explanation

The influence of the Cold War and foreign aid has been the focus of a number of scholars, including Terrence Lyons, Walter S. Clarke, Robert Gosende, Ahmed Samatar, Ken Menkhaus and John Prendergast. Lyons has tied the collapse of the Somali state to the withdrawal of external assistance and the increased demand for improved political goods (Lyons and Samatar, 1995:1). Clarke and Gosende (2000:129-158) agree with Lyons, but not entirely. To them,

'Somalia's failure may be only partially related to the end of the Cold War.' Samatar has related the collapse to a triple burden:

> Bearing the triple burden of defeat in the war and accompanying humiliation, an economy on the skids and a lack of super power patronage, Somali politics turns inward. The national focus became the regime and the state, which were caught in an enveloping atmosphere of acridity and suspension (1994:117).

Menkhaus extended this point, though perhaps overemphasising the role of external assistance:

> It may be an exaggeration to claim that the Somali state is a creation of external assistance, but it is indisputable that the state has never been remotely sustainable by domestic sources of revenue. As far back as the 1950s, observers worried that an independent Somali state would not be economically viable.

With, Menkhaus, Prendergast went even further:

> There was never in Somalia's history a sustainable basis for a viable central state authority. In the past, the Somali state was funded almost entirely by Cold War driven foreign aid, leading to a bloated and artificial structure which collapsed soon after that aid was frozen in the late 1980s (1995).

The Theory of Somali Irredentism and the War with Ethiopia

The Somali irredentism and the war with Ethiopia have been raised as factors contributing to the collapse by Lyons, Jeffrey A. Lefebvre and Peter Woodward. Again, Lyons emphasised the historicity of the causes of the collapse, pointing to the Somali national aspiration for unity:

> The point here is [nationalism] as an ideology; it encouraged leaders in Mogadishu to pursue foreign policies that inherently led the state into conflict with neighbours that had rival claims to the Somali-inhabited territories. Somalia's arguments under the principle of greater Somalia were antithetical to Ethiopia, Kenya and Djibouti's insistence on the principle of territorial integrity and sanctity of

colonial border, principles these states were prepared to defend by force if necessary (1994:193).

For Lefebvre,

Siad's demise and the disintegration of the Somali state were not only a consequence of clan politics but are attributable in part to Somalia's irredentist foreign policy, principally that aspect of it aimed at Ethiopia (1993:47).

On the other hand, Woodward related the Somali state failure to domestic factors, while describing border permeability as only a part of the problem:

While destruction of Somalia state as constituted from 1960 was primarily due to domestic factors, the issue of the permeability of the state's border was also relevant... Border permeability was to work against Somalia from 1978 as Ethiopia hosted Siyad Barre's growing number of opponents (1996:82).

Woodward also argued that the opposition's struggle to overthrow the regime developed into the destruction of the state.

In terms of state collapse, Somalia appears to be the most complete experience in the Horn. The building of Somali socialism in the 1970s contributed much to making state and regime increasingly synonymous; the reverse of that coin was the long political narrowing of the regime after the 1977-78 war with Ethiopia, which finally brought the destruction of the state with the overthrow of the regime (1996:81).

The Theory of Primordialism

Proponents of the primordialist theory include I. M. Lewis, Said Samatar, Anna Simons and Okbazghi Yohannes. This approach is based on the argument that the segmentary lineage social system is antithetical to the state. As Lewis argued, "the collapse of the colonially created state represents technically a triumph for the segmentary lineage system and political power of kinship" (1994:223). Indeed, Samatar stretched the clan factor to dominance: "Somali polity is

51

shaped," he argued, "by a single, central principle that overrides all others, namely the phenomenon that social anthropologists call 'the segmentary lineage system'" (2005). Finally, Yohannes takes the concept of primordialism to the end. In his view,

> In the first place, there has never been a State in Somalia in the strictest sense of the term. Somalia is a country of clans where the beginnings of a modern State have been only in the making in the midst of capricious forces of history within the context of a unitary capitalist order and yet politically compartmentalized system (1997:225).

The Resource Overextension Explanation

Ambassador Mohamed Osman once criticised the Somali leadership on their planning goals. He saw overextension reducing the capacity of the state by undertaking too many tasks too quickly. Osman what the priority for the new Somali state should be: consolidating the state or focussing on the Greater Somalia project? For him, building domestic institutions ought to be the priority. 'Perhaps,' he wrote:

> We devoted too much of our attention and resources to overcoming the disabilities, problems and disputes which we inherited from our colonial masters and which, naturally, led us to involvement in external struggle, giving us no time to consolidate the gains of our national freedom by creating and developing the institutions without which no nation in modern times can survive (Osman 1992).

The Moral Degradation Theory

Few scholars in the available English literature have focussed on the role of moral degradation in the collapse. This concept is, however, widely employed by Somali Islamic scholars. For many, the collapse was due to the Somali state's secularism, moral degradation and the unprincipled expediency of the leadership. Others have recently begun to voice similar sentiments. For Ahmed Samatar 'it is one of later arguments that at the heart of the Somali catastrophe is a full breakdown of culture (e.g., Heer, Islam)' (1994:129).[1] In my view, as I

---

[1] *Heer* means Somali traditional laws on which social order is based.

have discussed elsewhere in an attempt to see how the indigenous ideologies – Islam and clanism – were suppressed and perverted and how they became radicalised in the late 1970s:

> Only Islam possesses [if not used as radical ideology] the essential ingredients for successfully integrating the various elements of Somali society and providing stable government capable of meeting the urgent social, political and economic needs of the country (Abdullahi, 1992:122).

Moreover, in the Somali situation, immoral state policies including not offering enough weight to the Islamic factor had finally contributed to the collapse of state institutions (Abdullahi 2004b). Mark Huband remarked that

> Throughout the civil war, Somalia's religious leaders argued that the application of the shari'a was the sole route by which social order can be restored; they contend that the clan-based political structure, which endured colonialism and dictatorship, has failed to achieve a political resolution at a national level (1998:33).

The Eclectic Explanation

Proponents of the "eclectic" explanation of the Somali state collapse include Bradbury, Kieth, Mukende, Samatar, and Hussein Adam. When asked why Somalia collapsed so completely as opposed to its neighbours, Bradbury answered:

> There is little value in identifying single causal explanations for war and state collapse in Somalia. To focus solely on the contradictions between a foreign imposed colonial system of government and an indigenous political system would be to overlook the impact of the oppressive, corrupt and violent system of political patronage that marked the 21 year military rule of Mohamed Siad Barre (1969-1991), the influence of Cold War and post-Cold War politics in the region, the impact of structural adjustment and economic liberalization policies in the 1980s and the character of the armed movements in Somalia (cited in Feldman and Slattery 2003).

Kieth and Mukenge also saw complex causes behind the collapse:

The Somali civil war is the product of the synergy of contingent and proximate factors. In the case of the former, the factors are the evolution of the Somali state, its incorporation into the global capitalist system, and the failure of the first experiment at state-building... The latter factors are the repression, exploitation, economic deprivation, social malaise, and manipulation of primordial identities visited on Somalia by the dictatorial regime of General Mohammed Siad Barre (2002:124).

Thus, Adam has criticised single factor analysis by arguing that

One cannot satisfactorily explain problems of political disorder by using an anthropologically determinist approach.... Recently, perhaps angered by this emphasis on primordial sentiment, some scholars have turned to class analysis within the context of global development and under development but have tended to fall into another form of single-factor analysis (1992:11-26).

Therefore, he posits that Somalia collapsed because of "personal rule, military rule, clan rule, poisoning clan relations, urban state terror, neo-fascist campaigns against the north and dwindled international aid" (Adam, 1995:69-89).

Ahmed Samatar has echoed these sentiments, organising the causes of the collapse as follows:

... a dictatorial regime which created a bad culture of governance, a lack of national leadership as a result of prolonged dictatorial rule, and low education and the poverty of the population as a result of the failed developmental programs (cited in Mao, 2004).

Mapping the Perspectives

The above perspectives display a number of related themes regarding the collapse of the Somali state. To recapitulate, the major causes described in the literature are (1) the end of the Cold War and withdrawal of foreign aid; (2) Somali irredentism and war with Ethiopia; (3) primordialism and rampant political clanism; (4) cultural decay and moral corruption; (5) dictatorship based on clanism; and (6) state overextension. Putting all factors in a continuum, we can classify them into three categories.

Original Causes or Genesis

These include the colonial division of the Somali territory into five parts, the offering of a great portion of this territory to Ethiopia, and segmentation of the Somali society into clan-based mini-states. These two factors could be considered objective factors underscoring the collapse, as they caused the formation of a weak and deformed state. To these points we might also add economic underdevelopment and the lack of adequately trained human resources. The historical period relevant to these causes is the time prior to the independence of Somalia in 1960. It is worth noting here that only the clan-based system is indigenous to Somali people; the other three factors are inherited from the colonial rule.

Operational Causes

The subjective factors that deepened the conflict include state policies of irredentism; the negative impact of the Cold War on the Horn of Africa; unresolved conflict with neighbouring countries; the low capacity of leadership; and socio-political and economic under-development. The military dictatorship, socialist rhetoric and moral decay also contributed greatly. These factors led the Somali state from a weak state to a failed state. This situation prevailed from Somalia's independence (1960) until its defeat in the war with Ethiopia (1978). These five factors were partially inherited from the colonial era, yet Somalis missed opportunities to deal with them. Irredentism seems to have caused militarism and the war with Ethiopia, which in turn affected socio-economic programs. All this happened, however, due to the low capacity of leadership and problematic state policies.

Proximate and Efficient Causes

Proximate and efficient causes are the direct causes of the collapse. These include: the war with Ethiopia and defeat of the Somali army, the end of the Cold War and the cutting off of foreign aid, the continuation of militaristic clan-based dictatorship and the emergence of clannish armed factions. These causes began with the Somali defeat in the war with Ethiopia and continued until the total collapse of the

Somali state in 1991. The government of Somalia failed to use political democratisation and economic liberalisation to absorb the effect of its defeat in the war with Ethiopia. Instead, it opted for more repressive measures that targeted specific clans. These policies provoked the formation of more armed factions in Ethiopia.

Conclusion

The above analyses have shown that the Somali state was a deficient hybrid of Somali historical states from the precolonial era and an imposed colonial system of governance. The resultant organisation produced a political, economic and social system inadequate for governing the Somali society. It neither succeeded in suppressing the traditional system nor accommodated it within a new hybrid. As a result, the colonial rulers left Somalis jubilant at independence in 1960, but also vulnerable to the ramifications of a very weak state.

Examining the various perspectives, it is evident that the collapse of the Somali state occurred during its search for a final state identity, a "Greater Somalia." Pursuing that nationalist goal, successive Somali governments created military parity with Ethiopia, and entered a devastating war in 1977-78. The defeat of the Somali army in the war was indeed the beginning of the downfall of the very idea the army was founded upon: Somali nationalism. The aftermath of the war was catastrophic, with much fighting between the government and Ethiopia-supported armed Somali oppositions. Thus from a resource management perspective, it could be surmised that the over-stretching of resources in the quest for a "Greater Somalia" – without consolidating the immature state – was the major contributing factor to the collapse.

There are, however, many states in the third world on the verge of social fragmentation and economic disaster, yet few have reached the point of total breakdown. Some have experienced violent civil wars and regime changes while also remaining intact. Some collapsed states have recovered within a short period of time. So what makes Somalia a unique case? Somali distinctiveness, in my view, is grounded in its double segmentation: the natural primordial divisions and externally created divisions. Its clan segmentation developed into political clanism, divisive in nature and destructive to the state, while external segmentation triggered the emergence of irredentist Somali

56

nationalism. These two segmentations were exploited and deepened by the elite to achieve political power and by external actors during the Cold War great power rivalry to further their national interests.

The ultimate responsibility for the collapse lies primarily on the shoulders of Somalia's leadership. Every country faces challenges, which leaders ought to deal with. It is evident that during this particular period of its history, Somalia lacked capable and competent leaders. Both the ruling regime and the leaders of the armed opposition groups failed to find ways of preventing the state collapse.

Chapter 4

INCLUSIVE BUT UNEQUAL: THE ENIGMA OF THE 14TH SNRC AND THE FOUR-POINT-FIVE (4.5) FACTOR

Mohamed A. Eno

Lose the support and dedication of the people, and you lose all possibilities for building the community and the nation."
– Mohamed Eno

Introduction

After about 13 futile national peace and reconciliation conferences, the regional member states of the Inter-Governmental Authority on Development (IGAD), with assistance from well wishers of the international community, considered yet another attempt to convene a Somali conference (2002), the objective of which was to reconcile that country's communities and overcome the curse of statelessness. It was a poor decision because there was no credible authority to tackle the insecurity, illegal migration and other social evils the region was experiencing – from the smuggling of illegal arms and narcotics (Adan, 2003), and trafficking of illegal immigrants (human cargo), to the fighting in Somalia of "Proxy wars between Ethiopia and Eritrea" (Farah, Hussein, and Lind, 2002) – as a consequence of Somalia's lawlessness.

These ills and evils being the realities in the region, compounded by disaffection with the Arte initiative of Djibouti (which raised Abdikassim Salad to power in 2000), Ethiopia's multidimensional campaigning for the convention of the conference and its ensuing multifaceted manoeuvring and manipulation of proceedings in Eldoret and Mbagathi were discernible. The effort regarding the convention of the conference was a compliment to the IGAD Council of Ministers, who charged the Frontline States of Ethiopia, Djibouti and Kenya to jointly plan and organize the conference, and Kenya was to be the host.

Ills of an Amorphous Conference

The flow of the arriving contingents of delegates escalated commotion and crises that persistently haunted the receptionists and the organizers alike, especially in the provision of accommodation and catering. Within a short period, the number of the delegates sprouted up from the "official" 400 or so participants to a soaring 800, most of whom were equipped with official invitation letters. As one delegate remarked, "Participation has become for purchase."

Within the first three days or so, it appeared that the majority of the participants in IGAD's original list had most likely been selected on terms of "who is for" and "who is against" a certain Frontline State. Another mystery was how certain names got onto the list, while others were sinisterly expunged from it. It seemed there were no proper criteria used in the selection of the delegates to the various categories of participation. An example of this is the civil society category, which consisted of participants from diverse walks of life, from former warlords and war financiers to former ministers in Barre's failed regime.

"Mafia-like gangs and syndicates" were colluding with officials of the IGAD Technical Committee in garnering support of one kind or another. As Elijah Mwangale, the first Chairman of the IGAD Technical Committee of the Frontline, once admitted in a plenary, "a lot of things are going on. Dollars have reached even my doorstep." It was an open secret that collusions and business transactions were looming in the corridors of the hotels and offices; every financially capable warlord or prominent personality of a clan or sub-clan bought their way through to the inner circles of the Conference in order to defend their interests.

Uganda's president, Yoweri K. Museveni, once a warlord himself, referred to the conference as a "...long and torturous process..." Short of mentioning that it was due to collective foul-play by IGAD, representatives of the international community as well as members of the Somali delegates all played a part in the undesirable circumstances leading to the prolongation of the process as an amorphous exercise. It was even more torturous to the oppressed, unarmed communities like the Jareer and the outcasts who were denied social or human equality in the eyes of the international community.

There were no proper instructions to inform the participants beforehand about what meetings to attend and in which hall. Most of the meetings were arranged in a humdrum state, either following short notice or, in most cases, communicating to the delegates overnight through the bulletin board in the Sirikwa Hotel, which accommodated the offices of the IGAD Technical Committee and a section of the delegates. The other participants, who were lodged elsewhere, had to be informed by a friend or find out about events if chance brought them to Sirikwa the following morning.

In the course of the exercise, especially in the early stages, each member of the TC focused on a specific area of interest. Ethiopia focused its effort on recruiting a formidable group to subscribe to its policy toward Somalia in order to secure a large number of votes for its preferred candidate in the event of the presidential election. Commenting on this, Samatar and Samatar (2003) remarked, "Ethiopia and allies continued to try to gerrymander both the composition and quantity of the delegates." Adan Mohamed's statement comes in clear support of Samatar and Samatar as he writes, "The latest center of dispute was the claim that Djibouti and Ethiopia were unduly interfering with the talks for their specific interests" (Adan, 2002).

Kenya being the host country and seeing its partners' undiplomatic attitude, focused its attention on the misappropriation of funds by entering into dubious business deals with the hoteliers and transporters of the delegates. As the local media later reported, unscrupulous agreements were signed and fattened bills and invoices were concocted and paid for, eventually leading to shame and scandal prompting donors' reaction and displeasure. The scandal was assuaged in diplomatic corridors and through the replacement of the chairman and part of his team, ushering in the appointment of career diplomat ambassador Bethuel Kiplagat. Subsequently, the conference was moved from Eldoret to Mbagathi, on the outskirts of Nairobi, marking the completion of the Six Committee work deliberated on in the Second Phase.

Djibouti, the mentor and host of the 13th Somali National Peace Conference project, which groomed Abdikassim Salad for the presidency after a 4-month long meeting in the town of Arte, was also playing soft and shadowy diplomacy in its quest to help reinstall Salad, but not as openly or as visibly as their rival Ethiopia.

Deficiencies Disdained

The shifting of the conference to Mbagathi, Nairobi, envisaged a strategic move to reflect a shift in significance, following regime change in Kenya. Another viable reason was, according to the newly appointed Ambassador Bethuel Kiplagat, "...to change the image of the conference and give it wider and positive media coverage." True to his word, the conference was in a desperate need of a good samaritan the nature of events in Eldoret were deplorable, comparable only to the routine activities in the lawless Bakaraha Market.

Although Kiplagat's scheme to minimize the cost of the conference and improve its image could be commendably attributed to both his professionalism and good intentions, he couldn't save himself from falling into Ethiopia's trap of manipulations. In his lenient manner he once indicated to the Harmonization Committee that, "...whatever the case, I want to keep Ethiopia on board." Perhaps he did not consider at the time how costly it was to keep Ethiopia on board.

Furthermore, Ambassador Kiplagat's long career in the diplomatic and international relations arenas proved short when he could not persuade or convince Ethiopia to appoint professional reconciliators/mediators who could apply a meaningful, ethics-based, unbiased and actual form of reconciliation. After the commotion and complains became unbearable, it was no longer a secret as a Nairobi-based daily reported that, "Critics have accused the moderators in the Nairobi talks of concentrating more on power-sharing than reconciling the various factions" (Karoney, 2003). Obviously, the agenda IGAD had put in place was about power-sharing. Deficiency from the lack of reconciliatory measures ripped off all the institutions in the conference without sparing the well-respected Somali primates.

The Somali clerics arrived, already split into factions (or sects?): Babu-Sufi, Islah, Itihad, Ahlul-Sunna Wal-Jama'a, etc. They criticized and frequently called each other names, behavior which does not augur well with objective reconciliation. Astonishingly, in the opening sessions of the meetings, especially in the plenary and civil society gatherings, the clerics were at the forefront reciting verses from the Holy Qur'an; they supplicated and advised the delegates to maintain unity and Somaliness. But when it came to manipulation and nomination to committees, they would put the Holy Book aside and settle their differences the temperamental Somali way before returning to the verses and traditions.

At a glance, a disparity arises between the misleading 4-word title or theme, 'Somali National Reconciliation Conference,' and the actual occurrences that prevailed in the course of the conference, especially when taken into consideration the points elaborated below.

Owing to massive foreign domination and manipulation under the umbrella of IGAD, the conference was not Somali-driven. Worse, it was contrary to the original concept which reads: "The IGAD Council of Ministers emphasized that the Somali Peace Process should be Somali-owned and Somali-driven".[1] In his words, chairman Mwangale confirmed IGAD's role by retorting, "The approach of the Frontline States is not to prescribe solutions but create a basis for dialogue," though unfortunately, it remains common knowledge that no dialogue for reconciliation has taken place. Instead, as Hussein Aideed emotionally stated on a local TV, "The whole process is driven by circulars of instructive statements," and that the IGAD TC should remain "...as facilitators, not as managers," which portrays the hoodwink and twist administered on the initial guidelines given by the IGAD Council of Ministers. Aideed even went further, censuring the IGAD Frontline States as people who have "...neither will nor desire to continue the conference."

A major stakeholder and part and parcel of the Union of the Republic of Somalia, the administration of the Northern brothers was not officially present. Many farsighted Somali delegates and notables reiterated the necessity of Somaliland to the conference. Though earlier reports confirm IGAD's willingness to bring Somaliland on board, it was later undermined. According to the initial proposal,

> The Ministers re-affirmed a need to invite Somaliland to the conference and requested the TC makes efforts to invite Somaliland to attend the conference. They however recognized that Somaliland is not to be equated with factions and that the invitation to Somaliland

---

[1] See "Somali National Reconciliation Conference" at www.somali-civilsociety.org

be worded differently from that of other Somali parties (Somali Civil
Society, see website at the foot of the page)

Sheer reluctance and a hidden agenda on the part of the IGAD
Frontline States kept the conference from being nationalized. The
controversial case surrounding Somaliland's participation suggests that
the invitation was probably withheld as a last resort 'lucky-card' to be
used for subversive bargains for the future gains of a particular
member state of the IGAD Technical Committee.

(c) Because the Conference began with the factional philosophy of
gaining numerical supremacy of participants, which overshadowed all
other sectors of the proceedings, and consequently ended with the
same, there was no reconciliation, convened or achieved, worthy of
mention. Professor Abdi I. Samatar (2003) issued a clear comment on
the episode in a workshop in Nairobi, affirming, "We had facilitators,
not reconciliators."

In the 2-year life span of the conference, neither the organizers
(IGAD) nor the donors fulfilled requirements of reconciliation
necessary to put on track a society so divided and disgruntled along
tribal lines, polarized by centuries of feuding vendetta that funneled
xenophobia impregnated with hatred and antagonism.

(d) Although it was dubbed a conference, the proceedings of the
gathering left a lot to be desired to call it one. The lack of a workable
day-to-day agenda, the delegates being locked out of their rooms,
denied meals on several occasions for delay or lack of payment, the
pulling out of several of the warlords, the settlement of conference-
related disagreements on wars inside the country in contravention of a
cease-fire agreement[21] undertaken at the early stage of the conference
and signed by all the warlords and faction leaders, and the
contemporaneous dissonances and dissensions within the midst of the
IGAD Frontline States, all provide us with a sober contemplation that
the Somali Reconciliation Conference, despite the thematic title, was
derailed from the course expected of such an exhausting and expensive
meeting.

On the other hand, while not entirely disagreeing with Abdi I.
Samatar's statement that IGAD was a facilitator and not a reconciliator,
because the frontline countries preferred to be seen as such, my own
experience and observation as an official participant reveals more than
that. In a broad spectrum, "Facilitation is the process of helping a

group complete a task, solve a problem or come to agreement to the mutual satisfaction of the participants" (Kelsey & Plumb, 1999:7). Facilitation, in this paradigm, requires some tools and skills, which are essential to equip the facilitator so that he/she is aware of the process' multiple implications. Secondly, considering the importance of the conference and its input in human and material resources and the aspirations entwined in the intrinsic national morale, IGAD should have foreseen the prerequisite for professional facilitators and mediators to manage and consult the proceedings of the conference to attain the desired goals.

From day one, the Frontline States have compromised the traditional principles of facilitation. By this, I mean to note that IGAD's role during the two-year long process of the Conference was in no way focused on the tradition of "what would serve the group best?" (ibid), but rather what would best serve an individual faction subscribing to a particular member of the Frontline States and its interests. As such, the true qualities for the achievement of effective facilitation were lacking in their totality. Rather than act as pure facilitators, certain members of the IGAD Technical Committee and other 'friendly' countries misconceived their role, putting themselves in rivalry with each other and again with the disputing Somali factions. Practically, the nature of gerrymandering has made IGAD another stakeholder in the status of a faction, facilitating their own participation in multiple roles, maneuvering and manipulating the proceedings and influencing the decisions. Obviously there is a bulk of evidence to support their biases against certain factions and individual participants, while at the same time serving as consultants to the opposing rivals. Copies of complaints to the Technical Committee and press reports suggest persistent anomalies of bias and ring-leadership (Koroney, 2003).

Extrinsic Moral Integrity versus Intrinsic Moral Hypocrisy

Upon completion of the First Phase, marred by complaints, irregularities and confusion, Six Committees were formed to discuss, deliberate and report on respective areas of important national interest. Of these, Committee One, charged with the task of drafting a Provisional Charter, split into two sub-groups. The Committee, which included heavyweights in the legal profession, failed to consent on three issues:

a. Classification, interpretation and acquisition of citizenship.
b. Adoption of the Federal system of governance.
c. Adoption of the national language.

In brief analysis, Group A was in favor of the defunct theory of Greater Somalia, according to which, Somalis born in the periphery of the Somali Republic – born in Kenya's Northeastern Province (formerly N.F.D – Northern Frontier Districts), Ogaden in Ethiopia (which makes the part called Zone Five) and Djibouti (former French Somaliland) – would enjoy equal citizenship rights and status with Somalis born in the Republic. The rival subgroup B was against this idea, as those Somalis make up a constituent part of other jurisdictions, which are independent sovereign states in which ethnic Somalis hold cabinet as well as top decision-making positions.

The other contentious issue was the language. Group A preferred Arabic to be on equal footing and importance with Somali Maxaatiri as an official language, an issue which does not reflect a proper societal justification except on interest basis to please the Arab League countries. Group B had a case to press for Maay language, which is spoken as a mother tongue and lingua franca in almost all the Southern regions of the country, rather than the importation and imposition of Arabic, a language that is alien to the Somali people.

Group B, the Digil-Mirifle proponents of the Federal system of governance, had a long dream for federalism that was rooted in colonial days, when the political leaders of the community unequivocally expressed their sentiment to delegates from the Four Power Commission visiting Somalia for opinion-gathering and fact-finding mission regarding the UN Trusteeship and subsequent independence. Touval visits the federalism political ideology of the Digil-Mirifle:

> On the question of the constitutional form of the proposed union, however, the H.D.M.S. (Hizbi Democratic Mustaqal Somali) retained a distinct point of view, advocating for a federal constitution for the future Somali state. This position was reiterated in 1958 when Jelani

> Sheikh bin Sheikh, at that time the party president, said in a speech to the party convention that the party has become convinced that the only method of unifying the Somalis...is through a federal constitution which accords full regional autonomy (Touval, 1963:96-97).

Touval brings to our attention another community/political leader, Sheikh Abdullah, then the party president, who when asked by the Soviet member whether "he is not interested in the political activities of the country," replied, "I have only interest in the Digil Mirifle." In answer to another query, he stated, "When we asked for the trusteeship, we only meant for the country where the Digil Mirifle live, not the rest of the country. We do not mean the rest of Somalia" (ibid).

The controversial division of the Charter Committee into two polar sub-groups is historically laden in the pre-independence political philosophies. Group A, therefore, stood for the reminiscent ideology of the SYL, whose members were opponents of the federal system, with a tendency for a centralized unitary system of government and a Greater Somalia ideology, which Hussein Ali Dualeh (2002) claims "died a natural death" when Djibouti declined to join the Somali Republic upon attainment of independence in 1977. In any case, one year preceding independence, July 1959, then Prime Minister Abdullahi Issa was quoted as saying:

> In the interest of union among the Somali and in the interest of the very safeguarding of the Nation, the Government herewith declares that it does not pursue any regionalist or federalist goal, because unity alone can ensure the durable existence of a Somali national life (quoted in Touval, 1963:97).

These two faculties of thought had a hard political tussle for over 12 months, a scenario which on several intermittent occasions brought the Conference onto the verge of collapse. To save the situation, an arbitration committee, various harmonization committees and a retreat session were established as approaches toward a solution, but the contention was solid. Eventually, a harmonized Charter was agreed upon. The Digil-Mirifle won the day, particularly with the adoption of two key elements: 1) Maay-Maay as an official super-ordinate language parallel with its Maxaatiri counterpart, and 2) Federalism as the administrative political ideology of a Federal Somali Republic.

Maay and Maxaatiri Languages: as Equal as Distinct

In another dynamic socio-political turn-around, the Digil-Mirifle, traditionally despised for their distance from the location and genealogy of 'nobility,' emerged with tremendous victories in the social, military and political domains, achieving respect and recognition they would have never aspired to before taking up arms and liberating the Reewing land from Aideed's Habar-Gidir sub-clan of the Hawiye clan. After Aideed's defeat and other preceding triumphs over certain Darod sub-clans, the Reewing Resistance Army (RRA) and its community became a robust group to reckon with. In Conferences convened prior to the last two or three meetings, the Digil-Mirifle confederation was not deemed of equal participation and posts as compared to the Dir, Hawiye and Darod, owing to the invasion and subsequent conquest of key areas of their territory by troops of the late Mohamed Farah Aideed.

Understandably, therefore, the adamancy on the Federal system and the official super-ordination of the Maay language were invigorated primarily by the military might that erected the Reewing community as equals, rubbing shoulders with their Samale brethren. Only after ethno-political equality was realized were the other social issues tabled for debate, discussion and consequent approval. All other things being unequal, it would be beyond imagination for the northerly to have lifted the Maay language to official status and equal to the Maxaatiri language adopted as the official national medium in 1972, when the nomadic northerners were at the helm of their dictatorship.

The charter theme drove a precarious wedge between the Maay and certain communities of Maxaa speakers, creating a dreadful standoff and a stalemate that almost disbanded the conference. Thus, the proposal that each group work on its preferential draft charter has enlivened the inspiration of the multi-ethnogenetic Digil-Mirifle confederacy and the will for their political identity through the exercise of their age-old federalism ideology – a prestige in vertical identity mobility by virtue of their language of culture. Among other things, the factors lending a back-up support to the Digil-Mirifle argument were:

(a) Their acquisition of a militia power-base, which made them militarily equal to the other armed militia, and

(b) The logical dilemma of which language qualifies to the status of lingua franca – the vastly spoken local Maay language acquired as first and mother language by communities of native Somalis, or the alien and imported Arabic which has to be learned as a third or foreign language?

Most of the proponents of the mythical monolinguality faculty of thought shied away from responding to this question. The Reewing have used the logicality as a main instrument to push for their case. Eventually, Maay had to be recognized as a national language.

Four Communities and a Mesh of 'Half' of a Community: 4.5

Notwithstanding the disputations, disparities and disinclination over the subjects mentioned above, both sub-groups of the Charter, including several of the other committees, were inclusively unequivocal about the question of officially legalizaing the inequality of the divergent communities of the Somali society, particularly where the stakes related to the Negroid/Jareer. With the exception of the Committee on Economic Recovery, Institutional Building and Resource Management and the Committee on Regional and International Relations, all the other Committees, including the divided two sub-committees on the Charter believed in the 4.5 social inequality system, tutelage of dubious members at the 13th Somali Reconciliation Conference held in Arte, Djibouti.

Ironically, the draft reports of these Committees, which were to map out guidelines for the way forward, were decoratively enriched with terms such as "justice," "equality," and "rights" not less than thirty times, but were without the morality to consider the controversy within their respective documents, as the infamous 4.5 clan power sharing formula contrarily purported injustice, inequality and the rightlessness of a section of the society. It becomes more deplorable particularly when you consider that some of the proponents of the discriminatory 4.5 phenomenon of Apartheid are personalities with long careers in the legal and jurisprudence professions, some of them and alleged to have participated in the construction of Somalia's 1960 constitution.

Dissonant to the ethics of their profession and knowledge, they imprudently spearheaded the culture of betrayal and violated the human and civil rights of a section of the society by compromising the preservation of rights and dignity of the people. Somali delegates from all walks of life, without the exclusion of high ranking officers, women, intellectuals, religious leaders, clan leaders, notables, lawyers/advocates, politicians, medical doctors, engineers and representative members of the civil society, were not only unanimously silent about the inexplicable marginalization of the Jareer/Bantu population, but indeed all have firmly advocated for it.

Other "intellectuals" who harmonized several versions of the two disputative Charters have also celebrated the adoption and operationalization of the 4.5 clan power sharing formula ceremoniously as though it were the Holy word of God (Kusow, 2004). Remarkably, it was only after its omission and denunciation by the first official and IGAD appointed Harmonization Committee under the co-Chairmanship of Professor Abdi I. Samatar of the University of Minnesota and Professor Mohamoud Jama of the University of Nairobi, that the figure 4.5 ironically disappeared from the final draft of the Charter, which was enriched with code and content transposed from the Samatar-Jama Harmonization Committee's version. But the system was effectively in practice as a major formula for appointments at all levels.

In order to overshadow the sensitive topic of inequality and injustice, the IGAD Technical Committee, in conjunction with Somali armed clans, embraced the Apartheid method of clan categorization and adopted the dubious term "all inclusive", betraying to the international community that in actuality, the lacklusterly named 14th Somali National Reconciliation Conference was devoid of any equality for the Jareer community from day one. Underneath the superfluous "all inclusive" pronouncement was, in many respects, an innate ideology of segregation: "inclusive but unequal." The context lodges in its underbelly a Jileec modified version of the American racial policy of "separate but equal."

The clans that share inclusivity as well as equality, irrespective of their internal fission or fusion and recognized as "pure" Somalis by all standards permissible, were classified as Dir, Hawiye, Darod and

Digil-Mirifle. Regardless of the geographical and genealogical distance of the other clans from the birthplace of the Somali-Arab contact and origination of Somali nobility, the northerners had to force down their throat the bitter pill of parity with the other armed clans, especially after a show of military power had ousted them from the prestigious Villa Somalia.

After their military supremacy symbolized the removal of Dictator Siad Barre, the Hawiye won the recognition of genealogical mobility, a status whose prerogative to determination previously stayed within the jurisdiction of northern "nobility," which had stationed itself at the top. But this mobility, according to the ousters of Barre, would render insufficiency without employing an excessive push of downward mobility against the Jareer, so that the status gap, rights and equality between the "very" Somali and the "less" Somali would be as visibly demarcated as it was extensively widened. The Jareer, the Reer Xamar (Banadiri) and the outcaste groups of several sub-groups were lumped together to share half of the equivalent of one "pure" Somali clan's share, with the highest group garnering less than 0.2 of the envisaged 0.5 allocated to the totality of the "minority" groups.

The concept of 4.5 was designed in Djibouti and effectively implemented during the 13th Somali Peace Conference held in Arte under the auspices of Ismail Omar Guelleh's regime. It was the brainchild of certain Hawiye notables who wanted to exercise supremacy against unarmed communities. Unfortunately, neither Guelleh and his government, nor the so-called civil society stage managing that conference, nor the so-called 'Cuqaal' wisdom of the tribes, nor the power-hungry intellectuals cautioned against the ill effects of inequality and discrimination to the image of the Somali society in general, and the un-Islamic social inferiority status the system would afflict on the concerned discriminated people in particular. To add injury to insult, the participants at the Arte (Djibouti) conference were divided into Somali clans and OTHERS, a term which cut open the deepest hunch of Somali racialisticism and ethnocentrism. In fact, it was in this nihilistic ambiance that Abdikassim Salad's Transitional National Government (TNG) was incepted.

Although South Africa has succeeded in eradicating the Apartheid form of administration, Somalia has embarked on legitimating one in a new phenomenon developed under a pastoral philosophy called the 4.5 clan power sharing formula. The puzzle, however, lies in the avoidance to substantiate the basis for the introduction of the 4.5 system, rather than the goal it is to achieve. But what can be deduced from the system is that the socio-political goal of the so-called 4.5 clan power-sharing system is a clear indication of the Apartheid nature of the Somali society. It is a new device for mental oppression. Its aim is to foster in the Jareer mind the acceptance of socially imposed inferiority in comparison with self-exaltation of the "nobility," suppressing them into a situation that some call "a politically and socially limited life" (Christian Action, undated, accessed in the Kenya National Archives in Nairobi).

In this system, the Jareer survive under stiffly controlled social and economic segregation, and are associated with chronic disabilities "from the crade to the grave" (ibid). An experiment of this type is probably the testing ground for an eventual introduction of decrees and laws that will constitutionalize "…systematic and quite definite policy of Apartheid," (ibid) leading to the execution of acts such as The Somali Bantu Inferiority Act, The Jareer Re-enslavement Law, The Bantu Education Act (like in South Africa), The Right to the Bantu Land Expropriation Law, the Jareer-Animal Equality Act and many other laws that will enhance the supremacy status of the non-Jareer populace of Somalia, particularly the 'tanned' Arab Somalis, borrowing from the literary fashion molded by Ali Jimale Ahmed (1995).

The 4.5 system is a typical replica and nomadicized version of the defunct South African Apartheid policy, where Black natives were allowed to elect Native Representatives of White-European origin to the houses. In essence, when one limits the political participation of another group, it is nothing but effectively legitimized subjugation. It encourages segregation, which is paradigmatic in racist societies where "Onto the neck of a subject people they daily add a yoke which increases to unbearable limits the strain already caused…" (Christian Action, undated, accessed in the Kenya National Archives in Nairobi).

A large number of Somalis and others who think of Somalia as an egalitarian pastoral democracy may not agree with my contentious coining of Apartheid to Somali social life, which brings us to define the terminology "Apartheid" as it was put by the natives of where it originated. In Moses Mabhida's definition, among others:

71

> The word means segregation, discrimination and so-called separate
> development...The idea of segregation is based on a fallacious theory
> derived from Calvinistic religion, which is very widespread among
> the Boer population, who do so far as to claim, on the basis of
> quotation from the Bible, that the black man was created to be the
> slave of the white man (Mabhida, 1962:7-8).

An observation of the above definition presents a very rich degree
of similitude between the system of segregation and discrimination
against the Bantu/Jareer ethnic community in Somalia and those in
Apartheid South Africa. The most vivid similarities are (a) the belief in
inequality between the different races of Jareer and Jileec, hence Bantu
and non-Bantu peoples; and that (b) both dominant groups also base
their subjugation and slavery philosophy on theological grounds,
Christianity in the South African situation, and of course Islam in the
case of Somalia (Val Cismon, 1935:10). Whatever the sphere and
magnitude, the common denominator for both situations rests in the
exploitation of a self-dignified group against the autochthonous
population.

Recent historical fact demonstrates, however, that whereas after
national and international condemnations of Apartheid (Somalia being
among the anti-Apartheid forces) South Africa has achieved the
eventual hand-over of rule to the natives, Somalia has, in retrogressive
contrast, shamefully and callously moved onto a legitimating process
beginning with the adoption of a 4.5 clan stratification and clan
supremacization scheme, abominable evils that are now history in
South Africa. The objective of the system is instrumental to the
experimentation process through which an ultimately legal Apartheid
policy might be formulated and implemented in the Somali peninsula.

The 4.5 mechanism is framed in the context of an erroneous but
general myth of clan division, in which all the people are categorically
put into significant and insignificant tribal groups. The so-called
Somaloid groups (Cushites turned Arabs), the significant tribes, are
said to contain 4 'major' clans constituting the separate entities of
Hawiye, Darod, Dir and Issak, recognized as being of pure Somaloid
blood, excluding the occupational outcast groups that I discussed in
another study. Hypothetically, this major-minor clan myth is based on
a non-demographically proven but rather count-of-the-thumb
imagined and executed by a lustful Somali society.

More Retrogression than Reconciliation

The nature of the Somali conflict is as complex as the citizens themselves are. In that context, it was shortsighted and a grave misconception to treat the multi-layered crisis in the manner of a contemporary war instigated by inequitable distribution of insufficient resources perpetrated by colonial doctrine, and continued afterwards by neocolonialist rulers of civil and military regimes. As Dee Kelsey and Pam Plumb have observed, "Often we jump the gun by trying to solve a conflict before we have identified its roots" (Kesley & Plumb, 1997:20). As Committee Six confirms in their report, "The underlying sources of conflict have their origin in the precolonial period" (SNRC report, 2003). Thus, the misapprehension of 'straight-jacketing' Somalia's undoing into a "resources and underdevelopment" dispute, which is believed by even some African Presidents, is in strong contradiction to the scholarly observation of "...the superiority complex of one group over another, mainly based on cultural differences" (Jong, 1999:13) and lays bare another aspect of the root causes of this particular conflict. There is truth in the argument that the divided loyalties were partly provoked by mismanagement, greed, nepotism and ethnocentrism indulged in by those at the helm. It also lures a synchronous combination with other segments and series of cultural predicaments, which trail down the line of Somali social history.

Looking back into the history of Somalia, one may deduce that inter-clan and intra-clan animosities and a living culture of war were the order of the day. As Douglas Collins reminds us, "The Auliahan are fighting the Marehan, the Garre are fighting the Galgail, the Uadan are fighting the Geledi, the Omar Mohamud are fighting the Habr Ghidir and the Shifta are fighting for the hell of it" (Collins, 1960:23). This statement is only one out of many more written about the bellicosity of the Somali people and the depth of the roots of their antagonism against one another.

The Somali antagonists were born into a culture of war, and more often than not, battles fought in rural areas extended to urban towns, executing vengeance on innocent citizens for crimes committed elsewhere by unknown kinsmen. Likewise, minor personal urban grudges shifted to remote villages "away from the law" and bloody wars flared up as a consequence. Looking at the problem only as a conflict over resources was the first mistake, while the lack of expert facilitators and reconciliators supported by expert Somalists (Somalis and foreigners) [43] was another of IGAD's deleterious and premeditated discrepancies. This attitude of one-eyedness has led to the unnecessary prolongation of the Conference and the formation of a government in structure but not in function; eight months after its inception, it has yet to decide the location of its seat, despite the legitimation of Mogadishu as the capital in the Transitional Federal Charter of the Somali Republic adopted by the Conference.

Months after the formation of the cabinet, Nairobi was still the operational base of the Somali Transitional Federal Government, despite persistent calls from Kenya and the donors for its relocation in Somalia. Only after serious pressure from IGAD and the international community did Ali Gheddi's government relocate to Somalia, namely the agricultural town of Jowhar, about 92 km from Mogadishu and a stronghold of his close kinsman and renowned warlord Mohamed Dhere, who for an unending span was holding the local agrarian people at ransom. In other words, the Transitional Federal Government did not dare set foot and operate in Mogadishu, the national capital, an indication of a socio-political gap between the outcome of the so-called 14th SNRC and the aspirations of the masses claimed to have been represented at the Conference. A temporary accommodation of the TFG in Baidoa was not successful either, creating more political bloodshed and ideological distance among the clans. And after arriving in Mogadishu under the protection of Ethiopian troops, the shedding of Somali blood, especially the civilians and the unarmed, has become the order of the day.

Under the pattern of this reality, acute delusion is undermining discussions to unearth the nitty-gritty of the above social dynamics, and the crux of the matter still remains unattended to. The thesis of my argument is supported by incidents that created more havoc than reconciliation, as new factions were formed and others married into coalitions and alliances during the process of reconciliation!

The IGAD Factor in the Emergence of New Alliances in the Reconciliation Conference

1. The Transitional National Government (TNG) split into two: a faction led by then Interim President Abdikassim Salad, and its rival arm called TNG (Asali), which was headed by then Prime Minister Hassan Abshir Farah.

2. What was once a strong alliance comprising 8 factions, well-known as G8 (Group 8), suffered an abrupt political puncture, shrinking its membership to a teethless three, leaving Mohamed Kanyare and Omar Mohamed 'Finish' of the Hawiye clan and Mowlud Ma'ani of the Jareer community bewildered as the stout foundation of their coalition was pulled off its balance.

3. The civil society splintered into two parties spearheaded separately by Asha Hagi Elmi (Hawiye) and Shariff Salah (Digil-Mirifle).

4. The National Salvation Council, which was also an "offspring" of the 14th SNRC in Kenya, was dominated by the Hawiye with the exception of Jama Ali Jama and Ahmed Omar Jees, who both belong to sub-clans of the Darood clan family.

5. Abdikassim's section of the TNG was also a Hawiye control-zone save one member each from Ortoble, Lelkase and Dhulbahante, all Darood sub-clans, and an insignificant number from other clans.

6. The Jowhar administration of strong man Mohamed Dhere and the Puntland administration (a faction of ex-Colonial Abdullahi Yusuf) made a tactical coalition with the robust Somali Salvation and Reconciliation Council, formed after Arteh with strong backing from Ethiopia, to counter-balance and frustrate the Djibouti-backed Abdikassim and his dormant interim government. The two newcomers (Jowhar administration and Puntland) increased the SSRC coalition's subscription to a strong membership of 17 factions.

7. Out of the 25 signatories (including Abdikassim) of the National Salvation Council, 17 factions united into a separately independent coalition. Five of the remaining eight factions, chaired by Abdikassim Salad, Bihi, Muse Sudi, Atto and Barre Hirale, instituted an amalgamation, with Abdikassim Salad's TNG arm standing as the powerhouse. The other three consisted of the factions left aloof after the crumbling of the G8; their leader was Mohamed Kanyare Afrah.

75

8. A noteworthy elaboration here is that, although the National Salvation Council was composed of 25 groups or signatories, they tolerated differences elsewhere on an interest and ideological basis because 17 of those factions were automatic subscribers to the Abyssinian philosophy and school of thought, while 8 groups were inclined to a Djiboutian school of thought, i.e. TNG thinking.

9. The Digil-Mirifle confederation of communities was also affected, although some of their prominent leaders were cautious and secretive to give an impression of 'neutrality.' However, Sheikh Aden Madobe, Deerow (note that Deerow was killed in his hometown of Baidoa by a gunman) and Shariff Salah were opined as having a tendency toward the Ethiopian camp. Habsade, a prominent figure in Moallim Madobe's territory, was emitting signals of affiliation with Abdikassim. Ex-Colonel and RRA factional chairman Mohamed Hassan Shati-gadud had a devastating head-on collision with Ethiopia after an RRA splinter group was midwifed against him in his own area during the course of the conference. Shati-gadud blamed his former ally, Ethiopia, for masterminding the intra-RRA division at a time when he was in Kenya participating in the reconciliation conference. Later, Sheikh Aden Madobe had to be invited as a faction leader alongside Shati-gadud.

To sum up, there was an overall subscription to a certain member of the IGAD TC that made the whole conference a stage for a recruitment exercise to pledge loyalty to the country. This movement was so huge that even most of the Bantu/Jareer participant groups enrolled their loyalty. The oppressed and marginalized groups, the "unequals" and/or the "second-class citizens," in other words, the 0.5 communities, mainly supported the Ethiopian-backed fraternity. Of the three Jareer-Weyne groups, approximately a 2/3 majority was for Ethiopia, as a political tactic to (a) "encounter Mowlud Ma'ani's treacheries and alliances," and (b) "...have a strong wall to lean on against Somali antagonism that was continuously frustrating Jareer participation!"

Under this background, Abdullahi Yusuf's election as President was not a surprise, considering his campaigning from day one of the conference, the political back-patting and blessing he enjoyed from a very strong member of the IGAD Frontline States, his close relation with some of the Hawiye factional leaders and his generosity and 'open-handedness,' (thanks to foreign funding). All of these contributed to his majestically projected ascension up the ladder where the Hawiye clan had failed to protagonize in the management of milking Maandeeq.

Project 14

The long, hard and controversy-ridden Somali peace process culminated in the formation of a Transitional Federal Parliament, which elected an interim president. Inauguration, oath-taking and ululation marked the outcome of the conference in spite of its paradoxicality, and Siad Barre's army colleague ex-Colonel Abdullahi Yusuf Ahmed was crowned as the interim president in October 2004. In the sprawling Eastleigh estate, however, opposing crowds of Hawiye and Darood demonstrated in the streets at night. One group was welcoming the outcome and the other denounced it. It was a near-clash as flying stone-bullets were exchanged before elders moved in immediately and restored tranquility. This inimical emotion was a clear surfacing of the Somali clan animosity brewing and prevailing over the years, which the 'Reconciliation' conference had failed to carry on aboard. My premonition related to this episode is that yet another bad omen awaits Somalia.

A well perceived dialectic chronicling serious criticism opened among certain circles of the Hawiye, depreciating the result of the process as "from Darood to Darood," adducing that the time, lives and resources devastated in the war to overthrow Barre (a Darood) and its effects over the past decade and half as undeservingly incommensurate with the result. On the other end, the Darood expressed satisfaction and jubilation as they re-established themselves unobtrusively in a position they adore for its prestige, a seat which they have always believed their divine right.

There was a lot more to this conference than meets the eye. Indeed, it continued with an indefinite time limit. Associated with it were colossal funds, consumed to the tune of millions of U.S. dollars. Therefore, the exercise was a political project of regional as well as international dimensions.

The IGAD Technical Committee of the Frontline States on the one end, and representatives of the international donors on the other, had a load on their back and a duty to implement a project whose end product was anxiously awaited. Wreckage of the conference might have cost certain officials their jobs. Enquiries into the causes of the collapse would have revealed devastating discrepancies and the destinations of monies unaccounted for, which now are covered under the shadow of the visible indicator, the morphological existence of a parliament, an ineffective president and of course a white elephant in the form of cabinet structure to steer the government institutions and their obligations. These remain no more than structures installed for circumvention, which are now in dire perplexity of how and where to commence the required institutional functions expected of a government.

The traumatic pressure at the forethought of the precarious consequences entangled in the demise of the conference preoccupied the officials appointed to manage the 14th Project dubbed Somali National Reconciliation Conference. The devastating heat from the abortion of the Conference would have jeopardized the credibility of the entire IGAD membership under whose auspices the international community voluntarily committed enormous amounts of domestically needed resources. In a sense, therefore, the propitiation and appeasement with which the warlords and factional heads were approached every time they pulled out of the conference had an underlying strategic connotation to pre-empt the opening of Pandora's box.

With no tangible reconciliation eminently undertaken during the two-year period of the Conference, there is no doubt that century-old wounds were left rotting below the visible surface, while 'prestige' Project 14 dealt with only the dressing of the puss saturated on the external. In doing so, IGAD had to create an opportunity to conclude the Project and, again borrowing the words of Ali Jimale Ahmed, "opted for the easy way out" (Ahmed, 1995:140).

The International Community

The international community responded commendably to requests to help curb the debacle the regional countries and the world community was having difficulty coping with as a result of Somalia's anarchy. They responded with an intervention in financial sponsorship for the conference and they lived up to their word in their tolerance for the hefty amounts of funds expended.

Although this was a justified good gesture of human philanthropism, they should have also made sure that the exercise was carried out smoothly, in accordance with the principles of facilitation, mediation and reconciliation. By doing so, the financial sponsors would have stood in a better position to conduct the monitoring and evalutation of the program according to the successive stages and their outcomes. If anything, they should have provided experts in the divergent areas encompassing the process to steer, consult and advise in the various aspects of the Conference in order to help it follow the fundamental prerequisites for a successful reconciliation.

From an external viewpoint, the Somali National Reconciliation Conference, alias "Project 14," consummated more a game of robotics than it accommodated the true ideals of desirable reconciliation or purposeful politics. Technical and financial blockades have on several occasions pushed the exercise almost to an end. On several occasions, the delegates were abashed and disgraced as hoteliers kicked them out of their hotel rooms in demand of payments for earlier services, accommodation and meals.

Considering the magnitude of the conference, the international community should have taken the responsibility and provided expertise in conference management, mediation and reconciliation methods – in general, the engagement of Somalist scholars with the diversity of the Somali community of nations and their respective cultures was a necessity disdained on the part of the donors. They should have also welcomed and appreciated the expertise of distinguished Somali scholars from both inside the country and the Diaspora so as to allow the interplay between the local and foreign expertise to benefit the conference. Hypocritically, this opportunity was not seized because the intellectuals were elbowed out of active participation, at times mistreated and often disgracefully humiliated, owing to the heavy handedness of an IGAD TC member. The negative attitude toward the Somali scholars' input was premeditated by the Frontline States, who made it their mandate to further deepen the Somali clan hostilities. In fact, intellectual participation was initially limited, and the importance of their presence was eventually withdrawn and ignored altogether. The principled among these scholars have pulled out of the exercise, while others had their role reduced to (*kutuba-qaad*) personal secretaries to the warlords.

With the neglect of these useful factors, the good intentions of the donors have been thwarted by the monopolization and manipulation of IGAD stage-managers. But the donors were not unconscious of the obstructive impasse in the Conference. They received numerous copies of complaints by the factions and individual participants, informing them of the fruitless path of the exercise and the emotions inherent in the intense political climate. This was an inexcusable and unprecedented neglect on their part.

There is no question that the conference has widened the multi-dimensional psychosocial trauma excruciatingly afflicted on the Somali people. The solution, in my opinion, does not lie in the formation of a state, but rather in the creation of a viable reconciliation process in which every person could overcome his or her grief. Competition for resources, identity and cultural supremacy only make way for bias and hatred, factors through which social confianza and societal bonds cannot be enhanced. For Somalia, the way forward is in the restoration of the lost love, in rebuilding trust – regardless of one's ethnic background – and the preservation of the uncompromisable unity that was once the symbol of the country.

For the 14th Somali National Reconciliation Conference, the idea was initiated by IGAD, the conference was managed by IGAD the 'facilitator' was IGAD, and the Interim Somali government was molded by IGAD, yet the officials IGAD delegated to the the conference were diplomats with no reconciliation record in their portfolio. This factor is another clear representation of the conundrum that haunted the exercise. If under this reality we ask the question: Has any praiseworthy reconciliation been conducted in the SNRC? The true answer is NO. Reversibly, if we may please ourselves metaphorically with an end product, we can reframe the question to suit our illusive dogma and put it this way: Was a government installed? The answer is YES. Then to the latter response we may ask: why is the government neither functioning nor seated in the national capital if indeed it was born out of an effective reconciliation conference?

As Eno (2005) enlightens, "We have to evaluate the situation in pursuance of what the variable was before the conference and whether the conference as the vehicle has achieved that. If the variable in our search prior to the conference was in the structure of an institution, one was indeed formed; but if it was laid in reconciliation and a functioning institution, veritably this is yet very far from being achieved any time in the near future." This argument is clearly true, particularly considering the current Ethiopian occupation of Somalia in support of the TFG under the guise of fighting international terrorism.

Conclusion

This chapter presented a descriptive reflection on ethnic divisions, social discrimination and marginalization. From the general Somali claims of self-sameness, same culture, same language, etc. and the turbulent squabbles within them, this discussion has led us to the very recent phenomenon of Apartheid coded the "4.5 clan power-sharing formula". When we scale these hypotheses against the universal belief in Somali homogeneity, monolinguality, monoculturality and monotheologicality, we may deviate from our past understanding in order to observe the other version: that of a more realistic Somalia, a Somalia that is multi-ethnic and multicultural. This version exposes us to yet another extensive debate of who is a Somali and by what criteria is the paradigm of Somaliness determined? The ethnic marginalization, segregation and discrimination defined in this study portray the reality that Somalia is a truly ethnocentric racist society (Ibid). On the other hand, despite the 4.5 Factor and the grabbing of positions, Somalia literally has no functioning authority. This failure should not be blamed only on the Somalis' unwillingness to manage their affairs; it is also a consequence of a mismanaged and entirely neglected reconciliation conference. Upon its inception, the TFG was not born out of a Somali-driven reconciliation process, thus the lack of the Somali people's blessing. With a foreign-driven process and outcome, the TFG has entirely lost the support and dedication of the masses. The Somali people were left with no more meaningful option than to deny fellowship to a wicked leadership imposed on them by antagonistic foreign dominators.

Part II

Diagnosis of the Crisis

THE SOMALI INTERNAL WAR AND THE ROLE OF INEQUALITY, ECONOMIC DECLINE AND ACCESS TO WEAPONS

Abdulahi A. Osman

Ethnic conflict is caused by fear of the future, lived through the past
– Vesna Pesic (Quoted in Lake and Rothchild 1998:7)

The Somali war is a zero-sum game where warring
factions are fighting either to become Siad Barre, or not allow others to become
Barre
– A Somali Elder

The internal war in Somalia has proven to be difficult to explain thoroughly. As rightly noted by Abdullahi (Ch. 3), the majority of the literature suffers from a "single cause analysis," which concentrates specifically on the role and affects of Siad Barre's regime (1969-1990.) In order to understand this war one needs to understand the several factors that contributed to one of the bloodiest conflicts in recent African history. The current study will argue that the Somali internal war resulted from three interrelated factors: social inequality, economic decline and access to weapons. Unlike what many scholars have argued, Somalia has been a stratified society in which the political leaders and their clansmen, the majority of whom came from Mudug and Majertinia regions, have ruled the country. These clansmen were privileged by the state and have been literally above the law. Social inequality creates three problems: first, decline in the investment of social capital (i.e. education, health, etc.), second, political instability (i.e. military coup d'état), and third, severe poverty (i.e. high inflation that reduces the buying power of the people).

In addition to economic decline caused by years of inequality, the 1980s coincided with the end of the Cold War, reduced economic aid and introduction of the World Bank's Structural Adjustment Programs, all which worsened the economy of many in the third world, including Somalia. Tension also increased within these societies. More importantly, the capacity of the state to maintain its reciprocal relationship and keep its army intact fell apart. This created a severe case of merchandising, in which every person sold what they had in order to survive. Among the merchandise sold were weapons issued or stolen from the army's warehouses by starving soldiers to the general public. In these hard conditions, many people began to rely upon their tribal connections in order to survive, and this time they had grievances and weapons.

Introduction

At the dawn of the Somali independence in1960, Farah Sefey, a Somali poet, issued a satiric prophecy: "Be aware of the state midwived by travelers" (Jimale, 1995). By the early 1990s, after only thirty years of independence, his prophetic advice came true as Somalia laid in ruins, its government collapsed and destroyed. All aspects of central government and public services such as security, health, education and basic social services disappeared. Armed gangsters, locally known as Mooryaans (Jimale, 1995) or Jirrey roamed the country, robbing, raping and murdering senselessly. The majority of these armed bandits acted on behalf and with the instruction of brutal warlords battling for control of the state. The bloodbath that resulted from this brutal power struggle and the subsequent man-made famine claimed thousands of lives, sent thousands of refugees outside the country and displaced thousands internally. In the year 2000, a transitional government was created at Arta, Djibouti, but the lawlessness, chaos, mindless murders and rapes still continued unchecked.

Despite this human catastrophe and suffering, the literature on the causes of Somalia's internal war remains inconclusive. Literature claims the conflict stems from the problem of governance and bad leadership (Samatar, 1993, 1994; Mireh 1994; Hashim, 1997), the problem of resources (Kusow, 1993; Mukhtar and Kusow 1993; Besteman, 1994; Casanelli, 1996), or bad economic policy and lack of sustainable development (Wisner, 1994; Mubarak, 1996). Other analyses, especially journalistic accounts, portray the Somali conflict as "...continuing from Stone Age ancestral clan rivalries, but Star Wars military violence" (Besteman, 1999:4).

The majority of the literature that explains the Somali conflict, however, suffers from a "single cause analysis" syndrome vis-à-vis the role and affects of the Siad Barre regime (1969-1990). Kusow (1998) argues that this mode of thinking has not resulted from a shortage of imagination on the part of the scholars, but rather from "...conditions imposed by some generalized narrative cultures about the nature of the society" (Kusow, 1998:65). More important are the twin analyses of homogeneity and Somali segmentary lineage, which together portray a picture of an ethnically *homogeneous, democratic* and *egalitarian* society (Lewis, 1980; Laitin and Samatar, 1987; Touval, 1963; Samatar, 1988).

This chapter intends to examine the validity and effects of these twin analyses and how they jointly misguided many analyses of the Somali conflict. For example, Professor Samatar, one of Somalia's leading scholars, posed perhaps the most reflective question of this dilemma: "Why and how could this society, one of the few nations in the continent with one ethnic group, one culture, one language, and one religion, find itself in such parlous circumstances – verging on self destruction?" (Samatar, 1993). Yet Somalia continues to experience one of the bloodiest internal wars[1] in the contemporary history of Sub Saharan Africa.

This chapter will argue that internal wars in Sub Saharan Africa in general, and in Somalia in particular, result from three interrelated factors perpetrated by the colonial and postcolonial states: first, *social inequality* resulting from the policies and practices of the colonial and postcolonial state, which has been extracting the country's wealth. This extraction was accomplished either directly through state-owned enterprises or indirectly through domination of the country's economic activities. The Somali state created patrimonial paths to state benefits and became the creator and enforcer of social inequality within the society. The main criteria for benefiting from this unequal distribution of state privileges are based on clanism, tribalism and regionalism. The result has been a decline in investment in social capital (healthcare,

---

[1] Throughout this paper I will be using the term internal war as opposed to civil war. One main reason is that civil war refers to the war between an existing government and insurgents, rebel or non-governmental entities. In Somalia, however, the war has been directed towards non-governmental entities due to the collapse of the central government in January 1991. For details on this topic see: Henderson, Errol (1999). *Encyclopedia of Violence, Peace, and Conflict.* San Diego, CA: Academic Press, p. 279.

education, and so on), which then led to poverty and political instability. The second factor is the *economic decline* in the mid-1980s that resulted from, among other things, a reduction in economic aid, which had funded these states throughout the 1960s and 1970s and the end of the Cold War in late 1980s. The result was the disappearance or diminishment of the large and corrupt central government's ability to maintain its reciprocal relations with various groups (usually the relatives of the ruler) in the country. The third and final factor, civilians' *easy access to weapons*, occurred when civilians turned to weapons as a mode of survival and self-defense in the desparate economic conditions of the 1980s. The abundance of weapons was the result of Somalia's hyper-militarization after independence, coupled with the impoverishment of the armed forces, a situation due to the economic decline and soaring economic inflation of the 1980s. The rest of this chapter will follow these three factors: social inequality, economic decline in the 1980s, and access to weapons.

Social Inequality

Inequality is inherent to all human communities whether due to historical, geographical, situational or psychological differences. Social inequality, at least as it is understood in the industrialized world, is determined by how much control one has over the mode of production (Marx, 1887). Social inequality in Sub Saharan Africa, however, is determined by how one is related (usually through established blood ties) to the ruling elites. Similarly, in many societies, the process by which elties consolidate control over the mode of production is based on the control of state power and/or resources. In most Sub Saharan African societies, the state plays a vital role in consolidating the position of the dominant social group. Kasfir (1983:5) argues that "...a socially dominant class controls the productive asset, the bulk of the distribution and most of all commands a socio-economic pre-eminence." Also, Marx asserts that the state is instrumental in the creation and maintenance of the dominant class. Perhaps the most striking explanation for this state of affairs has been offered by the Italian sociologist Gaetano Mosca (1896), who argues that social inequality occurs when a small minority group within the society forms a monopoly over the instrument of *power*.

The issue of inequality in Sub Saharan Africa has been hotly debated over the years by scholars and politicians alike. Some scholars cite material or class-based inequality (Fatton, 1992; Kasfir, 1983; Sklar 1963). Others argue that ethnic differences, rather than class differences, are the most important factors in the creation of inequality (Ayittey, 1998; Young, 1982). More recently, however, a number of scholars have claimed that class and ethnicity play the same role in determining who belongs to the ruling elite, as well as inequality within the society (Adedeji, 1999, 1985; Bayart, 1993, 2000). Leadership in the region has often used the economic variable to justify their actions. The early leaders of independent Africa (e.g. Julius Nyerere of Tanzania, Kwame Nkrumah of Ghana and Ahemd Sékou Touré of Guinea) also addressed the issue of inequality. Many of these leaders adopted Marxism as a remedy for the inherent social inequality left by the departing colonial powers (Nyerere, 1968; Nkrumah, 1964; Friedland and Roseberg, 1965). Similarly, many later leaders, most of them from the military, used the equality parlance to justify the illegal seizure of state power.[1] In order to understand social inequality in this region, one has to examine how this inequality is created and enforced through *tribe, clan* and *ethnic lines.*

Ethnicity, Tribalism, Clanism and Inequality

The social inequality in Sub Saharan Africa is determined by one's closeness to the ruling elite, especially the head of state, which makes the difference when obtaining any benefits from the state. Berkhoff and Hewett (2000) surveyed the ethnic inequality of infant mortality in twelve Sub Saharan African countries. Their results indicated that, despite the claim of universal healthcare in most African countries, rates of childhood mortality and immunization depend greatly on a group's level of representation in the government. They found that in Ghana, the children of Ashanti women are 20 percent less likely to die than other Ghanaian children, in Uganda the Baganda have more than a one-third greater chance to survive than others, while the Kalenjin

---

[1] General Siad Barre of Somalia after his military coup in October 1969 gave three reasons for his action: *equality, justice* and *prosperity.* Yet, only few years into his presidency the Somali state became to be known as the Government of the Mareehaan (Barre's sub-clan).

children in Kenya are half as likely to survive as children in other groups.

In ethnic and tribal societies of Africa, inclusion or exclusion in the system, as illustrated in the three aforementioned examples, is determined by the control (or lack of it) of political institutions by a fellow tribesman. In order to understand the concept of exclusion, it is useful to begin its structure, in the sense of the overall order of social relations, specifically in a historical context. In the colonial period African populations were politically and economically excluded. The British colonies treated the Africans as "subjects" rather than "citizens," whereas the Africans in French colonies could progress from the status of "indigène" towards citizenship through the assimilation of French culture and civilization. Similarly, the Africans in Portuguese colonies could advance and become Assimilados. The major goal behind the nationalist movements in Africa after the Second World War was to end this exclusion. Mazrui describes the nationalist movement as "the right to self-rule rather than rule by foreigners." Mazrui further argues that in the colonial liberation movements "it was more often the ethnic conception of 'majority rule,' rather than the orthodox liberal one, which had pride of place in African nationalistic thought" (Mazrui 1967:23). But the issues of ethnicity, citizenship and nation-state soon became conflict-ridden after independence.

The modern states possess some core features of what Max Weber identified as "modern bureaucracy". Among the features of a bureaucratic state, according to Weber, "public moneys and equipment are divorced from the private property of the official" (Weber, 1978:957). In most African states, however, "particularism" is the norm; they lack both the Weberian characteristics mentioned above and, more importantly, all the ingredients necessary to promote societal development. In these states, public officials serve their own interests rather than their employing organizations (Médard, 1996; Callaghy, 1984; Hydén, 1983; Bratton and van de Walle, 1997). Almost by definition, the state has a low degree of capacity resulting from the lack of distinction between public and private entities. The public services take a particularistic rather than universalistic character. Thus, corruption is endemic, which in turn hinders the state's ability to implement policies that are favorable to the whole nation.

To fathom this disparity one must examine the role of the socio-cultural setting in which many African societies, their leaders and bureaucrats function. Ekeh (1975:92) suggests the existence of two public realms with two different types of moral linkages to the private realm in postcolonial Africa. The first is the *primordial public,* which is identified with primordial groupings, sentiments and activities (ethnic groups). The primordial public is moral and operates on the same moral imperatives as the private realm. The second is the *civic public,* which is historically associated with the colonial administration and is identified with popular politics. The civic public in Africa is amoral and lacks the generalized moral imperatives operative in the private and primordial realms. It is based on civil structures such as the military, civil service, police, etc. Ekeh suggests that these two publics define citizenship differently than it is understood in the West. In the African setting, *citizenship* acquires different meanings depending on which realm (primordial or civic) it is conceived of (p.106). On the one hand, in the primordial public realm, the individual is morally obligated to sustain his identity with his group. The individual, in turn, gains huge benefits in the form of identity and psychological security (p.106-7). On the other hand, in the civic public realm, the individual seeks to gain in material terms and does not have any moral obligations and duties, which "are de-emphasized while rights are squeezed out of the civic public with the amorality of an artful dodger" (ibid:107).

Ekeh (ibid:108) argues that the educated Africans belong to both of these realms, which puts them in a dilemma due to the dialectic tension between the two. This tension manifests itself in the uniqueness of African politics in the form of an unwritten law according to which "it is legitimate to rob the civic public in order to strengthen the primordial public." It is this dilemma of identity that provides the mechanism from which social *inclusion/exclusion* is created and enforced. This mechanism is the postcolonial state in Africa, which gives advantage to some groups while it deprives others. Therefore, the idea of "government" is at the heart of the process of social exclusion in Africa (and elsewhere). This exclusion is never the result of a spontaneous process; rather, it is the result of historical manipulation and the practices of the more powerful group[s] in the society.

In Sub Saharan Africa, as already argued, the most important aspect of inequality is the very close relationship between holding positions of power in the state and the acquisition of wealth. The African state and its leaders have an advantage over the ethnic groups within the country. Lonsdale (1986:141) compares these groups and argues that "states have some moral force in the modern world and some international standing; they are licensed to use violence against their citizens and to incur debts. Ethnic groups are allowed none of these strengths...and Ethnic politics is stigmatized as tribalism." Lonsdale further argues that the morality of new forms of social inequality was the "tribe," in which the included persons took on "the duties of patronage" and justified their actions by "creating communities in which they had a moral standing and beyond which they acted as brokers of political alliance within the new arena of the state." (143).

Bayart (1993) asserts that the key to understanding political action in Africa is "the quest for hegemony." This quest is realized, in most cases, through the control of the state institutions. One main reason is the salience of the relationship between ethnic identity and the acquisition of any state benefits. One such benefit is obtaining gainful employment. Ekeh (1990:660-700) indicates the contrary ways in which access to different types of *formal employment* is affected by ethnic identity. Kinship networks are inevitably used in the search for jobs; moral pressure to support kin and individuals of the same ethnic origin is put on those who have the power to hire people.

Somalis: Egalitarian or a Stratified Society?

Many scholars and students of Somali studies describe the Somali society as fundamentally egalitarian. The British anthropologist I.M. Lewis describes it as "fundamentally democratic" because, he argues, "traditionally, decisions are made by councils of men. These councils are egalitarian... Somali egalitarianism permeates all aspects of society. In Somalia, it is not at all unusual for a poor and uneducated nomad to approach a high government official as an equal and engage him in a discussion about the affairs of state." Lewis however goes on to admit: "While Somalia's political culture is basically egalitarian, social and political changes have created new patterns of social life. In recent years, a new urban group, educated in Western-type schools and working as merchants or in government, has emerged. These urbanites enjoy more wealth, better access to government services, and greater educational opportunities for their children than do other sectors of society."[1]

In the above paragraph, Lewis establishes the existence of both an egalitarian and stratified society in Somalia. The question is then: who are these Western educated elite who enjoy the disproportional access to wealth and influence in this "egalitarian" society? A careful analysis reveals that some groups disproportionately make up the majority of this elite club. As established, the arenas in which Somalia's inequality and social exclusion are also noticeable are clanism and tribalism. It has been shown that the Somali political and economic arenas have been dominated by the nomadic clans of the Mudug and Majertinia regions since independence.[2] The members of these clans made up the majority of the ruling class throughout the short-lived Somali state (1960-90). Moreover, the members of these clans are on the forefront of the current devastating internal war in Somalia.

Colonial Legacy

Colonial rule had a negative impact on the long-standing independent rule in Sub Saharan Africa. Colonialism strengthened particularism and divisions based on ethnicity, language, religion, etc. by amalgamating peoples of different traditions, languages and cultures or dividing groups in "new" countries with artificial boundaries. The postcolonial indigenous elites continued to rule their respective states in ways that resembled the old colonial rule, notably through clientelism and patrimonial rule (Mamdani, 1996; Medard, 1982, 1996; Braathen et al., 2001). The elites followed the colonial politics of extraction and operated the state as a source of personal enrichment. Therefore, extractive politics, high rates of corruption, the lack of a technical class, and dependent/peripheral economies are the legacies of European colonial state.

Additionally, colonial states had no interest in promoting a viable state in Africa. Bruce Berman (1998:305-341) describes the colonial state

---

[1] http://www.culturalorientation.net/somali/ssoc.html
[2] These regions are based on the six regional administrations that the Italian colonial administration used, which the government of Siad Barre (1969-1990) sub-divided into smaller regions. Also, parts of the former Majertinia region were renamed as the Northeastern region.

as "an authoritarian bureaucratic apparatus of control ... not intended to be a school of democracy." Few indigenous peoples were educated beyond the primary grades, and those with administrative experience were limited to the most menial clerical posts within the colonial administration. These authoritarian measures, unfortunately, were copied and used by the leaders of the postcolonial states in Africa. Most Africans had little or no opportunity for any political participation until the very end of the colonial period, when elections were held. Therefore, the African elites were not the product of their own efforts, but rather they were handpicked by the colonial state for various reasons. Once they were established, they usually became elites for life. Max Weber (1949)'s advanced *loaded dice* analogy perhaps explains the longevity of the African elites. The loaded dice analogy says that once a dice is rolled and comes up in a certain combination this pattern would be repeated in the following rolls. In other words, once history decides who the members of the elite will be and the division of the country's political and economic pie, it will maintain the same pattern.

Italian Colonial Administration and its Impact on the Somali State

Colonial administrations provided the blueprint for the postcolonial states in Africa. Italy was specifically contributed to the failure of the Somali state by recruiting its future elites. These elites were not recruited for their ability to advance the interests of the Somali people, neither political nor economic, and less so their social interests. Rather, they were selected, as in many colonial states, for their contribution to the functioning of the extractive colonial states. Therefore, historicism and the loaded dice analogy (implicitly or explicitly) established the Somali postcolonial political and economic structure and the subsequent conflict that followed after the collapse of the state in 1991.

The seeds of the current suffering, especially in the southern part of the country, were planted at the end of the 19th century. This is when the European colonial administrations of Britain, Italy and France were established in Somalia. However, for the purpose of this paper we will specifically examine the role of the Italian colonial administration in setting up the current clan hierarchy of the country. The end result was the domination of the Somali political, economic and cultural arenas by the nomadic clans of the Mudug and Majertinia regions.

Italy first established its authority in Somalia in 1889, when it created a small protectorate in the central zone. Italy expanded to the south and northeast, a territory deserted by the Sultan of Zanzibar. In 1925, the Jubaland treaty moved the area east of the Juba River from Kenyan to Italian hands; it became the westernmost part of the Italian colony. In 1936, Italian Somaliland combined with Somali-speaking districts of Ethiopia to form a province of the newly formed Italian East Africa. During the Second World War, Italian forces invaded British Somaliland. The British, however, operating from Kenya, retook the whole region in 1941, including Italian Somaliland, which it ruled until 1950.

Italy renounced its claim to the rights and titles of the territory in 1947 under Article 23 of the 1947 peace treaty. However, on November 21, 1949, the General Assembly of the United Nations adopted a resolution recommending that Italian Somaliland be placed under an international trusteeship system for 10 years. Italy, using tremendous local maneuvers, won this trusteeship and the General Assembly granted Italy the authority to administer its former Somaliland territory (Mukhtar, 1989). Italy established the *Amministrazione Fiduciaria della Somalia* (AFIS), which led to Somalia's independence on July 1, 1960. Immediately, the northern British territory of Somaliland, which gained its independence on June 26th, 1960 joined the South and formed the Somali Republic. This union has been broken since 1991, when the former British colony of Somaliland declared its separation. However, this breakaway republic is yet to receive international recognition, despite many efforts by its authorities. Franco Henwood's chapter in this volume strongly advocates for this recognition (see Ch. 9).

During its administration, Italy promoted the members of the nomadic clans from the Mudug and Majertinia regions and groomed them as local elites. One main reason for this was that the Italians needed agricultural products, which were available in the south. Italy therefore created a system that helped the Southerners to fulfill their exploitative ambitions, while at the same time using them as cheap Italian manpower. Following a general colonial practice, as Rodney (1977) shows, Italy established patrimonial path to state, in which it hired members of the Mudug and Majertinia clans to fill up the subaltern and mid-level positions in the colonial administration. The promotion of clan members from these "chosen" regions enforced the exploitative and extractive practices of the colonial and post-colonial states. Additionally, the extractive nature of Somalia's governance spilled over into the anarchy that followed the collapse of the state in 1991. Many members of the Habargidir clan, for example, the clan that dominated the Somali politics by the barrel of a gun, continue to occupy farmlands and enslave members of the southern agrarian community into forced labor. Perhaps this is why members of these clans acquired the name of "Dawlad Ku-Nool" over the years, which literally means to live on state property.

The Nature of Africa's Postcolonial State

Mamdani (1996) argues that the postcolonial state in Africa has its roots in the patrimonial state ran by colonial powers. Specifically, the colonial institutions of 'indirect rule' continued in the postcolonial state transformed as "reactionary" direct native governance. These postcolonial states created what several scholars call the neo-patrimonial state[1], blurring the boundaries between public and private spheres. Though these states are described as "weak," they still proved to be capable of maintaining themselves in power for long periods of time (Robert, Jackson, Rosberg, 1982:177-198; Bienen, 1993:271-282). Power was retained partly because these states were able to extract resources and redistribute reward among the society. However, the means for this redistribution has always been private, hence personalized. To Braathen, et al. (2000:11), "the independent states created a specific patrimonial path of redistribution which divided the indigenous majority along regional, religious, ethnic and at times familial lines." For example, those related to the ruling elites always

---

[1] Neo-patrimonialism is a hybrid of a patrimonial and legal-rational state. The patrimonial state is characterized by strong familial ties between rulers and the ruled usually found in colonial states. The legal-rational state, on the other hand, is characterized by impersonal or unbiased transactions and adherence to the rules of the state. In many African states only the legality exists, and the impersonal and unbiased aspect is non-existent. For details see: Mamdani, Mohamoud (1996), *Citizen and subject: contemporary Africa and the legacy of late colonialism*. Kampala, Uganda: Fountain Publishers. See also, Crawford Young (1994), *The African Colonial State in Comparative Perspective*. New Haven: Yale University Press.

had more privileges than other clans. All benefits from the state, including jobs, government contracts, scholarships, etc. were set aside for members of the elites and their kinsmen.

The elites in Africa, however, have always had a connection to the rest of society. Jean-François Bayart (1993), using the history of Africa's states, examines the interdependence between the *state* and *society*. Since many African societies are ethnic or clan-based, he argues that ethnicity provides the arena for the competition for wealth, power and prestige, and that state behavior is shaped by this very competition. He further argues that the elite do not function in isolation, but rather through the formation of alliances with traditional rulers. Thus, the postcolonial "bloc" consists of Western educated bureaucratic cadre in alliance with the traditional ruling elites (Young, 1988:25-66; Blanton, Mason and Athow, 2001:471-491). Adebayo Adedeji (1993:7), one of the leading scholars in Sub Saharan African politics, describes this alliance as "a small urban based but rurally connected middle class. A tiny group of actors in the unproductive and often illegal sector of the economy is setting the beat." In Somalia, the state was always given the name of the president's sub-clan. For example, Siad Barre's government (1969-90) was known as the "Marehaan" government after his sub-clan of Marehaan.

Braathen and others argue that this patrimonial process created a huge social inequality, which is not a debate between the *haves* and *have-nots* or between other social classes as understood in the West. Rather, it is day-to-day survival under political institutions that are above and beyond the Weberian legal coercion. Under this system, the state occupies a central role, from which it commands the largest portion of all economic activities in the country. More importantly, states are strengthened by large militaries acquired over the years for protection and extractive ambitions. Therefore, the state became the arbiter of both security and economic activities within the country. This control over the economy and military, coupled with tribalism, nepotism and favoritism, made the state both the creator and enforcer of social inequality. The inequality in the Somali state could be observed in the cultural hegemony of the ruling clans, where the language and culture of the Mudug and Majertinia has been

maintained as the culture of the whole nation (Mukhtar, pp. 35-36).[1]
Additionally, the inequality in Somalia was economically beneficial to
the state rulers and their tribesmen. Since 1960, several policies,
including the 1975 Land Reform Act, were introduced, leading to the
seizure of ancestral lands from many landowners in southern Somalia.[2]
However, the inequality in Somalia was most visible in the political
system of the country.

Politics and Inequality in Somalia

As argued, Somalia's elites are overwhelmingly from the Mudug
and Majertinia regions, despite the fact that these clans are minority in
number. According to the the 1958 census, which is the only census
available, the Somali population was estimated at 1,263,584 in the
entire Italian Somaliland's six regions: Majertinia (82,653 or 7%),
Mudug (141,120 or 11%), Hiiraan (176,528 or 14%), Banadir (387,600 or
31%), Upper Jubba (362,234 or 29%) and Lower Jubba (113,449 or 9%).
This makes the Southern regions of Hiiraan, Banadir, Upper and Lower
Jubba the majority with 82% of the population (Mukhtar, 1989:26).
These regions remained intact until the Barre regime (1969-1991)

---

[1] The nomadic clans of Mudug and Mjertinia regions speak the Maxaa
language. Before 1961, the Mogadishu radio news was read in Maay and
Maxaa languages until Maxaa was adopted as the only language. Another
indication was the creation of the Department of Culture in the Ministry of
Education during the 1960s. In the 1970s, the Department was elevated to the
Ministry of Culture and Higher Education. Mukhtar, Mohamed H. *Islam in
Somali History: Fact or Fiction*, pp. 35-36. See also, Lee Cassanelli, *The Shaping of
Somali Society.*

[2] One of these policies was the establishment of the Agricultural Development
Corporation (ADC) in 1970. Under this policy, the individual farmer and his
family were only permitted to keep enough grain to last until the next harvest
season, and the rest had to be sold to the ADC, usually at a price below the cost
of producing them. This policy caused many farmers to abandon the
profession of farming. Another policy was the 1975 Land Reform Decree. This
law intensified the confiscation of fertile land from its owners. The law
declared all land resources government property. Any sale or lease of land had
to be registered with the government. The government began levying heavy
taxes on these farmers, which caused many farmers to lose their ancestral land.
The government redistributed the confiscated lands to the members of the
Barre's sub-clan of Marehan.

subdivided them into eighteen regions. This division was mainly intended to create administrative enclaves for the Muduigan clans and to facilitate the Darood expansion to Southern Somalia. The Upper Jubba region was divided into Baay, Bakool, Gedo and parts of the current Middle Jubba region. The Gedo region was created specifically for Barre's Marehan clan. The capital city chosen for the region was Garbaharrey, small, mountainous and literally empty, instead of the larger city of Bardhere, a booming city on the banks of the Jubba River that has a long history, going back more than 500 years.

These clans reached their elite position through the Italian colonial state. In 1960 Somalia established a unitary government, with a parliament that had 123 members from all the regions of the country (at the time these were 8 regions, including two regions from the British Somaliland). On October 15, 1969, a member of his own clan of Majerteen killed President Shermaarke. On October 21, 1969, army units took over the control of the government. The commander of the armed forces, Brigadier General Mohammad Siad Barre, assumed leadership (although he is not regarded as the author of the military takeover) of the officers who deposed the civilian government. President Siad Barre, himself from the Mudug region and a member of the elite clans, installed a governing body, the Supreme Revolutionary Council (SRC), and became its president. The SRC arrested and detained at the presidential palace leading members of the democratic regime, including Prime Minister Mohamed Ibrahim Igaal.[1] The SRC banned all political parties, abolished the National Assembly, and suspended the constitution.

The regime identified itself as a Marxist revolutionary regime with the aim of radically transforming the Somali society through the application of "scientific socialism." The regime promised, among other things, an end to tribalism, nepotism, corruption and misrule. The new motto became: *maxaa taqaan* and *not ayaa taqaan*, which means "it is what you know, and not who you know." In 1970, Barre's government immediately organized a huge public rally during which a dummy symbolizing tribalism was burned and buried. Barre established a totalitarian regime complete with indisputable absolutist power. His regime constituted even more of a polarized clan-based

---

[1] Mohamed Ibrahim Igaal later became the president of the breakaway Republic of Somaliland.

structure than the previous regimes. For example, Barre's first cabinet in 1969 consisted of 14 ministers, of which 7 (or 50%) were members of his Darood clan, up from the 32% of the late Abdirsahid Sharmaarke's government. As time progressed this domination became absolute.

The Darood have dominated Somali politics throughout the post-independence existence of the country, and that is true for all successive Somali governments. Between 1960 and 1990, there were 26 governments, which nominated a total of 567 ministerial and senior cadre posts. The Darood clan took 216 posts, Hawiye 125, Isaaq 102 and Digil-Mirifle 31. Despite Siad Barre's overthrow of a Majerteen (a sub-clan of Darood) government in the 1969 coup, the Darood still continued their dominance of the Somali politics. The Majerteen gained 78, or 36%, of the Darood's 216 nominations. During the same period, the Hawiye clan members were nominated 125 (or 22%) times out of a total 567. A closer look, however, reveals that the Habargidir sub-clan, which resides in the Mudug region, received 45 (36%) out of those 125 nominations. Another sub-clan of the Hawiye, the Abgaal, which resides both in Mudug and Banadir regions, got 32 (26%) of the 125 nominations. However, the majority of these nominations went to the sub-clans that reside in the Mudug region, i.e. Siad Barre's Vice President the late Hussein Kulmiye Afrah, a Wa'aysle sub-clan member, who was nominated 10 out of the 32 times the president made a nomination. Notwithstanding the fact that members of the Mudug and Majertinia clans were a minority in the former Italian Somaliland, they still received roughly 67% of the nominations between 1960 and1990.[1] This was a direct result of their control of the country's political system in the period between 1960 and 1990.

Overall, members of the Darood clan and its sub-clans made up 40% of the total nominations in successive Somali governments between 1960 and 1990, followed by the Isaaqs with 30 (19%), including

---

[1] To get these figures, I deducted the share of each clan from the number of total nominations of 567 made by the successive governments in this period. I thus found that the Northern Somalilanders, Isaaq and Gedabursi, together took 125 nominations. This left 442 posts out of the total of 567 nominations. The clans from Mudug and Majertinia took roughly 297 nominations, or 67.25%, of the total of 442 nominations. For details on these figures and the rulers of the Somali state, see: Hagi, Aves Osman and Abdiwahi Osman Hagi (1998). *Clan, sub Clan and Regional Representation in the Somali Government Organization 1960-1990: Statistical Data and Findings*. Washington, D.C.

twice as Prime Minister from 1967-69 under the late President Sharmaarke and in 1990 under Siad Barre (see figure I).

Figure 1: The clan and sub-clans of individuals who held posts, including presidents, vice presidents, prime ministers, and ministers between 1960-90.

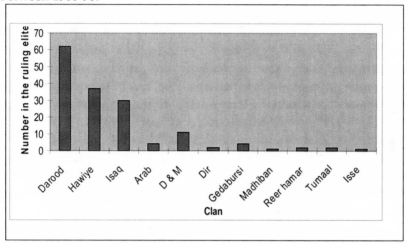

Source: constructed from Hagi and Hagi, 1998:118-131.

Inequality Leads to Conflicts

The link between inequality, poverty and conflict has been weak. Inequality and poverty are not necessarily causes of conflict and violence. However, the propensity or vulnerability of a society to conflict and violence increases when inequality becomes horizontal and is associated with ethnicity or regionalism. Such inequality manifests itself in political, economic and social marginality and the denial of basic human rights to specific groups. This leads to what Galtung (1990) named "structural violence," which results from a disparity in the distribution of power. Inequality in Sub Saharan Africa is the result of internal mismanagement of the state property and the creation of social inequality, hence bad governance. One main reason is that these states are too independent for their citizens. They have, since independence, had the ability to function much of the time without resorting to taxing their citizens. Their operating budgets were mostly provided by the international community through foreign aid, or the availability of natural resources such as agricultural commodities, minerals and oil.

Therefore, little incentive exists for these states to provide adequate public services (Herbst, 2000). In fact, Reno (2000) argues that in many cases, some states in Sub Saharan Africa use poverty, which in some cases is their own creation, as an instrument to control the state. In 1970, for example, the Siad Barre regime established the Agricultural Development Corporation (ADC). Private sale, purchase or distribution of any agricultural commodities, especially maize, sorghum and sesame were made illegal. This practice resulted in a 20% decrease in grain production between 1969 and 1980. In fact, Somalia, which until then produced almost 100% of its grain, had to import an average of 8.4% annually between 1975 and 1984 (The Economist, 1986). The state's disincentive, coupled with the dilemma of citizenship as established by Ekeh, created huge social inequalities. Social inequality brings three major problems, all of which are associated with conflict and violence within the society. These are: economic decline, political instability and poverty.

First, social inequality brings decline in the country's economy. The decline usually results from a reduction in investment in social services such as public education and healthcare. Therefore, inequality is inherently an ingredient in the slow growth of social capital (Bardhan and Urdy, 1999). Secondly, inequality has been associated with political instability in most states in Sub Saharan Africa, as evidenced by the number of military coups d'état that have occurred in the continent since independence. Alesina and Perotti (1996) argue that inequality correlates with political instability, measured in the number of political murders annually. The authors argue that political instability in turn creates disincentive to invest in the country both internally and externally. This is evidenced by the reduction of the Direct Foreign Investment (DFI) from 15% in 1970 to 8% in 1989 (UNDP, 1992:37).

Third and finally, the end result of political instability and economic decline is poverty. Moore (2000) links bad governance to poverty, particularly in Sub Saharan Africa. By the end of the 1960s, the majority of newly independent countries had experienced either a civil war, military intervention, or both. Consequently, by the end of the 1970s, a study by the World Bank found that of the 34 world's poorest countries, 21 (60%) were from Sub Saharan Africa. And by the 1980s, the African continent would harbor 82% of the world's poorest nations, with 93% of the countries reporting the lowest levels of standards of living in the modern world.

Economic Decline

The economic decline in most African states, including Somalia, is a result of social inequality coupled with the reduction in international donation during the 1980s. Somalia has been the darling of the international donor community. This was partly the result of the ideological war between the East and West during the Cold War. Over the years, the Somali ruling elites had received millions of dollars in foreign aid from both camps of the ideological divide, which kept them in power for more than three decades. Between 1965 and 1987, despite the fact that the country's economy stagnated, Somalia received over U.S $800 million dollars from the U.S. alone (Ayittey, 1994, p. 3). The main reasons for the stagnation were corruption and the misguided economic policies of various governments ran by regional and clan-based elites. This was especially true for the Barre regime, which received large amounts of aid (military and economic) from international donors.

This aid gave the Barre regime the ability to maintain its grip on the state and keep its challengers at bay. Thanks to its strategic location, Somalia was a magnet for the combatants of the Cold War. Specifically, the port city of Berbera on the Red Sea was a point of contest and cash cow for the regime. The former Soviet Union first established a navel base in the area and in return provided plenty of military hardware for the regime, making Somalia's military one of the strongest armies in Sub Saharan Africa. In 1977, however, during the Ogaden War between Somalia and Ethiopia, the Soviets switched their alliance to Ethiopia. The regime then turned to the United States for help. In 1980 the Carter administration promised support for Barre on the condition that he sever relations with the Soviets. During that same year, Washington and Mogadishu signed an agreement that would allow the U.S. navy to use the naval facilities at Berbera in exchange for military and economic aid. The Carter administration provided a package of about U.S $45 million in military, economic and budgetary support (ibid).

The Barre's regime also received aid from its former colonial power, Italy, through its aid agency *Funda Aiuto Italiana*. Italy invested more than one billion dollars in various projects, and the majority of these projects were wasteful and misguided. Among the many projects was the 450 km road project in the sparsely populated and barren desert area between Garowe and Bosaaso (ibid). The over U.S $250 million allocated to this project and funds assigned to other projects were spent in a very wasteful and corrupted fashion. Ironically, the Italian government was aware of it. According to an employee at the Italian Embassy in Mogadishu, "[the] Italian aid program was used to exploit the pastoral populations and to support a regime that did nothing to promote internal development and was responsible for the death of many of its people" (quoted in Ayittey, 1994:3). This aid increased inequality among the Somalis. For example, the number of luxury cars in Mogadishu increased, to where it was not a surprise to see Mercedes and Toyota Land Cruisers in the streets and markets. More important was the increase in the number of luxury houses complete with swimming pools, air conditioners and modern amenities. In fact, a whole area in southern Mogadishu came to be known as "Booli Qaran," meaning "extra-legally obtained people's money."

By the end of the 1980s, however, the large amount of aid that went to many African states, including Somalia, became devastating to their already weakened economies. Keen (1998) argues that poor social services and poverty fuel conflict from below. Historically, marginalized parts of the society tend to turn towards banditry and other illegal activities. For example, in the late 1980s, the city of Mogadishu saw an unprecedented increase in the number of bandit groups and unruly teenagers from the poor parts of the country. One such group was a gang of former orphan children called *Ciyaal Faay Cali*, "the children of Faay Ali."[1]

The violence that social inequality brings coupled with economic decline (internal or external) may also lead to society-wide conflicts. Bayart (1993) argues that in the conditions of extreme poverty, scarcity,

---

[1] The name comes from a lady who raised bunch orphans. These children reached adolescence during the 1980s, which coincided with the weakening of the Siad Barre regime. The gang was famous for brutal actions including robbery, rape and even murders. But, importantly, they were partially responsible for the dismantling of the regime and the creation of public dissatisfaction and apathy towards the regime. This information is based on interviews this author conducted in 1993-94 in Mogadishu.

insecurity and political instability that exist in Africa, everyone is engaged in life-and-death struggles, both to survive and to accumulate wealth and power. In this struggle, both rich and poor strategically attach themselves to networks and organized factions based primarily on one's family, tribe, ethnic alliance or friends. This struggle is central to understanding political action in Africa. Its objective is to control "the distribution of the possibilities of realizing a primitive accumulation, in the strict sense of the concept, by the confiscation of the means of production and trade" (234). With these factions engaged in the rivalry of obtaining acceptable livelihood and security, conflict and violence are predictable. Bayart concludes that, "today, as yesterday, what is being fought for is the exclusive right to the riches claimed by the holders of 'absolute seniority'" (241).

Overall, there is little doubt that the number of violent conflicts and internal wars has increased in the poor countries of the third world. There is also little dispute that the increases in the number of these conflicts were severe for Sub Saharan Africa, and that they coincided with an era of economic decline due to, among other things, the end of the Cold War. Steward and Fitzpatrick (2000) assert that the high incidence of conflicts in poor countries result from three interrealted factors: (1) a widening inequality in wealth and income between *vertical* (social groups) and *horizontal* (territorial groups) in the country; (2) an increase in the uncertainty of the future prospects; and (3) the weakened capacity of the state.

Arms Accessibility and the Somali Conflict

The economic decline that resulted from both internal social inequality and a decline in foreign aid, combined with the consequences of the Structural Adjustment Programs, created an environment of economic and physical insecurity. We will consider military expenditure, determined by the amount of money a country spends on its military, as the indicator for weapons availability in the country. At the heart of military expenditure is the issue of state security. Hutchful (2000) argues that, among other things, the state is created as a "security racket." To him, "the relationship between governance and security is at once intimate and obvious. First, governance is both about creating and the management of the instruments of violence that at the same time necessarily underpins assuring conditions of security. Second, governance involves the effective administration, regulation and control of the instruments of violence" (Hutchful, 2000:211). However, Jackson (1992) argues that the security of African states in the post-World War II era has been guaranteed by external forces, e.g. former colonial powers, Cold War superpowers, international and/or regional organizations (UN, NATO, ECOWAS, OAU etc.), and that the state is protected from external threats. Despite this minimal external security threat, the African militaries expanded tremendously. In 1963 the average African state had 0.73 soldiers per 1000 people; by 1979 this figure had jumped to 3.10 per 1000 people (Herbst, 2000:105). Over the years the state militaries became palace guards, a tool for the ruling elite to dominate the rest of the society.

Since its independence in 1960, Somalia has spent a great deal of money and talent in military and military-related activities. Most of the expense was provided externally by world powers, due to Somalia's strategic importance. First, it is geographically close to all-important oil production centers of the Middle East. Secondly, it controls the important trade route through the Suez Canal and the Red Sea. Therefore, Somalia received huge amounts of military aid over the years from the rivals of the Cold War. During the early 1970s, Somalia was a client of the Soviet Union. The Somali dictator Siad Barre (1969-1991) established this relationship in response to the large-scale American military support for Somalia's rival Ethiopia under the rule of the feudal emperor Haile Selassie.

In 1974 however, a military coup by leftist Ethiopian officers toppled the monarchy and declared the country a Marxist-Leninist state. The superpowers switched their allegiances, with the Soviet Union backing Ethiopia and the United States siding with the Barre regime in Somalia. From the late 1970s until his ousting in January 1991, the U.S. sent hundreds of millions of dollars worth of arms to the Barre regime in return for the latter's permission to use the military facilities at Berbera (ibid) (see table II). The U.S. government ignored all warnings of Siad Barre's brutal regime and its violation of human rights throughout the 1980s, and when it finally withdrew support in 1989, Somalia plunged into chaos.

In addition to the former Soviet Union and the United States, Somalia received major weapon supplies from the Muslim world. This assistance reinforced mutual interests shared with several Muslim states, most notably Egypt, Saudi Arabia and Iran, and provided the basis for military cooperation between Somalia and these coutries. In the 1960s, Cairo trained the Somali army and navy.

Most postcolonial leaders in Africa have used the military to recruit their clansmen. In Kenya, for example, the Kamba and Kalenjin made up 34% of the military in 1961, while these tribes together accounted for only 9-11% of the total population. Similarly, during Siad Barre's regime (1969-91), the Somali security apparatuses were controlled by three groups: the Marehaan (Barre's clan), Ogaden (his mother's clan) and Dhulbahante (his son-in-law's clan), all of which fall within the larger clan family of Darood, an alliance labeled among the Somalis as MOD (Laitin, 1987). Over the years these large and tribalized militaries created an insecurity dilemma, where the average citizen was afraid of the military of his own country. Additionally, military expenditure dragged the economies of many Sub Saharan African countries to the ground. As a result, the responsibility for the security and welfare of individuals and groups that were not part of military and bureaucracy fell to other social organizations, e.g. tribes, clans and kinship groups.

The high military spending led to economic decline in many Sub Saharan African countries. As a country's economy declined, so did its security and the banality of access to weapons by the civilians. Where a bad economy was coupled with the availability of arms, the state became weaker and incapable of providing security (physically and economically); this can lead to chaos and possibly the collapse of the state. As the central authority weakens, and in some cases collapses, emerging groups must pay attention to the amount of power they have relative to other groups. Balance of power races ensue as these groups prepare and pool their resources in order to preserve their existence. The groups must organize themselves, choose leaders, set up bureaucracies to collect taxes (or sometimes loot others) and organize security forces in order to enforce internal cohesion and insure external security (Posen, 1993:110). The power resources of the old regime, especially materials (e.g. weapons, money, etc.) and contacts (e.g. diplomatic relations), then become spoil for the contesting groups. In the Somali internal war, for example, the clans with heavy representation in the military and administration were best positioned to benefit from the disintegration of the state, both materially and politically. These groups consisted mainly of clans in Mudug and Majertinia, in other words, Darood and Hawiye.

After Barre was ousted, factions that intended only to replace his absolutist and dictatorial powers with their own brand came to the scene. Only this time, instead of one dictator, the country was initially compartmentally run by fifteen clan and sub-clan-based factions, a number that has swollen to as many as forty. The loaded dice continued because the overwhelming majority of the new *so called* leaders of these factions were high-ranking officers in the Barre regime, e.g. the former chief of the armed forces and the son-in-law of Barre, General Mohamed Said "Morgan" of the SSDF (a Majerteen-based faction). Thousands of Somalis suffered in this regional-based madness. During this period, government buildings and offices were destroyed and telephone and electric cables were dug out and sold for cash. Manufacturing machines were taken away. One example is the sugar factory located in Mareerey, a town in the Middle Jubba region, worth U.S $240 million, which was sold to businessmen in Tanzania for U.S $1 million.[1]

This robbery of public property has locally become known as the *Aboor* (meaning termite) looting system, in reference to the high speed with which the looting and destruction of property were accomplished. One of the main figures behind this looting was Osman Ali Hassan (Atto), a member of Saad, a Sub-clan of Habargidir, who was the financier of the late General Aideed's war machinery. However, Somalia's internal war has been far more devastating for the settled majority communities of southern Somalia. The combatants of the war are the minority clans from the Mudug and Majertinia who were fighting for the control of the fertile lands and their occupants.

Conclusion

This chapter argued that the internal war in Somalia resulted from three interrelated sources: social inequality, economic decline and easy access to weapons. Despite the tendency of many scholars to describe

---

[1] This figure is based on an interview conducted by the author in 1993-94.

Somalis as egalitarian, huge social inequalities still existed. These inequalities were not based on the control of production nor educational attainment, but rather on tribalism and clanism that takes its roots, as in most African states, from the colonial era. The Italian colonial state chose the clans from the Mudug and Majertinia region as their helpers and later passed the baton to them. The latter ruled the country from independence in 1960 to its collapse in 1990. The political leaders from these clans used the state as personal property for their own and their clansmen's enrichment. This state lacked any resemblance to the Weberian legal-rational state, and more importantly lacked any accountability to the public. All that one needed was to be a member of the ruling clan, or in some cases, know one member from that clan in order to receive any benefits. The members of the ruling clans, who are locally known as *Dowlad Ku Nool* (those that live off state property) enjoyed a disproportional amount of wealth and privilege.

Social inequality leads to three factors, which in turn lead to social breakdown. First, it leads to a decline in investments in social capital such as healthcare and education. Second, due to the waste of public money, it leads to economic decline. Finally, it leads to severe poverty.

In addition to social inequality, the Somali conflict resulted, as is the case of many conflicts around the globe, from the decline in the amount of donations from donor states and organizations. Also harmful were the World Bank and International Monetary Fund-imposed Structural Adjustment programs. Finally, the end of the Cold War made Somalia and many in the third world less desirable. These three factors together severely weakened the state's reciprocal and enforcement capabilities. The poor economic situation created a heightened situation of survival, in which everybody had to sell what they had in order to supplement their salaries, which were severely weakened by high inflation. Doctors and nurses sold medical supplies, teachers sold grades, and worst of all, soldiers sold their weapons, which brings us to the third factor. Over the years, Somalia has spent a large amount of its budget on military and military-related activities. Additionally, the country received one of the largest military aids in the continent due to its strategic geographical location. Thus, by the time the government collapsed, the country was saturated with too many weapons.

In a final analysis, one may argue that the Somali conflict stems from bad governance that crippled the realization of the country's economic potential. This bad governance also perpetrated and enforced severe social inequalities. As a child in Mogadishu, I remember a culture that discouraged one to show off his wealth, power and privilege. But by the end of the 1970s, this culture gave way to a new and more flamboyant culture, where building better houses such as those at Booli Qaran and driving luxurious expensive cars like the Mercedes Benz and Toyota Land Cruiser (Geela Mareehaanka) became the norm. More importantly, the clan members of the ruling elite, especially those of Barre's Marehaan, became the Sultans and its members were literally above the law. For example, Abdi Hoosh, who was also known as *Hoosh kibray* (the arrogant Hoosh) had his own jail where he arrested people without due process and detained them. He also slapped people at will, including high-level ministers in the cabinet. This practice can be traced back to the 1960s, when during the Majerteen reign, the famous daughters of Musa Mataan, who were the sisters of the first lady and chief of the police, General Mohamed Muse, slapped people in the streets.

The quest for the monopoly of the state is at the center of the conflict in Somalia. The majority of the warring groups came from the Mudug and Majertinia regions. The current interim government headed by Colonel Abdulahi Yusuf Ahmed, a Majerteen, is falling apart as a result of its incompetence and the appearance of a new phenomenon, the Union of Islamic Courts, which controlled Mogadishu until January 2007. Both the leaders of the courts and interim government are members of clans from Mudug and Majertinia.

The conflict in Somalia presents a dilemma whereby everyone wants to become the new Sultan so he/she can accumulate more wealth and privileges than others. On the other hand, one does not want to re-witness the severe maltreatment that many in the country experienced under the "sultanship" of another clan. Therefore, everyone strives to prevent the emergence of a strong state ran by others. It is this dilemma that both scholars and policy makers need to address in order to end the Somali internal war and create a viable state.

Chapter 6

SOMALIA: A FAILED STATE GOVERNED BY A FAILING GOVERNMENT?

Gerrie Swart

One core element of good governance is a capable democratic state – a state embedded in the public will, relying on legitimacy through the democratic process, with strong institutions promoting the public interest (see Chapters 2, 3 and 5). Good governance is considered to be a process, a work in progress that all countries strive to achieve. It is the product of deliberate policy choices, which countries make in managing themselves and creating a vision for the future (UNECA, 2005:26). Yet the exact opposite has transpired in Somalia.

Governance in Somalia

Somalia is in a state – a state of transition, a state of uncertainty and in a state of impending crisis yet again. Somalia tragically remains in a state of failure. Failed states seldom return to normality and Somalia has become a textbook example of state failure in action. That the situation in Somalia is precarious is self-evident. The real danger is that Somalia is entering another potentially dangerous phase characterized with its own set of complexities.

Very few observers would argue against the notion that the crisis in Somalia is far from resolved. In fact, the events of late 2006 and early 2007 point to a worrisome trend: Somalia is entering yet another phase characterized by severe instability, the risk of yet another civil war and the potential for further loss of life. Violence continues and in 2006 nearly 500 people died. As this chapter was completed, Somalia remained a country that effectively continued to exist without a government. Despite the various attempts at preventing a return to full-scale war, the country remained a failed state, failing to come to grips with much-needed reconstruction efforts. To add to the plethora of woes, Somalia's much vaunted transitional government was failing in carrying out its most crucial mandate – to lead Somalia to peace.

The former U.N. Secretary-General highlighted the dire situation in Somalia in a 2005 report:

> There has been no progress in ameliorating the contention between leaders of the transitional federal institutions on four broad issues: the relocation of the transitional federal institutions, a national security and stabilization plan, national reconciliation and the peace support mission envisaged by the African Union/Intergovernmental Authority on Development (IGAD) (Annan 2005:3).

As Mohamed Eno rightly shows in this volume (see Ch. 4), it is clear that progress has been slow, if not non-existent, on the salient issues crucial to ensuring a peaceful transition in Somalia. Without an agreement on reconciliation efforts, the location of the seat of power and governance, and the lack of a much needed national security and stability plan, it can rightly be asserted that Somalia will continue to be a failed state with scant prospects of changing status in the very near future, unless serious efforts are made to bring crucial actors in the crisis to the negotiating table.

Despite the move of the Transitional Government (the country's first government since 1991) to Mogadishu, the Somali capital remained a war-zone at the end of February 2007. It remained captive to the brutal civil war that was threatening to resurface. The capital was a scene of day-to-day carnage and violence and it appeared that the situation may be the start of yet another dark chapter in the country's futile attempt at achieving semblances of stability, let alone the arduous task of returning to statehood. In early 2007, the optimistic observer of the situation in Somalia was easily frustrated to note that war continued unabated. Sadly, the reality of war has proven more lucrative than the reconstruction of the Somali state. Years have passed and reports emanating from Somalia have cast an ominous shadow on peace. A number of recent developments have placed Somalia on a dangerous course of prolonged confrontation and crisis. This chapter will highlight recent developments in Somalia that continue to thwart reconstruction efforts. Attention will be given to the attempts by the Transitional Federal Government (TFG) to restore order to Somalia as well as the crisis that led to the emergence of the Union of Islamic Courts (UIC) as a viable alternative to the weak government. In the final analysis, I will argue that the greatest obstacle to the success of efforts aimed at reconstituting the failed state has been the government that was elected to reconstruct it.

A State of Emergency – the War Continues

Somalia continues to exist in a state of emergency, a country at war with itself. The hostilities witnessed in Mogadishu in late 2006 and early 2007 bear testament to the utter chaos and carnage that continues unabated, despite the fact that a transitional government has been elected to lead the country to peace. The already tense situation was exacerbated by an upsurge of violence that saw warlords and supporters of the Union of Islamic Courts fight for control of the battered Somali capital of Mogadishu. Given the importance of having the capital under one's effective control, Mogadishu had become the battlefield for groups with their own political ambitions.

In the third round of fighting in 2006, the warring factions were gunmen allied to Islamic courts and militia from a self-styled anti-terrorism alliance of powerful warlords known as the Alliance for the Restoration of Peace and Counter-Terrorism, allegedly backed by the United States. At a point of the conflict, many thought that the creation of an Islamic state ruled by extremist elements was a worst-case scenario that could not be avoided any longer.

The Rise of the Islamic Republic of Somalia?

Supporters of the UIC are a mixture of people or groups with different agendas and doctrinal orientations. They include progressives who embrace democratic values; opportunists who used the Courts' power for personal advancement; socially conservative *salafis* whose agenda is focused on public morality (leading to the periodic efforts to close cinemas); those who want an Islamic state but do not advocate political violence; and jihadis whose use of assassination as a tactic of choice has led to dozens of deaths in what amounts to a silent war in the streets of Mogadishu (International Crisis Group, 2006:15). As Osman illustrates in the previous chapter, tensions are also present across the clan spectrum, which adds another troubling dimension to the prospects of political leadership under the Islamic Courts should they regain control of the country.

The Islamic Courts are heterogeneous, encompassing a range of religious traditions and political perspectives almost as varied as those within the broader Somali society. Simplicity is the key to their popular appeal. A typical court has three main elements: a *majlis shura* (council), which includes respected political, traditional, business and religious leaders from the clan; a chairman appointed by the Council; and a militia commander appointed by the chairman, subject to the Council's approval. Their ostensible lack of political ambition makes them more broadly acceptable than other forms of local administration or factional authority, and their forces' relative discipline makes them preferable to other militia. The court's resources usually come from a combination of private contributions and taxation via militia checkpoints (International Crisis Group, 2006:9).

The first Islamic Courts appeared in Somalia during the early 1990s, shortly after the fall of the Barre regime. These were essentially local initiatives intended to provide a degree of law and order in an anarchic situation. But in 1998, a new brand of court was established under the leadership of Sheikh Hassan Dahir Aweys, a former vice chairman and military commander of the Islamic organization *al-Itihaad al-Islaam* (AIAI) and a member of the Habar Gidir Ayr clan. The court at Marka, headed by Sheikh Yusuf Indha'adde, became a vehicle for the expansion of Ayr political and commercial interests in Lower Shabelle region; the court at Ifka Halane, in western Mogadishu, emerged as a platform for Muslim extremists.

Shortly before the establishment of the old TNG at Djibouti in 2000, an overarching "Sharia Implementation Council," largely on Aweys' initiative, was established to coordinate the actions of the courts and provide a platform for political engagement with the TNG. The Council failed to persuade the TNG cabinet that its members should become the core of the regular judiciary and soon began to unravel. Aweys traveled to the Galguduud region, where he busied himself with setting up courts in the homeland of his own Habar Gidir Ayr clan.

In 2004, as the TFG was emerging from the deliberations of the Somali National Reconciliation Conference in Kenya, a new umbrella structure for the courts was established in Mogadishu: the Supreme Council of Sharia Courts. Aweys retained influence as a vice chairman. Under the leadership of the Supreme Council, several courts were persuaded to contribute troops and technicians to a combined militia force some 400-members strong. In the interim, allegations began to emerge of links between leading figures within the Courts and some terrorist activities at home and abroad. As a senior AIAI leader, Aweys was accused of involvement in bombings in Ethiopia in 1995-1996; testimony by al-Qaeda suspects in U.S. courts reportedly linked him to the team that bombed the U.S. embassies in Nairobi and Dar-es-Salaam in 1998 and suggested a relationship with Bin Laden himself. By early 2006, it was increasingly apparent that the Islamic courts were asserting greater autonomy from their clans (International Crisis Group, 2006:11). In 2001, the U.S. officially designated Aweys an individual with links to terrorism.

The growing assertiveness of the Courts did not go unnoticed on the international stage. For example, in April 2006, a UN arms embargo monitoring group called the Courts a "third force" in Somalia and described the dramatic enhancement of their military capacity through arms purchases and training. Two months later, Islamic leaders achieved victory over the warlords and in a statement indicated, in the words of Sheikh Sharif Sheikh Ahmed, chairman of Mogadishu's Islamic group, that "The Joint Islamic Courts do not want continuation of hostilities and will ensure peace and security following the change attained by the victory of the people with the support of Allah" (Crilly 2006). The establishment of the "anti-terror" alliance was seen as an attack on the courts and on Islam itself.

The International Crisis Group (2006:14) described the Islamic Courts as the "biggest wildcard in Somali politics today." Before their overthrow by the forces of the TNG, backed by Ethiopian troops in early 2007, leaders of the Courts presented themselves as a viable alternative to the ineffective Transitional Government. They proved themselves ready, willing and capable of exerting power and restoring security, which had, and perhaps still has to some extent, the potential of even further broadening their appeal to a war-weary Somali society. The Islamic Courts were also praised for their military prowess, possessing what were considered to be the most effective militias in the capital and indeed in the entire southern part of the country. There was, however, the fear that this military precision could be utilized to eliminate political opponents if necessary. This could engulf Somalia in yet another civil war situation.

It had also become clear that the Islamic courts had aspirations for control of Somalia well beyond just Mogadishu, and that large swaths of the country had already fallen under their control. Though first and foremost an Islamist movement, the Islamic Courts were/are also a manifestation of the interests and resistance of the Hawiye clan. Thus, one may argue that unless the TFG is reconstituted into a true government of national unity, it will face continued resistance from the bulk of the Hawiye, which had denied it access to the greater Mogadishu area and parts of central Somalia (International Crisis Group, 2006:2).

A country that has literally lacked a central government for more than a decade can ill afford for any new political vacuums to emerge. The Islamic Courts have already seized upon an opportunity where the transitional government did not exercise effective control. The danger is that more intolerant and violent groups could emerge to further undermine the transitional government's weak authority. While the discussions and negotiations that were going on at the time this paper was completed were crucial, they would be useless without considering the lingering tensions that led to the conflict.

Peace in Pieces: Talks about Talks?

In late 2006, Somalia's Transitional Federal Government (TFG) called for talks with the Islamic court leaders to chart a way forward, but observers rightly noted that this could prove difficult, as President Abdullahi Yusuf Ahmed is perceived as having an anti-Islamist agenda. These observations became a reality when Somalia's transitional parliament voted in mid-January 2007 to sack its speaker, Sharif Hassan Sheikh Adan.

Mr. Adan was opposed to Ethiopia's intervention in Somalia and, most importantly, had called for peace talks with the UIC before the latter lost control of Mogadishu. Obviously, neither of these positions had gone over well with the Interim President.

The Arab League had attempted to reconcile Somalia's transitional government with the Islamic leaders when they still controlled Mogadishu. This initiative received considerable support from the international community, including the International Contact Group on Somalia. The European Commission offered to establish a task force to facilitate inter-Somali dialogue.

The Intergovernmental Authority on Development (IGAD), at the forefront of attempts to end the conflict, backed Kenya's decision to impose sanctions on the warlords in an attempt to encourage the return to the negotiating table with the transitional government. Kenya hosted and played a key mediation role during the lengthy reconciliation talks between Somalia's numerous factions, culminating in the formation of the TFG in 2004 (see Ch. 4). The African Union had mandated the IGAD to deploy a peace-support mission to Somalia. However, the deployment of such a mission proved problematic and cumbersome, as the Union of Islamic Courts fiercely opposed the decision to initiate such a deployment, stating that further internal divisions would be amicably addressed within Somalia. On the other hand, the head of the transitional government refused to negotiate terms for the formation of a new, unified government with the UIC, saying he could not enter into talks with what he called "the UIC's radical leader, Sheik Hassan Dahir Aweys."

Eventually however, the transitional government and the Islamic courts signed a deal in which they agreed to recognize each other. Somalia's transitional parliament also voted in favour of the deployment of an African peacekeeping force to support the interim government in its efforts to restore law and order and re-establish state institutions. The International Crisis Group issued a stern warning that the proposed U.S.-UN Security Council resolution, which was to be presented by 29 November 2006, would be tantamount to a declaration of war. The proposed resolution would authorize the deployment of a regional military force (IGASOM) in support of the TFG and would exempt troop contributing countries (i.e. Ethiopia, Uganda and possibly Kenya) from the existing UN arms embargo. While the objectives were to strengthen the TFG, deter the Union of Islamic Courts from further expansion and avert the threat of full-scale war, it was likely to backfire on all three counts (International Crisis Group 2006).

The initial round of talks scheduled in July 2006 between the government and the UIC did not materialize. The two sides had met on 22 June in Khartoum and agreed to meet again on 15 July. The transitional government boycotted the talks on the basis of what it perceived as the Islamic courts' violation of the Khartoum agreement by engaging in fighting and capturing further territories in Somalia. The International Contact Group, which was created by the United Nations after the Union of Islamic Courts seized control of Mogadishu, launched initiatives to encourage a process of inclusive dialogue amongst Somalis in order to seek means through which the conflict could be ended.

The second round of peace talks between the two parties opened in Khartoum in September 2006 under the auspices of the Arab League. On 4 September 2006, the Transitional Federal Government and the Supreme Council of the Islamic Courts signed an accord in which they agreed to reconstitute the Somali national army, work towards the reintegration both entities' forces and practice the principle of peaceful coexistence between Somalia and its neighbours. Shortly afterwards, still in September 2006, a summit meeting of IGAD member states endorsed a deployment plan for the proposed IGAD-led peace support mission for Somalia. The Supreme Council of Islamic Courts had continued to voice its objection to the deployment of what it termed "foreign troops" on Somali soil.

However, in November 2006, the mediators called off another round of talks that were scheduled to be held in Khartoum. In late November, the Transitional Federal Government (TFG) rejected an agreement reached in the capital between the Union of Islamic Courts (UIC) and a delegation of members of parliament led by speaker Sharif Hassan Sheikh Adan. A return to war appeared inevitable and, in December, the two parties engaged in fierce fighting, which ended in the victory of the TFG backed by Ethiopian troops. The UIC had not lacked supporters either (Lynch 2006:A13). One is therefore frustrated to note that, despite the apparent high-level diplomatic manoeuvrings that were seen and the efforts made by different well-wishers, Somalia continues to take three steps back for every one small step towards peace. But the explanation appears glaringly obvious. Any peace process demands bold and steadfast leadership. It should be a peace process owned by the Somali people, yet continued pressure from outside has always imposed peace plans. Conflict prevention did not form part of the core solution when tensions first led to the brutal civil war. The greatest Achilles' heel of Somalia's attempts at successful transition and return to statehood is ironically the very institution elected to lead the country, a weak and ineffective transitional government.

A Government in Exile from Within

The creation of Somalia's Transitional Federal Government in 2004 was heralded with much optimism and hope. The creation of the country's first functioning government in 15 years would be crucial in ensuring that peace efforts were to succeed. This was purely symbolic. The realization was that the advent of a government in itself was not going to be enough to ensure a smooth transition. The birth of Somalia's new government regrettably took place from outside the country, in Kenya, a decision that should have signalled that the arrangement was destined to failure. The creation of the Somali government was supposed to herald the advent of a new era, in which security and stability would be returned to the embattled nation. Instead, conditions within the country proved far too dangerous to allow for the formation of the new government even from within. It was apparent from the outset that the elected leaders were at odds with each other. Tensions between President Abdullahi Yusuf Ahmed and Prime Minister Ali Mohammed Gedi, based then in Jawhar, on the one hand and the Speaker of Parliament, Shariff Hassan Sheikh Adan, on the other became evident.

Eventually, in June 2005, the Transitional Federal Government relocated to Somalia and a decision was made not to return to Mogadishu, citing a continued lack of security. In July 2005, President Yusuf indicated his intention to move the seat of government to Jawhar. Warlords threatened to attack the President and President Yusuf himself was said to have very little support in Mogadishu. He thus refused to move to the capital as long as his rivals remained in control. The Speaker of Parliament, along with 100 members of the 275-strong parliament, decided to relocate to Mogadishu in an attempt to restore order.

The seat of parliament became the next contentious issue. Under an agreement that was signed after talks held in Yemen, the parliament managed to convene its first session on Somali soil in February 2006, following an agreement between President Yusuf and the Speaker of Parliament. Divisions continued and Prime Minister Mohamed Ali Gedi criticized the fact that he had not been consulted on the decision of the time and venue for the first parliamentary session in Somalia. Both President Yusuf and Speaker Adan indicated that the assembly session would be held in the town of Baidoa. Further tensions arose after the assassination of Abdalla Deerow Isaq, the Constitution and Federalism Minister in the Transitional Federal Government (TFG). The effective functioning of Somalia's first parliament became crucial in light of the vast and seemingly insurmountable task that lay ahead in reconstructing an entire country ravaged by brutal conflict. It became apparent that, even on technicalities, the government would be deeply divided, thereby casting doubt on its ability to oversee the return of the country to statehood.

Transition Impossible?

As I completed this paper, it was still premature to entertain notions of reconstituting a state such as Somalia, not because the need to do so was not urgent, but because the conditions for making genuine strides in this direction were not met. Firstly and most importantly, the country remained at war and the root causes of the conflicts that had ravaged the country remained unresolved, leaving the country vulnerable to a return of war at any time. For effective resolution of the problems Somalia faces, far greater attention must be paid to the effects of state failure on regional dynamics and relations and vice versa. Yet these considerations were not properly taken into account when peace efforts were launched.

Secondly, it is not yet clear what implications a fully reconstructed Somalia might hold for regional security. As a failed state Somalia posed a definite security threat, yet what will a strong Somali state look like? Is the reconstruction of Somalia in the interest of its neighbours? A strong Somali state, depending on who is at the helm, could pose equally severe security risks to overall regional stability. If it can be deducted from this that not all regional countries are on board as genuine partners for peace in Somalia, does this make the transition impossible?

Conclusion and Policy Recommendations

To salvage the peace process, even though the Transitional Government seems in control of the situation after its victory over the UIC, a number of crucial measures need to be taken. The need to see the implementation of a reworked Mogadishu Security and Stabilization Plan is vital. Following the March 2005 walkout, the

Mogadishu Group announced an ambitious initiative to enhance security in Mogadishu. The Mogadishu Security and Stabilization Plan (MSSP) included an impressive proposal for demobilizing 1,400 militiamen and 60 technicals from eight militias in two camps outside the city; efforts to eliminate militia roadblocks in the city; and preliminary plans to establish a regional/municipal administration. The plan succeeded in fostering some semblances of cooperation, which had been sorely lacking in the transitional period.

Regrettably, the plan was hijacked by some groups for their own selfish political gains and failed. The alarming rate at which arms continue to flow into Somalia proves the weakness of the arms embargo and the need to ensure greater compliance. This requires a revised and strengthened National Security and Stabilization plan that provides for a credible and united military and police force ready, willing and able to guarantee national security. Initiating talks on the future of Somalia's constitution will have to include frank and sobering discussions over the Somali state and rebuilding the country from its very core. Reconciling the vast ethnic, clan and religious groups will be central to achieving statehood. The acute refugee crisis that persists also warrants greater attention.

Discussions and the debates about the revival of the Somali state must take place within Somalia, for if the Somalis take responsibility for their own future and assume ownership of the outcomes, this could produce a state that is vibrant and ready to function once more. But should genuine external assistance be offered, especially by regional (IGAD) and continental (AU) institutions, such offers should be welcomed. If Somalia decides to isolate itself entirely in its quest to return to statehood, we may see the emergence of a more defensive, closed, and secretive state that only communicates with the outside world if and when it deems it useful and not necessarily in an accommodating manner. The Somali people ultimately must have a greater share in the kind of state that takes shape at what hopefully will signal the end of the brutal civil war.

Somalia has embarked on a very difficult road to peace that is likely to take many more detours before the final destination is reached. While Somalia continues to be characterized as a failed state, it remains a state nonetheless, and returning the country into the fold of nations at peace with the world is now crucial more than ever. The government and whoever may assume that role in the end has to be accountable to the most important and often sidelined group in this crisis, Somalia's citizens, who have had to bare the greatest brunt in the loss of their freedom, security and lives. Faced with such a huge responsibility, the leadership will have to come to the stark realization failure is not an option.

The carnage, however, continues.

The rest of the developments during the first quarter of 2007 have produced further cause for concern. The conflict situation threatened to engulf the entire region with the presence of Ethiopian troops in Somalia. The conflict furthermore threatens to draw Eritrea into the fray and the possibility of a regional conflict involving Somalia, Ethiopia and Eritrea should not be ruled out. Analysts have expressed fears that Ethiopia and Eritrea, still at odds over their unresolved 1998-2000 border conflict, may initiate a proxy war in Somalia, which could further undermine any and all efforts at securing peace in the embattled nation. Towards the end of April 2007, fighting continued unabated in the Somali capital of Mogadishu. Heavy shelling rocked the Somali capital as fighting raged between Ethiopian forces and Islamist insurgents. The prospects of securing a definitive negotiated settlement to the conflict appear increasingly dismal.

The perceived threat of Somalia becoming the epicentre of Al-Qaeda's operations in East Africa adds another troubling dimension to an already dire conflict situation. The most extreme elements of the Islamic insurgency are said to remain intact. It is reported that more than 1,400 people were killed in the country between January and June 2007, of whom 400 from violence largely caused by the militants. The government, supported by Ethiopian troops, declared victory in late April 2007, but the extremists appear to be infiltrating towns across the country. The government's failure to restore order may yet again provide an opportunity for a takeover by radical Islamic elements who grabbed power for nearly six months in 2006. The United States has also entered the fray, which could add further complexities to the Somali conflict. A U.S. warship shelled what the Americans claimed were suspected Al-Qaeda targets in northeastern Somalia at the beginning of June 2007, after resurgents clashed with troops from the country's semi-autonomous region of Puntland. The current U.S. operations are unlikely to deter the most determined segments of the insurgents operating in the region. These extremist are likely to continue to exploit the precarious security situation that persists in

Somalia. Somalia remains a failed state governed by a failing government, entering yet another turbulent and ominous phase in its tumultuous history.

Part III

Actors and Tentative Solutions

Chapter 7

SOMALI RECONCILIATION CONFERENCES: THE UNBEATEN TRACK

Mohamed H. Mukhtar

Introduction:

Since 1991 there has been 15 major national and an uncountable number of regional and clan reconciliation conferences, most of which took place outside of Somalia. Ethiopia hosted four, three in Addis Ababa in 1992-1993 and one in Sodere – a hot spring resort about 100 kilometers southeast of Addis Ababa – in January, 1997. Djibouti hosted three, two in June-July 1991, and one in May 2000 in Arta, a summer resort near Djibouti. Sudan is hosting the Khartoum conference which began in July 2006.

What are most striking are the similarities in the way these peace and reconciliation conferences were conducted. Each of them attempted to lay the groundwork for a comprehensive peace, and each supposedly represented the entire nation. Most were hosted by a friendly neighboring country, supported by the Somali public, the United Nations, international organizations and nongovernmental organizations (NGOs). Key participants included representatives of armed factions, collaborators of faction 'leaders,' and former civilian politicians and army officers who clearly helped put the country in the position where it is today. At the start of each meeting, there were great expectation and hopes that there would be no more missed opportunities for peace. But these conferences were all doomed to fail, leaving Somalia without a functioning government.

The time has come to reconsider the basic ingredients of peace and reconciliation. According to Somali tradition, *"Ol nebeda ku dombooyty,"* every war gives way to peace. *"Dagaal wiilbaa ku dhinta ee kuma dhasho,"* war results in the death of a son, but not in the birth of one. *"Nebeda naas la nuughy leh,"* it is only peace that can give you milk. To make peace the following are required (ICRC & Somali Red Crescent Society, 1997):

a) Trustworthy participants:

For stateless societies recovering from periods of massive atrocities, reconciliation efforts can easily be doomed by disputes over who has the right to represent whom in the peace talks. It is necessary, therefore, to ask what would it take, and what the current or imagined institutions need to do, to help Somalis come to terms with the past and to help heal the victims, bystanders, and even perpetrators of violence? What could build a nation capable of preventing future massacres and the rise of new regimes of torture? The most effective way is to embrace the rule of law and to set up a tribunal. Somali victims are entitled to full justice, namely trials of perpetrators and adequate punishment for those found guilty. There must be due process.

The trials of the 1994 Rwandan massacre in Arusha, Tanzania, in December 2003, almost a decade after the massacre, convicted many Rwandans of genocide and crimes against humanity. The prosecutors called the verdicts an historic victory of good against evil, and Rwandans started to pursue their life regularly, to forgive and forget. The South African Truth and Reconciliation Commission (TRC) of 1995 is another good example of the positive recovery of a society from a deeply divided community to a future founded on a peaceful coexistence for all South Africans irrespective of color, race, class, belief or gender.[1] Imagine World War II without the Nuremburg trials; what would have been the fate of Europe?

Somalia has not conducted its own tribunals of reconciliation, but the door is still open. Such a procedure has the added advantage of identifying or "short listing" the number of potential participants in any future peace negotiations and gives the public a clear conscience as they choose future leaders. The United Nations and friendly nations should assist Somalia in implementing this process.

---

[1] The TRC was set up by the government of national unity in 1995 to help deal with what happened under apartheid era. The commission, after so many years of fact findings, concluded to grant amnesty in respect of acts, provide reparations to victims and hope the sufferers to come to terms with the past and finally lay to rest the trauma and pain associated with it.

b) Impartial or disinterested negotiators:

According to a Somali saying, *"Habar lang fadaw mal ha ku weidiyaw,"* ask not for the hand of a bride from one who want her himself. So far most conference participants have viewed the meetings more as vehicles for enhancing their own status or that of their clan than for advancing the cause of peace. Many of them went to the gatherings without an invitation and managed not to miss a single meeting. For participants, it was for the *"dhaadhac"* daw – per diems, travel expenses and hotel accommodations generously paid by the UN, the Intergovernmental Authority on Development (IGAD) and other international nongovernmental organizations (INGOs). Indeed, the 275 members (parliamentarians) of the current Transitional Federal Government TFG would not convene in Baidoa in February 2006 unless the UN Development Program (UNDP) promised to pay each parliamentarian a monthly allowance of $1,800 and other per diems for chairing a committee or international travels (ICG, 2006:7-8). The longer the duration of the conference the more *"dhaadhac"* involved, and thus, the more participants. Of the 15 Somali National Reconciliation Conferences from 1991 to 2002, the First, known as the Djibouti I, lasted for only one week, from 5-11 June 1991, and only leaders of four faction groups participated. The 15th, known as the Mbagathi, Kenya, lasted for over two years (2002-2004) and attracted more than twenty factions.[1] Most participants were also jockeying for political positions, i.e. President, Prime Minister, Speaker of the Parliament, Cabinet member, or at least MP.

Participants in future Somali peace and reconciliation conferences should be composed of individuals, invited by a plenary committee, with no vested interest in holding political office.

---

[1] It is worth noting that throughout the period, not only did the number of factions and representatives increase, but also the number of parliamentarians. In the 1993 Addis Ababa Conference, the number of Transitional National Council (TNC) agreed upon as the transitional authority was 74, whereas in the Arta or the Djibouti III Reconciliation Conference of 2000, numbers jumped to 245 MPs, and in the Mbagathi Conference of 2002, the agreed members of the TFG came to 275. For further details see Mukhtar (2003: 2-5, 76-77).

c) The need for some alternative ideas:

For decades, the political rules in Somalia have been set by the rulers, first a dictator, then a series of warlords or Islamicists. In both cases, to maintain their power, these rulers eliminated competition and restricted participation, since any enlargement would likely have disturbed the prevailing status quo. Future peace and reconciliation conference needs new players willing to accept new entrants. The political reforms required for the future Somalia should not be conditioned or imposed by external donors. The country needs cultural and economic adjustments before it is ready for sustainable ideologies.

d) Reinterpretation of sovereignty:

Since Somalia currently does not fit the meaning of "sovereign state" in its modern political parlance and has no official standing in the global world order, all that exists is a patchwork of regional authorities in different stages of lawlessness, anarchy and chaos. The Northwestern region declared itself an independent state on May 18, 1991 as the Somaliland Republic, the Southwestern regions as the Reverine State in 1995, and the Northeastern region proclaimed itself Puntland State in 1997. From 2004, there is also the government of national unity known as the TFG based in Baidoa and their rival the Union of Islamic Courts (UIC) based in Mogadishu. All of the above authorities are clan-based and none were able to bring about Somalia's unity. All transitional mechanisms recognized by the international community and supported by the Somali public are doomed to fail.

It may be necessary to reconsider the possibility of "tutelage," if that term is reinterpreted to mean "temporary custodial care" by the UN, for a state that has given up or lost its sovereign nationhood. If the current Transitional Federal Government (TFG) fails to bring about governance for Somalia, the UN may be obliged to develop a mechanism for intervening in situations where a state's fundamental institutions have collapsed – not with the aim of institutionalizing foreign control but with the goal of creating stronger domestic institutions. The Somali people may even be ready to welcome such temporary recommitment to the UN.

Some success stories:

And yet while Somali peace and reconciliation conferences have so far not managed to achieve their ultimate goals, they have not all been abject failures.

Regional Autonomy

The Addis Ababa Peace Conference of March 1993 promulgated for an idea of fundamental importance, the proposition of regional autonomy. The Somali people have been moving toward that form of governance for the past thirteen years, and there is still a chance for its success. The regional factional conferences of 1994, such as the Cairo Accord, the Nairobi Declaration, and the Somali National Alliance (SNA) Mogadishu Conference brought about alliances of factions to perhaps forge such regional authorities. The Cairo Accord was signed by leaders of 12 factions, dubbed as Group 12 (G 12), and the Nairobi Declaration was initially signed by the SNA and later welcomed by the signatories of the G 12. The Mogadishu Conference was undertaken exclusively by the SNA, which declared an interim "national" government. Similar experiences took place earlier in Somaliland, which proclaimed itself a republic in 1991 but has not gained international recognition, and later Puntland, which became an "autonomous" region in 1997.

The Digil and Mirifle people also established, in March 1995, the Supreme Governing Council (SGC), a bicameral council, as an autonomous legislative body for the Reewin people called the Reverine State, which was overthrown by Mohamed Farah Aideed seven months later. The Reewin land covers former Upper Juba, Lower Juba and Banadir regions. The Reewin (Rahanweyn) Resistance Army (RRA) also established a regional administration over what it called the "liberated" territories of Bokool and Bay in 1998 and 1999 respectively. This could also be considered an accomplishment in governance, though one not widely accepted because the concept of Somalian occupation of a Somali territory was not comprehensible and was not an issue previously addressed in Somali politics.

It was after Aideed's occupation of Baidoa in 17 September 1995 that some Somalis started questioning the right of invading clans to govern. In fact, there were many regions that had been occupied by new clans, among which were the Lower Shabelle, occupied by Habar Gedir, the Lower Juba by Majerteen, the Middle Juba by Ogaden and Gedo by Marehan. These regions were historically Digil and Mirifle. During the occupation, local people found themselves negotiating not with representatives with whom they shared long common experience and social contracts, but with young, armed militiamen whose interest and actions placed them outside the pale of the Somali customary law. The RRA, by liberating the Bokool and Bay from Habar Gedir militias, opened up a Pandora's box, as they promised to continue the liberation movement until the last piece of the Digil and Mirifle land was freed. If regional authority based on local participation was the goal, then those RRA actions could be considered movements in the right direction despite the general stagnation of Somali reconstruction efforts.

Clan Size and Power

Another important accomplishment is the Sodere Accord of 1997, where for the first time Somali clans agreed about their relative size, power and territorial rights. The Sodere participants agreed that there are four major equal clans: the Reewin (known also as Digil and Mirifle), the Issaq (later called Dir), the Hawiye and the Darood. The conference also recognized another segment of the Somali society which included minority groups not identified with one of the above clans, i.e. the Banadiris and the Somali Bantus just to mention some (Mukhtar, 2003:225). After Sodere, the question of clan composition of any future Somali "conference" should not be a problem.

Empowerment of Women

In Djibouti 2000, the gathering agreed that 12 percent of the seats of the Transitional National Parliament (TNP) be reserved for women. This is a significant accomplishment as well, because women were conventionally excluded from the Somali political scene. Although both the *"Heer,"* Somali customary law, and the *"Sharia,"* Islamic law, strongly support women's rights, clan authorities and religious practice later stripped women of their basic human rights and excluded them from playing a significant role in politics. Since women rarely held leadership positions and, until recently, had only a marginal influence on politics, the 12 percent is a step forward to build upon further recognition for women.

Multiculturalism

Finally, the Mbagathi Peace and Reconciliation Conference of Kenya in 2003 acknowledged with sizeable majority the consideration of two Somali languages, Maay and Maxaatiri, as the official languages of the Somali society. The Transitional Federal Charter of 2003 states in Article 7: "The official languages of the Somali Republic shall be Somali (Maay and Maxaatiri) and Arabic.[1] Who is not delighted to see, after decades of silence, a more complete discussion of the roles of women, minorities and alienated or marginalized cultures in shaping the history of Somalia? A multicultural approach to the past is long overdue. This is a challenge to the long-held view of Somalia's homogeneity and monolingualism that gives a more accurate account of Somalia's history and culture.

Conclusion:

Now the issue focuses on how Somalia can do better. Only by tackling the obstacles outlined here can Somalia expect to move forward on the slow road to reconciliation and renewal. To conclude, I will emphasize some of the most important challenges Somalia is facing.

First, Somalia needs to redefine the term "occupation." Today in the country – as I highlighted earlier – there are clans occupying other clans. Someone has to speak up for the voiceless, otherwise peace will remain remote.

Second, it is necessary to bring the war criminals to justice. It took Liberia many years to nail Charles Taylor. The international community must ban Somali warlords from coming to their countries by stopping the issuance of visas and freezing and shutting down their bank accounts. It is never too late. We can do it now.

Further, the rule of self-determination must be applied. We should not be obsessed with what form of government Somalia should adopt,

---

[1] See Draft Version 7.0, The Transitional Federal Charter of the Somali Republic, Nairobi: August, 2003.

be it unitary, a federation of regional states, or split into many independent states.

Finally, there is a need to indigenize the ethos of the reconciliation process. Future conferences should take place in Somalia. I believe if some of the "reconciliation" conferences had taken place in Somalia, the outcome would have been more promising and the chances for peace would have been higher. Somalia must draft its own constitution based on its needs and experiences under "*Geedka hoostiisa,*" the tree not the hotel. The time has come to employ and empower the "*Heer*" customary laws and promote the tolerant form of Islam.

Chapter 8

SOMALIA'S RECOVERY AND REFORMATION: TRANSCENDING THE RHETORIC OF CLAN POLITICS

Omar A. Eno

The following is an anecdote about a nomadic character: "The King of [Dahomey, now Benin] said that a country must be loved by its...[people] and that is why he has forbidden his people to migrate from one part of the country to another, since a [nomad] can never have a deep love for his land "(Polanyi, 1966).

Based on the King's description of a nomad, the current intra-tribal war in Somalia, caused and sustained by nomads, validates his predictions. Throughout the past 17 years the Somali nomads have showed no love or mercy for the land and its people.

Introduction

As we read in many academic texts, journals, and newsletters, Somalis are a traditionally nomadic society with a nomadic way of governing, a system some scholars have called a "pastoral democracy," which is traditionally geared towards "mythmaking," (Arthur, 1999) rather than peacemaking, among the warring Somalis. As part of an ongoing cultural genocide, the dominant nomadic Somalis have utterly denied to recognize the culture, tradition, languages, history, and values of the sedentary and non-nomadic societies.

In this chapter, I intend to transcend the politics of pessimism conducted by the warlords in conjunction with their clan affiliates, which continuously resists any viable resolution and reconciliation. By that note, the chapter intends to shed some light on, and discover new introductory options and alternative solutions that might help resuscitate and reinvigorate, Somalia as a nation that could once again function normally. Thus, this chapter gives an overview of the political structure and dynamics revolving around the nation state in Somalia from independence to 2006.

The chapter will be divided into three parts. First, I will provide a brief description of some of the events that transpired during the dictatorship of the late Siad Barre's military regime and the factors behind its collapse in 1991. Second, I will analyze factors behind the continuously frustrated and failed efforts to revive the Somali state. Finally, I will provide recommendations and way forward that brings a long lasting peace in Somalia by acknowledging the atrocities perpetrated by the nomadic clans of Somalia against non-nomadic Somalis.

Background of Somalia's Political Structure, 1960-2006

Somalia is a nation that binds together people of distinct cultures, customs, traditions, languages, values, as well as destinies. In theory, all Somalis practice Islam, although differences in practice can be observed. The existence of these differences does not in any way mean that they cannot live together in peace and harmony by respecting their differences and contributing to the dialogue to help discover the solutions to their problems.

Since the independence of 1960, Somali politics have been dominated by nomadic clans who, despite the existence of diversity in the country, continued to portray a homogeneous society in their image. The price tag attached to this unresolved festering problem has been high. Extensive damage has been suffered as a consequence of the sheer arrogance in nomadic self-grandeur, which prevails in the cultural dogma of their psycho-social thinking. The Somali people have inherited the devastation, which remains an enduring entity.

In the wake of European colonization, different territorial areas inhabited by Somali-speaking groups were administered separately. The concept underpinning the creation of a modern Somali state began as the brainchild of the British colonial administration Hussen A. Dualeh, who had political rivalry with Italy prior to Somalia's independence. The idea was to put all five Somali speaking territories under the same administration: British Somaliland, Italian Somaliland, the Ogaden of Ethiopia, the Northern Frontier Districts of Kenya and Djibouti (French Somaliland).

In 1960, two of the five territories became independent: Italian Somaliland in the south obtained its independence on July 1, 1960 from the Italian colonial authority, while British Somaliland in the north gained its independence on June 26 of the same year from Britain. Soon after independence, both states were conflated and formed "the Somali Republic" (Mukhtar, 1996). Aden Abdullah Osman, a pro-Italian and a non-founding member of the SYL (Somali Youth League) party, was inaugurated as the first president of the Somali Republic. Osman served the presidency as a provisional leader and later sought reelection that saw him in power till 1967. He was defeated in the subsequent election by Abdirashid Ali Shermarke who, in turn, served until October 1969 as the second president.

For unspecified reasons, his vexed kinsman, who at the time was serving among the presidential security staff, assassinated Shermarke in October 1969. Analysts, however, suggest that the ill fate of Shermarke was determined by his government's corruptness and other political sagas related to his party's vote rigging in the previous parliamentary elections. The late General Mohamed Siad Barre led a bloodless military coup d'etat following Shermarke's demise. Unfortunately, an unforeseen and bleak future was awaiting Somalia; it began a long and most arduous journey under general Barre's military dictatorship. From 1969 to 1991, Somalia experienced the iron fist of a malignant military administration, which was based on nepotism, human rights abuses, extortion, and hooliganism (Mukhtar, 1996).

Upon acquisition of power, Barre immediately became popular mainly for his cunning attitude and eloquence, and by vowing to restore equality, justice, and economic development for all Somalis. Barre shrewdly exploited the public desire for change while using tantalizing nationalistic themes such as achieving the Greater Somalia dream, amicable settlement of the feuding inter-tribal differences, enforcing the rights of women and minorities, and bringing self-sufficiency and egalitarianism that would satisfy the wishes of the general public. However, his strategy to please the general public did not last long as the government embarked on a long journey of suppressing opposing views and ideologies. Subsequently, Barre's clan and those loyal to him became the favored citizens above the law who enjoyed impunity and extensive privileges.

After 21 dreadful years, Barre's military regime collapsed in 1991, giving birth to a renewed wave of inter-clan and intra-clan conflicts, which in the process destroyed the country, particularly the southern regions, thus reducing entire masses to a shell-shocked society. What is the real cause of Somalia's destruction: the prevalent skirmishes between clans, or the difficulties arising from the process of setting up a state? To the nomadic groups who controlled the state for decades, the state was an imported institution, an unquestioned entity that lacked a strong link to the people.

Although the conglomeration of armed clan militias succeeded in the unceremonious ousting of the late dictator amid wide public admiration, mutual frustration developed in the inner circles of leadership. Like the Sri Lankans, Somalia's "failure to lay down the constitutional foundation of a multi-ethnic society based on equality, ethnic pluralism, and the sharing of power has exacerbated the ethnic conflict. As a consequence, [Somalia] has been besieged for years by ethnic fratricide and political violence" (Tiruchelvan, 1999). One thing that we should bear in mind is that authority, arrogance, and domination are tools subject to change, tools that should not have any legitimacy in front of human rights (Eno, 2001a). In short, this imprudently opportunistic sector of the society, constituting largely of unproductive clan-subservient, has ruined the southern Somali regions and their communities, putting their future in a stagnated limbo.

The late Siad Barre's war and the militias' subsequent takeover have resulted in mayhem in southern Somalia. They also contributed to the creation of one of the vilest and most venomous tragedies in Somali history, which failed to implement the restoration of trust, unity, and peace among the multi-ethnic communities. Unfortunately, this very theme of restoring peace and unity in Somalia has been the same over a decade or so since Siad Barre was unseated in 1991. It is also likely to be the theme of countless meetings and conferences that may be organized by NGOs, African States, United Nations and other bodies in future. Yet, the reality is that Somalia and Somalians are very far from the goal of comprehension, unity, peace and justice, in spite of thousands of pages in reconciliation, dialogues and the adoption of countless disarmament charters. Not only is Somalia a considerable distance away from unity and stability, it also exists today as the only stateless nation on earth and the most poverty stricken, tolerating the burden of carrying a record of the most criminal human rights abuses.

Also, corruption within the Somali de-facto regime and its loyalists is one of the incurable diseases today in Somalia. Maniacal leadership based on tyranny and trauma has become a way of life for many victims of war in Somalia. The educational system in Somalia has been shut down for over a decade and half, illiteracy has become the number one enemy of Somali society while hunger is the on-going threat to all Somalis. Because of the harassment and looting of crops by militia group, farmers do not feel safe on their farms. An ordinary person can not afford to buy the few medicines that get into the country – only the warlords and those loyal to them can – so diseases become epidemic quickly in the country. The denial of women's rights is another important and often ignored issue in Somalia. If Somalia really wants to prosper in the future, women should be included in the decision making. I personally believe that some Somali women are more intelligent, competent and sensitive than the brainless beasts and ideologically barren "warlords" and others that could not form a sustainable state with a viable system over a period of a decade and half.

Some of the Causes of State Collapse in Somalia

At this point it would be essential to define the "state" within the Somali context. After two years of reconciliation, reformation, resolution, and policy-making meetings in Nairobi-Kenya, the warlords and the nominated members of parliament have finally selected an interim government. However, the tribal rift within the interim government is still germinating and in multiple spheres. Since its inception, it has become evident that the elected quasi-government does not enjoy the blessing of the average Somali. What the Somali warlords have not realized is that, with the formation of a state in any given society comes an exciting extent of possibilities. These possibilities include challenges that test the prowess and patience of the most talented men and women in a society. This startling procedure necessarily implies the pertinence of fundamental philosophical questions that beg to be answered. For example, the rebirth of state institutions presumes a serious rethinking and remodeling of the ethos and circumstances of the people. It requires a resolute search to define the indigenous cultural, social and religious beliefs of a nation like Somalia, whose people are diverse. Regrettably, the newly elected quasi-government is not yet effective and still remains itinerant in Nairobi and Baidoa, unable to go back to the capital and other cities to implement national policies (Jamal Haji: 2006). This indicates that the political ideology within which this new government was founded is not well received by the people. In fact, one of the unusual policies adopted by the so-called Transitional Federal Government is the infamous modality used for the allocation of parliamentary seats, known as 4.5 (four point five); in other words four full groups and one that is 0.5 (half). The underlying astonishment in this episode is that the group that was given half representation consists of those who stayed neutral in the conflict and did not take arms against any clan; in other words, they maintained absolute restraint from killing, raping, looting, or robbing. The insinuation here is that, in order to qualify full representation, one has to have blood on one's hands.

"A state is, in a way, an expression of the people's way of life. The manner in which members of a certain community communicate and interact with one another, what they maintain as a value and what they view as important in existence, in short, their social and cultural values, ultimately surface in, and considerably influence, the institution known as the state" (Somali Newsletter, 1996). That said, it's logical to suggest that one of the best ways to create a state in Somalia would be from within the Somali culture. Since there are different and diverse cultures in Somalia, the big question will be: which Somali culture should the state be based on? So far, the only Somali culture that has been associated with the state is the nomadic culture. It is also the only culture that was arrogantly imposed on every Somali citizen directly/indirectly. Actually, it stands as one of the major contributors to the rot in the administrative machinery and failure of Somali state. In order to recover Somalia's reputation from its infamous past, what is needed urgently is a futuristic political vision based on an ethnically heterogeneous political partnership called the state. My disposition infers a state that recognizes and appreciates Somalia's cocktail and conglomerate cultures and traditions, where ethnic fairness and justice are the moral basis, where people are judged by the content of their character and not by the community and clan they belong to. Consequently, fairness and justice can secure the normative structure for a new egalitarian system in which Somalis of every ethnic background are treated equally and valued equally (Farah, 2005).

From another distinct perspective, the main ingredients that precipitated Somalia's civil war and the current political turmoil are entrenched in land and resources, particularly the agricultural fertile land between the Rivers Juba and Shabelle and the coastal cities of Southern Somalia. This land belongs to Somalia's victims and non-partisan groups. But feeble-minded, power-hungry Somali warlords and the mostly illiterate clan elders have armed barbaric nomadic youths to invade and conquer other regions in Southern Somalia. It is these nomads who, for decades, have manipulated and interrupted the democratic system in Somalia, licensing their clansmen to possess lethal firearms. And today, the flame from their firearms is beyond the control of normal human beings.

Instead of liberating the people from Siad Barre's tyranny after they took over, the militias became the new colonial powers through legitimating and forcibly taking over almost all of the arable lands in the south. It was part of the militias' ambitions to exploit the agricultural produce of the inter-riverine people and to build a gigantic economic empire in the region in order to subdue the rest of the nation with the gains from extorted economy. As a result, the resurrection of a virtual slavery against the inter-riverine communities became routine practice. Environmentally, cruel aliens from other regions occupy most of the inter-riverine region; they somehow found a way to stretch their territorial claims and wrest control of most of the land from its original owners under the pretext that "we have liberated you." Some of these aliens are today emphatically claiming themselves as the legitimate and sole owners of land as far as Kisimayu city and its surroundings. Others have claimed the territorial zones along the Shabelle River, including Bay and the coastal regions, while the landlords' "minorities" are either decaying in refugee camps abroad or live destitute in foreign countries.

We have presumed that slavery has been abolished in almost every corner of the earth. However, its presence has been revived once again in Southern Somalia under the joint collaboration of the warlords and multi-national entities. They've targeted the regions between the Rivers Juba, Shabelle, and its environs in Southern Somalia, since these are important to the backbone of Somalia's economy and are agriculturally the most productive lands in Somalia. These regions contribute heavily to Somalia's national income. Yet they are the least developed ones economically, educationally, and politically; in fact, they are neglected in distress and total dilapidation. The indigenous citizens are very angry at the exploitation they have suffered at the hands of the state, past and present, which has extracted wealth from their regions without investing it in return. As I said earlier, the victims are the unarmed and most vulnerable members of Somali society.

Militiamen loyal to certain warlords have been forcing farmers in the fertile zone of the inter-riverine region, including women and children, to work on plantations without any compensation save a meager diet of boiled beans upon completion of the day's work at sunset. Not only are these people denied their rightful earnings, but they have been turned into slaves and are denied and subverted of their personhood. The warlords and a few foreign companies continue to benefit from the sweat and travail of the forced laborers from the farming communities.

From sunrise to sunset, under the scourging heat of the tropical sun and in temperatures as high as 95 degrees, they have been subjugated to the back-breaking labor of digging and carrying thousands of tons of bananas with no compensation or wages at all. This is happening in the twenty-first century before the eyes of the civilized world. These poor farmers are living in the shadow of oppression, isolation, exploitation and permanent threat. Stories of humiliation, horror and ill treatment in Somalia are not isolated incidents. Yet the world has chosen to abstain and ignore dealing with this serious issue of slavery and land expropriation in Southern Somalia. In the meantime, the victims are desperately awaiting the intervention of the human rights institutions and foreign governments so that they can resume their normal way of life. Until then, the warlords and their militias continue to engage in slavery and extortion, a business that thrives best in lawlessness and the deprivation of human rights.

After hearing so many dreadful stories from the victims of war about their horrific experiences of mistreatment and discrimination, I realized that many of the people in Somalia who are trying to live a normal life are in fact carrying the burden of war and anguish. This is a burden inflicted on them by the warring nomads for no other reason than that they did not fit the Somali nomads' framework of Somaliness. The Somali warlords' actions are clear indications that, at present, Somalia's main problems are not solely due to clan rivalry but also by the rapacious ambitions of these war criminals. Despite their relentlessness, no one has taken effective measures to intervene and put on halt to the wanton human rights abuses and other forms of genocide against easy prey groups in Southern Somalia, in this case the unarmed inter-riverine communities consisting of the marginalized Jareer people.

Amazingly, these important issues are often overlooked and not conspicuously emphasized in any of the Somali reconciliation processes. Of all the past Somali reconciliation processes, none has clearly addressed or included methods that would bridge the gap between the evil deeds of the past that deeply divided the society and a future that promises justice for the victims. Like Desmond Tutu said in the case of South Africa, Somalia suffers from a past that was nourished by conflict, clan rivalries and untold suffering, and it needs a future that is firmly founded on the recognition of human rights, human respect, democracy and peaceful co-existence and development opportunities for all Somalis (For further reading see: Tutu, 1999).

Reformation and Resolution

In the past, attempts to resolve the conflict in Southern Somalia concentrated largely on the creation of a state and constitutional matters, without giving much consideration to how to heal the wounds inflicted on the victims of war. Another aspect that was overlooked by Somali policy makers was the lack of improvement in the relationship between the victims and victimizers. In a conflict of this magnitude, reconciliation does not come by either miracle or fluke, but rather through understanding, sacrifice and implementation. So far, the laws, reconciliation agreements and resolutions in concept have not been adequate; they must be put in practice and permeate the fabrics of Somali social life (Eno, 2001a). We must also recognize that the victims of war are human beings whose precious lives deserve to be consecrated by all through the utilization of laws that protect them. In this regard, an interpretation of the reconciliation and reformation process must be made clear in the legislation in order to avoid repetition of the past, in which small groups have monopolized Somalia's political power, giving them access to a range of unlawful privileges.

Although the intensity of the destructiveness and war seem to have subsidized, it does not necessarily mean an end to the conflict. Exclusion, uneven distribution of resources and uneven tribal representation in the Somali government and recent reconciliation process in Kenya, which was again repeated by the Islamist groups, continue to influence the anarchic situation in Somalia. With the uneven distribution of resources and nepotism, Somalia continues to retrogress, easily finding itself back to where it began but with different players this time. If Somalia is ever to reduce ethnic antagonism and violence and establish itself as a tranquil multiethnic society, it will have to find a way to implement constitutionally, politically, and socially the principle of equal rights and nondiscrimination based on a system of governance that is the choice of the people, one which is unlike those imposed on them by dubious foreign mediators.

Almost sixteen years have lapsed since the Horn of Africa nation disintegrated and fell into the abyss of social disarray heavily blamed on tribal warfare between uncompromising nomadic groups. Prior to the ouster of the military regime of late dictator General Mohamed Siad Barre, the amalgamated clan militia had felt excluded from the favors and preferential treatment of Barre's regime. Their determined action at the time configured the causative domain that their primordial rights as first class citizens were deprived. But after toppling Barre, the militia began to abuse innocent Somali citizens. From 1991 to date, the Somali society has been subjected to what seems to be an endless journey of misery. Several international institutions and a high-level peacekeeping operation have tried unsuccessfully to intervene and stabilize the situation.

Since then, Somalia has become a dependent variable for experiments in the search of solutions to its anarchy. Friendly states, well-wishers, experts on African affairs and others have suggested particular solutions for the Somali predicament, or for some aspect of it. These solutions, despite their merits and good intentions, are rarely based on Somali realities. For instance, some of the most controversial and ineffective aspects of these solutions have been the legitimacy and high considerations deemed to the very warlords who committed the atrocities and human massacre, war criminals who should have been hunted down to answer to charges of crimes against humanity in the International Tribunal Court (Baxaar, 2003).

As for the newly emerging Islamist faction (Islamic Courts Union) in Somalia, one should look at the structure of the leadership. A clear picture of this institution depicts nothing but a continuation of clan macabre and the unilateral tribal authority of one subgroup. If the proponents of the Islamic faction are really genuine in their mission to create a sustainable and stable state, they should have been more inclusive and transparent in the selection of their leadership. The prime skepticism is caused by the fact that almost all the top ranking leaders of the Islamic Courts Union (ICU) are from one sub-clan. Knowing the system of tribal affinity and affiliation in Somalia, should one say that this is a unique incident, independent of any deliberate strategy? Does this peculiar composition mean other clans in Somalia do not have religious clergymen of their own who could represent them? Or should we prefigure, for the sake of sheer pessimistic tendency, the notion that other clans might have been denied the right to be included in the Islamist top brass deciding the future of a more stable Somalia? As a result of the aforementioned anomalies, the future of the Islamic State in Somalia is bleak because, in my view, Islam is being misused for personal gains.

As for the Somali warlords, they are self-elected/self-styled kleptocrats who parade themselves as leaders, while the armed militia gangs are nothing but ramshackle groups presided over by political thugs and military adventurists, so-called generals who have never had the guts to lead in the battlefield. It is also most unfortunate that such brutal warlords receive support from some of their clan elders. As a result of militia transgression, the killing, looting and confiscation of properties of innocent people have risen dramatically, to the extent of holding a whole nation at ransom. Furthermore, the most important aspect of a resolution has either been ignored or overlooked: the restoration of the victims' trust and the healing of physical as well as psychological wounds and scars cut open by the war. Regrettably, the victims feel ignored and the magnitude of their grievances undermined. The attitude towards the victims must change from apathy to sympathy and concern over their ordeals must be raised as a measure to avoid grudges that may be triggered at a later date in retaliation.

In spite of being aware of a systems breakdown, Somalis stop short of acknowledging the negative consequences. As Chhanda and Chattopadhyaya (1998) wrote about Sri-Lanka, a trend relevant to the Somalia case, in any given society "social structure is said to be a network of relations between different groups, classes and roles, which forms a functional unity. Moral, legal, political, economic, religious, educational and linguistic phenomena hang together and are to be understood in their mutually supportive relation, not in isolation or abstraction" [Chhanda and & Chattopadhyaya, 1998]. With similar sentiments in mind, the fundamental concern of the war victims in Somalia is to find justice and equality on the path to achieving forgiveness, clemency, durable peace and fraternal co-existence. Unless these have been achieved, then the popular slogan that there is no forgiveness without confession and no confession without repentance may endure for possible future repercussions.

In one of my research trips to Africa and the Middle East, a considerable number of my interviewees reiterated that the victims and non-partisan groups have been seeking closure to the ordeals caused by racial discrimination, cultural genocide, murder and the imposition of nomadic culture. What we should always remind ourselves, however, is that condescension and disdain do not build a nation; it is mutual respect that builds a sense of unified national purpose, respect that transcends the nonsense of an ego or superiority complex. It is a matter of reality that Somalia, as a society, did not detribalize itself before she could expound into the rhetoric of Somaliness, nationalism, camaraderie and compatriotism. Unfortunately, the *xeer* (Tribal rule) and loyalty to the tribe was, and still continues to be, the pivotal element and principal sacrosanct the nomads adhere to. This kind of attitude was obvious among the less law-abiding and belligerent pre-Islamic Arab-Bedouins, with their rule "one for all -- all for one." At the heart of Somalia's conflict, then, is the question of state power. That simple fact makes mediation an infinitely complex exercise. Regardless of the warlords' non-altruistic motives in bringing the conflict to an end, we should all remain optimistic that a join sincere effort can turn around the precarious situation this morally and materially dilapidated nation has been experiencing for years.

Resolving problems of root causes, including the need to foster a vibrant civil society in Somalia, should have been mainly the responsibility of the elites and prudent citizens from all walks of Somali society. Experience over the past decade and half has taught us that because there is no legitimately functioning government in Somalia, this role has been seized by irresponsible humans without concern for the nation, ill-intended evils who believe that the nation's administrative gear should be left in the crafty hands of those who have the most destructive arsenal. Due to this erroneous opinion, violence and atrocities are looming among Somali society. Yet, as the warring nomads' situation envisages, violence will never solve a social problem forever; it merely creates unforeseen and more complex havoc. Occasionally violence is temporarily successful, but never permanently so. It may at times bring temporary victory, but never permanent peace or a solution to a conflict as deeply-rooted as the Somali experience.

Like any other African nation, leaders in Somalia enjoy exercising an enormous amount of absolute power in the government, with no accountability for their actions. An attitude of this nature is what has brought Somalia to its knees. It has endangered the well-being of every member of the society. Therefore, should leaders have too much power they should also have too much responsibility, and hence accountability.

Can the Somalis Borrow a Leaf from Nigeria?

In 1966, after the death of the head of state in Nigeria in a coup d'état, Nigeria was faced with the difficulty of selecting a viable head of state to replace the deceased president. However, after a long period of delving, grappling, gimmicks and rhetoric, the Nigerian Military Supreme Council could not decide who would be the next head of state. The reason for their failure in selecting a new president was based on a problem similar to that which Somalia is facing today: what tribe should the head of state belong to? Will the next president of Somalia be from Habargidir, Abgaal, Majerteen, etc.? The qualification given to such perception is that these are the dominant tribes who are at the heart of the country's problems. Likewise, Nigerians could not decide whether their head of state should have come from the Ibo, Hausa Fulani, or Yuruba. However, they were smart enough not to go the way of the Somalis, who shut down the whole nation for a period of fifteen or sixteen years in a state of anarchy. They (Nigerians) came to their senses by changing course and appointing Yakubu Gowon as the new Nigerian head of state.

This was welcomed as a win-win situation for the disputing Nigerians. The nation was saved from falling into a state of anarchy and all the competing major tribes were happy because Gowon belongs to the Angas-tribe, which is one of the smallest tribes in Nigeria. Gowon was also a Christian, yet the Muslims did not mind because Nigeria as a nation and society was at stake, hence the sacrifice of any other variable (Jumare, 1999). In comparison, can the so-called Somali "noble" tribes be nationalistic enough like the Nigerians as to nominate an outcast Midgaan or a Jareer as the new president of Somalia, in order to salvage the remaining rubbles of the wrecked nation?

Clemency

Somalia is long overdue to create a "war crime inquiry commission" to find out the truth about the gross human rights violations against the victims of the Somali tribal war. Although there is no consensus about the best way to deal with the past, surely humanity can do much better than to settle for a mere "let bygones be bygones" or simplistically cover up with statements such as "we cannot change the past." Even though we cannot change the past, we can influence the way it is remembered by constituting a war commission for the sake of national harmony, accountability and unity. As Tuomas Forsberg says about the conflict in the South African situation: "We should not forget about the past, but we can forgive, [the perpetrators because telling the] ...truth is the way to reconciliation." Forsberg further argues that in any given war-torn nation, "the best that a society can do is to generate various tactics of its own for reckoning with past evil" (Forsberg, 2001).

In fact, if Somalia is seriously seeking sustainable peace and reconciliation, the individual/group victims of the conflict must be addressed through processes of justice, reparation and psychological healing. Like the truth commission enterprises of South Africa, Rwanda, Argentina, Chile and El Salvador, the Somali process must also be public; it cannot take the form of *sotto voce* murmuring and private mea culpa. The fact that the non-partisan groups were murdered, maimed, raped, robbed and brutalized for opting non-partisanship must be affirmed and acknowledged. Thereafter, the perpetrators must be dealt with based on whatever punishment or pardoning procedures the commission and the victims agree upon, so that similar atrocities could be avoided in the future.

Due to the tawdry, shameless nature and arrogance of the popular Somali culture, the notion of seeking forgiveness from the victims and accepting culpability of abuse has not been adequately addressed in any of the past reconciliation forums. Thus, the perpetrators have not remorsefully expressed the seriousness of the unhealed wounds inflicted on the victims of war, both inside and outside Somalia. Up

144

until now, I'm not aware of any group or individual victim-of-war or war-related abuse that has received an official apology. I am not suggesting under this intonation that there should be a blanket blame on all war contributors for what happened. I believe that the perpetrators can either come forward voluntarily to admit their vile deeds to the commission or be identified by the victim (if still alive) or an eyewitness to prove the committed atrocities. The culprits have so far exhibited indifference to the pain of the victims by covering up their guilty consciousness in a hitherto "let's put this behind us" or "let's achieve closure," which is not conducive to healing the wounds of the victims, particularly the non-partisans.

I also understand the reality that there are wrongs suffered in Somalia that cannot so easily be put right, however, Somalis must try to reconcile. In one of my research sessions of this study, I asked one of my informants, "What was the most regrettable thing that you have ever encountered in Somalia?" His answer was "I feel my worst experience in the riverine and inter-riverine area was that I was gullible to have been duped into the notion of Somaliness and national compatriotism. In reality, it was our Somali compatriots who killed us and forced us out of our abodes into destitution" (Barrow, 2004). Often the victims are left perplexed by the fact that these devious and abominable treatments came not from a heathen or from an infidel unbeliever but from fellow countrymen who claim to be fellow Muslims who read the same Qur'aan and worship in the same mosque.

In order to achieve genuine reconciliation, Somalia should follow the basic fundamentals of reconciliation processes, which are: reaching out to the victims, creating a broad based system to accommodate all Somalis in the reconciliation process, naming a commission for public repentance and returning properties to the rightful owners. Like Hugo van der Merwe, who suggested in his article "National and Community Reconciliation" in South Africa, "If we recognize reconciliation as a long-term process that requires ongoing efforts of empowerment, confrontation, pain, dialogue, exchange, experimentation, risk-taking, the building of common values, and identity [acceptance]" (Hugo, Merwe, 2001), the work of any reconciliation commission might be valued, including in Somalia.

Different societies around the globe practice different cultures and have approaches on dealing with the past. According to Farida Mtengeti, for example, the Japanese maintain a shame culture, whereas

Western society is based on a guilt culture, while in South Africa the culture of dealing with the past is referred to as the African concept of *Ubuntu* (humanity) (Mtengeti, 2005; 2006). As part of the Somali and Islamic culture, repentance and forgiveness are well embedded within daily lives. Religion is also supposed to be one of the most effective tools in dealing with healing wounds of the past. Unlike the Japanese, the Westerners, and the South Africans, Somalis seem to undermine and consciously avoid dealing with past wrongdoings so as to devalue the victims' ordeals. Failure to successfully reconciliate the current problem in Somalia will, sooner or later, doom the country to another disaster. In her discussion about Ireland, Martha Minow describes the problem of Ireland as one which "...the Irish will never forget and the British will never remember" (Minow, 2001). In the Somalia situation, the victims will never forget their ordeals and the culprit murderers will never want to remember. Therefore, so as to focus on a beginning, the right tools must be employed to foster the renewal of healthy relations between the perpetrators and the victims and to avoid future fratricide and unnecessary massacre.

One needs to accept that reconciliation and forgiveness are not isolated single-carriage pathways; rather, their effectiveness implies and/or requires compromise, courage and the redevelopment of a new relationship between the aggressor and the aggressed. This will make available or help facilitate a transitive dimension through the process of reconciliation: be it reparation, restitution, joint project for counseling/healing, or commemoration. Asking for forgiveness is not a self-exculpatory act. Nor is it aloofness, nor the detachment of "just not giving a damn." It is about building a renewed trust between communities that need each other for a mutual coexistence in harmony and lasting peace. To the victims, the importance of apprehending the criminals should not be underestimated in this instance. Neglecting the apprehension of the perpetrators will only augment the pains of the psychological scars that haunt the bereaved and preyed upon. Therefore, we need to think well beyond tribal rhetoric by setting up a commission of inquiry into the war crimes committed, with the aim of achieving a restorative justice that generates no new victims of the sorts of societal misdeeds and criminality that destroyed the past. Somalia needs a restorative justice that addresses the legitimate concerns of victims and survivors while seeking to reintegrate perpetrators into the community.

What I found intriguing, though, is the relevance and similarities of the Somali warlords' attitude to the ideology of Niccolo Machiavelli, the famous Italian political philosopher, who was passionate about totalitarianism. In the 21st century, Machiavelli's ideology still has relevance in today's totalitarian leadership of chaotic nations such as Somalia. After committing every kind of atrocity, human degradation, and human rights abuse it seems that the Somali leadership — the warlords — found support in the advice Machiavelli gave in his book, *The Prince*, that a ruler "must not mind incurring the charge of cruelty for the purpose of keeping his subjects united and faithful" (Cecil, 1986). Although Somali leaders (warlords) used every cruelty in the book against their own people, they still could not keep their subjects united. Machiavelli further suggests that the root of political effectiveness and success is a force unrestricted by considerations of generally accepted values. It is therefore likely that Machiavelli's basic idea – that in order to achieve political ends one may lie, deceive, intrigue, conspire and use any kind of crooked means – has had great appeal for the leadership of Somali society.

As Mohamed Eno wrote back in the 1980s, "aggression is not a solution" to a situation where reform and recovery are required for a rewarding remedy. In fact, aggression and malgovernance have brought Somalia to its current backwardness. This has turned out to be chaotic, because military might and tribal allegiance can never be the sole source of communal strength, as many Somalis believe. For a society to succeed, it requires various attributes including the spirit of freedom, justice, patriotism, education, economic stability, etc. Under the Somali system and rules, some people have lacked the freedom to express views that may have challenged the deep-seated beliefs of selfsame Somaliness and compatriotism, for fear of censorship and suppression.

The axiom of the Somali society was, and still is, based on unilateral and intimidating tribal dominance, which can/may be corrupted. The people of whom it consists avoid culpability by suppressing and oppressing certain Somali communities to a status of 'less'--Somaliness or second-class citizenship. In this thick mist of confusion, can simple agreements between criminal warlords bring about peace in Somalia? Or are there a few more truths to be learned about the country and its people, so deprived of calmness over the long period of a decade and half? Somalis of every clan or creed have by now known the anomalous and aberrant behavior of the Somali warlords, and should therefore uphold the notion of compatriotism and Somaliness as values to be proud of but not as a threat to be avoided. As Burton suggests, conflict cannot be resolved unless basic human needs, such as security, autonomy and identity are met, which in the case of Somalia, are still absent.

Conclusion

I hold the belief that the responsibility for the present Somali tragedy lies primarily with Somalis themselves, although there are other external contributing factors as well. Bridging the gap between the offenders and the offended is a long-term effort that should be high on the list of priorities for those concerned with the resuscitation of Somalia as a functional nation and the laying of groundwork for a more peaceful Somalia. What is needed most is a broader, deeper and more sustained effort, and this need not wait for generations. Indeed, without laying the popular groundwork, the chances are that future negotiations will crash as well, leaving a dim future for a country that deserves a bright one.

In order to have a successful reconciliation process, one must make sure these elements are implemented as an integral part of the process: the perpetrators have to accept contrition, confession, and ask for apology through repentance and a nationwide acknowledgement of their roles in the evils with which they have bedeviled the country. To that admittance and brave acceptance of responsibility and apology, the victims need to be open-minded and realistic, because in some cases they have to forgive and move on to begin the healing. Within their inner emotional and psychological being, they need to cope with the scars of the past and, with reciprocal courage, to forgive and accept the apology for the sake of opening a new chapter in the history of a reunited Somalia and upholding the true spirit of Somaliness.

It is true that the conflict in Somalia created physical as well as psychological distance between neighbors, friends, siblings, acquaintances and relatives. This distance has exacerbated mistrust, which led to confirmatory biases that require a sincere soul-searching therapeutic remedy. In a situation of this nature, Somalia needs a solution guaranteeing the minimum conditions for peace and reconstruction by utilizing some of the following measures:

148

- Termination of the present war between factions through an agreement between them by all means necessary.
- A broad based political agreement based on equal inclusiveness, power sharing and satisfactory implementation.
- Since the Somali people are already deeply divided ethnically, and the reconciliation process seems to have failed to select a viable leadership, I suggest that Somalia could adapt what Ali Mazrui calls "ordered anarchy," so that each clan will look after their own affairs in their own ancestral region or location.
- Codifying and legalizing whatever community/customary laws and rules that are required to be in practice.
- As Martha Minow suggested with regard to those who have committed atrocities against their own compatriots in many parts of the world, Somalis should create memorials in the form of public monuments, sculptures, museums and days of memory. Atrocities against humanity, particularly in Somalia, should be included in children's public school curriculums to avoid secrecy, celebrate the transition, and warn against future recurrences of new atrocities (Minow, 1998).

Chapter 9

THE UNITED NATIONS INTERVENTION IN SOMALIA: A RETROSPECTIVE LOOK AND LESSONS FOR FUTURE AFRICA-UN PARTNERSHIP IN CONFLICT RESOLUTION

Issaka K. Souaré

The dramatic but anticipated fall of the Siad Barre regime in Somalia in 1991 led to a fratricidal war in the country that was still roaring at the end of 2006, with periods of intensification or relative tranquility. With no effective central government, warlords and their armed bandits have been controlling different parts of the country, with the northern part of the country unilaterally proclaiming its independence as the Republic of Somaliland. As other aspects of the crisis have been dealt with by other chapters, in this essay I will look specifically at the United Nation's military intervention in Somalia in the period 1992-95 following the overthrow of the Siad Barre regime. In order to put the analyses in their proper theoretical context, I will begin by providing a brief theoretical overview and discussion of the conflict resolution between international organizations, especially the UN, and regional organizations or arrangements. The idea behind this demarche being an attempt to see if there is anything in this which may help explain why the United Nation's intervention in Somalia ended the way it did.

This chapter is largely adapted from two previous publications of mine in mid and late 2006. The first is my book, *Africa in the United Nations System, 1945-2005* (Souaré, 2006a) and the other one is an article I published in the special issue of the journal, *African Renaissance*, whose main theme was "Somalia: Reconstituting A Failed State" (Souaré, 2006b). After a theoretical discussion of the chances of successful conflict resolution between international organizations and regional arrangements in Africa, the second section of the chapter will provide a concise historical background of the Somali conflict; previous chapters have provided a more detailed one (see Chapters 2-4). The third section looks at the United Nation's peacekeeping force and the circumstances that led to its formation and dispatch. This necessitates an analysis of the main characteristics of the force. Concluding that the mission failed spectacularly, the fourth section looks at the main factors that may have led to this failure. From this, the concluding section makes some policy recommendations as to what should be the conduct of future Africa-UN partnerships in peacekeeping.

The UN and Conflict Resolution in Africa

As far as the safeguarding or restoration of international peace and security are concerned, the United Nations Security Council is the prime responsible body. This was, in fact, the main purpose of setting up the United Nations. It is the entity that the international community has entrusted with this task through approval of the UN Charter. This is so especially when it comes to peace enforcement, which may necessitate economic sanctions, arms embargoes and the actual use of force. Moreover, the United Nations has such enormous resources and such a wealth of expertise in the field that no one can question it as being the best body to effectively deal with conflict issues around the world. Two main points are worth mentioning, however.

First, as a global institution, the United Nations has a global constituency. It thus has to be ready to serve all of its constituents. Yet despite its enormous resources, when the needs of many of these constituents arise at more or less the same time, it is difficult to deal with all of them effectively. Whenever this is the case, *Realpolitik* comes into play. This entails choosing between the different constituents and giving priority to some over others. Reading through the history of UN engagements and the responses and reactions of the international community to armed conflict situations around the world, one observes that these have been below expectations as far as Africa is concerned. Critical observation shows that these responses have been largely different when such conflicts occurred in parts of the world other than Africa. This may be illustrated, for instance, by the slow and poor response of the UN and the international community to the civil wars in Liberia, Sierra Leone and the Democratic Republic of the Congo or, most tellingly, the 1994 genocide in Rwanda. This is in sharp contrast with the more sophisticated and robust forces sent to Kuwait in 1991, Bosnia and Herzegovina in 1995, and East Timor four years later (Souaré, 2006a:208-209).

The other point is that even if the UN were to intervene in an armed conflict situation, the process of agreeing to this is slow, cumbersome and lengthy — of course depending on the location of the conflict (Zacarias, 1996:26-37). This excludes any realistic chance of early conflict prevention activity. In fact, depending on the location, many countries do not tend to consider a looming conflict a threat to international peace and security —which is the main requirement for UN intervention— until hostilities begin. Yet this is the most effective period of preventive diplomacy and conflict prevention that Boutros-Ghali (1992) rightly stressed in his *An Agenda for Peace*.

This state of affairs has led to an animated debate about the best way forward in conflict management in Africa. Should Africans continue to rely on the UN despite the increasing reluctance of the Security Council to commit itself to establishing effective peacekeeping operations in Africa because the Western countries do not want to commit their soldiers or resources to it? If so, what will be the consequences for peace and security in Africa? On the other hand, should Africa cease to be a "Prisoner of Expectations," to start being in charge of its own security independently of the UN? In that case, where will it get the necessary resources? And what will be the consequences of a poorly equipped peacekeeping operation?

Here emerge three main schools of thought, which are, in reality, only two. One school argues that, despite all the issues enumerated above in relation to UN peacekeeping operations in Africa, given that the continent lacks the appropriate and adequate institutional structures, managerial capacity and resources to properly manage peacekeeping operations, the task should still be left to the United Nations, which has the comparative advantage in this regard. The role of Africa, according to this school of thought, should be limited to providing troops to the UN operations under the command of UN force commanders. Another school argues that Africa should take the lead in preliminary negotiations, securing a ceasefire and committing itself to provide the troops. It should then ask the international community to provide the logistic, technical, transport and other support facilities. This could be through the UN or even through bilateral arrangements between Africa and different Western countries. This school of thought credits itself with guaranteeing African ownership of the process while avoiding the financial hassles that may hinder the operation should everything be left to the poor Africans (Vogt, 1999; Jones & Duffey, 1996).

There does not seem to be much difference between these two schools of thought. True, advocates of the second school may claim that their formula guarantees African ownership of the process and avoids the cumbersome process of securing a direct and full-fledged UN peacekeeping operation. However, the suggestion to seek secure logistical and other support facilities from the international community —if necessary through the UN— makes it no different from the first school of thought. To start with, it is clear and indeed understandable if the UN does not fund any peacekeeping operation which it did not create and/or set its mandate. On the other hand, putting the so-called bilateral arrangements under serious scrutiny reveals their risks, inadequacy and unreliability (Souaré, 2006a:209-210).

The reason behind this observation is clear and simple to grasp — not all outside actors have a bona fide interest in ending these conflicts. The so-called bilateral partners may never commit their resources if they do not have any significant geopolitical interest in the region or country concerned and thus have a stake — not of a humanitarian nature in most cases — in the outcome of the conflict. In any case, they will want to ensure publicity and public relations opportunities in their engagement and will thus be more focused on scoring diplomatic goals than on caring for the people they are being called upon to save. This will have its impact on the quality and the timing of the delivery of any assistance they may commit themselves to offer, and will lead many of them to seek a prominent public role in the whole process. Yet there are some actors who somehow benefit from these unstable situations, like fishing in troubled waters, so to speak (Souaré, 2006a:208-209; Ki-Zerbo, 2003:57-61).

These observations lead to the third school of thought. Some may perceive this as rather radical, but it is nevertheless the most reliable and realistic one, and the one that this author adopts. Africans should be in the driver's seat not only in mediation, but also in the whole process of peacekeeping and peace-building. Because there are countries always looking for a way to feel good, some will offer their assistance, be it logistical or financial, when they see Africans doing it alone and making good progress. Such assistance should be welcomed and duly credited should the donors ask for that, as they are very likely to. However, this should in no way allow that external "donor" to take charge of the operations or set up a parallel operation. In addition to the observations made above, this approach may be further explained, substantiated and justified by the following two considerations.

First, the AU or regional organization to which it chooses to delegate the task of conflict management in a given African country is considered an "insider," closely connected to the conflict at hand, with an intimate and profound knowledge of local conditions. It also shares norms and experiences with the parties involved and may even have personal links with some of them, which certainly facilitates their task. This is at the diplomatic level, but it also holds true if a military campaign turns out to be necessary. The local actors have the unrivalled advantage of knowing the terrain (Elgström, Bercovitch and Skau, 2003; Jones & Duffey, 1996; Souaré, 2006a:210-211; 2006:5-12).

Secondly, the conflicts in question are African wars and those dying are Africans. Armed conflicts cause the death of thousands of people. They also lead to massive refugee flows to neighbouring countries. These refugee populations in six figure numbers become a burden on host countries. Refugee camps tend also to be a breeding ground for rebel movements, as fleeing rebels may infiltrate the refugee populations and regroup their forces from there. This is to say that neighbouring countries have more at stake in the outcome of the conflict than any other actors. They are thus the only ones that can commit the necessary resources and make the necessary sacrifices to put an end to the conflict (Etzioni, 2004; Jones & Duffey, 1996). The role played by Tanzania in the Arusha negotiations to find a solution to the crisis in Rwanda prior to the genocide is illustrative of this. The performance of the African contingents of United Nations Assistance Mission for Rwanda (UNAMIR) during the 1994 genocide, especially the Ghanaian contingent, in comparison with that of the Western contingents that pulled out from the country following the path of the Belgians as the situation deteriorated is also illustrative of this.

Another example in West Africa occurred in Liberia in late 2003. There was intense fighting between the rebel group Liberians United for Reconciliation and Democracy (LURD) and troops loyal to the government of Charles Taylor. In Monrovia, the Liberian capital where the heavy fighting had reached, people, mainly women and children, were dying or being maimed on a daily basis by gunfire. There was a real risk of famine and the spread of killer diseases in the country. The rebels were demanding as a *sine qua non* for a ceasefire the departure of

Charles Taylor without conditions. Taylor was adamant against conceding, especially because the UN Special Court for Sierra Leone had indicted him for involvement in the country's civil war. Meanwhile, Liberians called for the international community, the United States in particular, to intervene to stop the violence and killing. They invoked their so-called "shared history" with Washington in a desperate attempt to persuade the White House to act. Economic Community of West African States (ECOWAS) and other African leaders urged Washington and the rest of the international community to at least help financially, saying that they would be ready to send troops. But both the Americans and the international community proved unwilling. The fighting was ended only by the intervention of ECOWAS, thanks to the good offices of President Olusegun Obasanjo of Nigeria and President Thabo Mbeki of South Africa, then the Chairman of the African Union. This is not to blame the outsiders for their inaction. It is just not their problem and they have many of their own anyway (Souaré, 2006c:5-12).

A Brief Historical Background to the Somali Crisis

In Africa, as elsewhere in the Third World, the end of the Cold War and superpowers' rivalries led to the withdrawal of the latter's unconditional backing for many dictatorial regimes on the continent. Many of these autocratic regimes that were supported by one camp or the other during the Cold War had lost their strategic value to their respective camp leaders, the U.S. or the Soviet Union. The political aspirations of their people that had hitherto been thwarted because of superpowers' backing came once again to the fore or were re-energized. Those leaders that were wise enough responded quite swiftly to this whirlwind of change and introduced — even if it was only theoretically— mechanisms for such a change. In particular, they embraced multi-party systems and agreed to political liberalization. However, those who had an illusion of power and ignored the calls of the masses continued in their obduracy and resisted pleas for change. Such positions led often to destabilisation and civil strife. Somalia was clearly one of the states that suffered the negative repercussions of the end of the Cold War due to the the lack of foresight of the leaders of its ruling regime.

At the end of the Cold War, the strong man of Somalia was a certain Mohamed Siad Barre. General Siad Barre had come to power through a military coup d'état in 1969. Shortly thereafter, he banned multi-party politics in the country and introduced an autocratic style of government. Playing the different clans and religious leaders of the country against one another, his policy of divide-and-rule and his mastery in playing the strategic carte between the two superpowers helped him remain in power until his overthrow in January 1991. Somalia's strategic location — situated along the oil routes from the Middle East — made it an important and sought after geostrategic ally of both superpowers. In the 1970s, Siad Barre professed socialism to win Soviet military support for his drive to annex Ethiopia's Ogaden region, whose inhabitants are predominantly Somali and some of whom clearly wanted to be part of Somalia but without emigration. As a Marxist regime came to Ethiopia, however, the Soviets found a better ally and the support shifted. However, Siad Barre did not encounter any difficulty in gaining support from the other superpower. American support for Siad Barre proved to be superior to that of the Soviets and continued throughout the 1980s. Such was U.S. aid to Siad Barre's Somalia that U.S. total military aid to the country during the 1980s is estimated at some U.S. $200 million, with hundreds of millions in economic aid (Sanjian, 1999:641-670; Woods, 1997; Schraeder, 1994:160; Ayittey, 1994). As Blaton (2005:647-668) notes:

> In the fight against Communism, arms transfers were both an instrument of influence and an indicator of U.S. political support. Within the context of superpower competition, U.S. arms transfers were part of a larger effort to promote patron-client relationships in the Third World and fortify Cold War political alignments.

Despite the unconditional American support to the Siad Barre regime, the country was never totally peaceful throughout the 1980s, as various rebel groups were operating in different parts of the country. The armed opposition to Barre's regime intensified towards the end of the decade and eventually led to the overthrow of Barre in January 1991. This led to further instability in the country. The faction of General Mohamed Farah Aidid, Chairman of the United Somali Congress in Southern Somalia, collided with the Interim President, Ali Mahdi Mohamed in Mogadishu, while Northern Somalia proclaimed the independence of Somaliland. Many smaller factions emerged. Violence ensued between the different factions over the control of scarce resources in their respective regions. Having lost their strategic relevance to the U.S., which was busy with the "rich man's war" in the Persian Gulf, Somalis were simply left to themselves to sort out the situation.

The continued hostilities led to widespread death and destruction, forcing hundreds of thousands of civilians to flee their homes and causing a serious need for emergency humanitarian assistance. While scores of Somalis crossed the borders to seek refuge in neighbouring countries, a significant number of them became internally displaced. According to UN estimates at the end of 1992, almost 4.5 million people in Somalia – over half of the population – were threatened by severe malnutrition and related diseases. While this was a general case across the country, those living in the countryside were thought to be the most affected. It was estimated that perhaps 300,000 people died since November 1991, and at least 1.5 million lives were at immediate risk.

This was the state of affairs in Somalia when the Organization of African Unity (OAU) initiated talks between the opposing factions in the country. The OAU's initiative was backed by a number of other concerned institutions. In particular, the League of Arab States (LAS or the Arab League), the Organization of the Islamic Conference (OIC) and the United Nations deployed significant efforts, Somalia being a member of all these organizations (Clapham, 1999). All of these institutions were involved with the political aspects of the crisis and were pressing for a peaceful solution to the conflict. It appears, however, that with the passing of time and in view of the worsening situation in the country, all these organizations gave way to the United Nations and contented themselves with hosting peace talks and carrying out background mediation efforts whenever the UN demanded.

The United Nations and the Somali Crisis

The first involvement of the United Nations in the Somali conflict came on 27 December 1991. The outgoing Peruvian Secretary-General of the UN, Javier Pérez de Cuéllar, informed the President of the Security Council that he intended to take an initiative in the attempt to restore peace in Somalia. With his request approved, he consulted with

the incoming Secretary-General Boutros Boutros-Ghali, and they
agreed that a team of senior UN officials should be dispatched to
Somalia for talks with the opposing factions with the aim of bringing
about a ceasefire and securing access for the international relief
community to aid civilians caught in the conflict. The Under-Secretary-
General for Political Affairs at the time was James O. C. Jonah from
Sierra Leone. Jonah was asked to lead the team on its visit to Somalia.
Apparently, all the Somali factions expressed to the UN team their
desire for the UN to play a leading role in the resolution of the conflict.
Aidid, however, made no secret of his opposition to the deployment of
any peacekeeping force.

Boutros-Ghali took over the Secretary-General post in January 1992
and the Somali crisis naturally became one of the very first dossiers he
worked on. In the same month (January 1992), the Security Council
passed a resolution in which it urged all parties to the conflict to cease
hostilities, and decided that all States should immediately implement a
general and complete embargo on all deliveries of weapons and
military equipment to Somalia. The Secretary-General was requested to
increase humanitarian assistance to the affected population and to
contact all parties involved in the conflict to seek a commitment to the
cessation of hostilities, to promote a ceasefire and to assist in the
process of a political settlement of the conflict (UN, S/RES/7333, 1992).
Despite the signing of a ceasefire agreement between the opposing
factions in March, hostilities continued in the country. Thus, following
two reports of the Secretary-General on 21 and 24 April, the Council
passed Resolution 751 (24 April 1992) establishing the United Nations
Operation in Somalia (UNOSOM) and agreed, in principle, to establish
a UN security force to be deployed in the country as soon as possible.
A unit of 50 UN observers was to be deployed immediately to monitor
the ceasefire in Mogadishu.

The Secretary-General was asked to continue his consultations with
the Somali parties regarding the proposed UN peacekeeping force.
Boutros-Ghali soon appointed the veteran Algerian diplomat,
Mohamed Sahnoun, as his Special Representative, but Sahnoun did not
last long in the post because of disagreements between him and the
headquarters in New York, as will be seen later. He was replaced in
November 1992 by the Iraqi diplomat, Ismat Kittani, whose mandate
also proved short-lived and ended when the Americans took over after
only five months (November – March 1993).

Led by Brigadier-General Imtíaz Shaheen of Pakistan as Chief Military Observer, the advance party of UNOSOM arrived in Mogadishu in early July 1992. The first group of security personnel arrived in Mogadishu on 14 September 1992 after considerable delays. Whilst one should not forget the difficulties with the Somali factions on the ground, the delays can also be attributed to the fact that the UN was focusing attention on the conflict in the former Yugoslavia. By the time the UN's mission arrived, the ailing institutional structures in Somalia had further collapsed. As Zacarias (1996:67-68) notes, the delay in the UN's intervention "forfeited the opportunity to support the failing administrative structures and those Somalis trying to prevent the disintegration of the governmental system."

The delicate political and security situation in Somalia, compounded with the desperate and urgent need for humanitarian assistance for the many displaced people, meant that the strength of UNOSOM was insufficient for the task on the ground. Following the advice of his Special Representative, the Secretary-General realised that there was an urgent need not only to address the above issues, but also to embark on a well-planned project of institution-building in the country. Moreover, widespread banditry and criminal activities in the country meant that the UN force not only needed to protect the Somali civilians from the gangs of thugs, but also to protect UN workers tasked with the transport and distribution of humanitarian assistance. Thus, in a report to the Security Council, the Secretary-General strongly advised that the United Nations rethink the strategy of its involvement in Somalia and that its efforts needed to be enlarged in order to bring about an effective ceasefire throughout the country while at the same time promoting national reconciliation.

This led to the Security Council authorising, in August 1992, an increase in the strength of UNOSOM. The total strength of UNOSOM was now to be 4,219 all ranks, including the unit of 500 authorised in Mogadishu and 719 for logistic units. As always, the Secretary-General was urged to continue working in close cooperation with the OAU, the Arab League and the OIC in "his efforts to seek a comprehensive political solution to the crisis in Somalia" (UN, S/RES/775, 1992).

Problems Within the UN Force

Despite all this, it would appear that UNOSOM was without any clear strategy. This stemmed mainly from the disagreement in tactics and strategy between Ambassador Sahnoun, the Secretary-General's Special Representative, and the UN headquarters in New York. While the latter advocated, doubtless because some troop-contributing countries pressed for it, a quick fix so that UN could be swiftly relieved, Sahnoun, with his vast knowledge of the terrain and the region, urged a long-term solution that required patience on the part of not only headquarters but troop-contributing member states. It also needed a special kind of diplomacy, engaging not only the politicians or warlords but also their supporters amongst the ordinary people (Clapham, 1999). At the end of the day, Sahnoun resigned and was replaced by an Iraqi diplomat, as mentioned above.

As a result of this, the political aspect of the crisis, the main issue behind the surface, was neglected by UN strategists. Instead, they saw the issue first and foremost as a humanitarian issue (Zacarias, 1996:69). This was also reflected in the nature of the mandate given to UNOSOM before the involvement of the Americans. UNOSOM's mandate had always been under Chapter VI of the UN charter, which does not have the enforcement provisions of Chapter VII. These came only when the Americans offered to contribute independently of the UN force.

The American Intervention

As noted at the beginning of this chapter, the outbreak of the Somali crisis coincided with the end of the Cold War and the ushering in of a new era in international relations. Indeed, the Americans had proclaimed a New World Order with them as the world leader. In other words, the multi-polar world order had given way to the *Pax Americana*, or the American hegemony, in world affairs. Thus, as Makinda (1993:69) observed, the American president George Bush (senior) "was embarrassed by the fact that the new world order . . . was now characterized by the mass starvation of Somali children," hence the American decision to intervene in Somalia.

In a resolution passed 3 December 1992 (S/RES/749), the Security Council approved the offer of the United States to lead a coalition force to assist the UN force in its efforts in Somalia. Whereas the overall strength of the UN force had never surpassed 5,000, this force, known as the United Task Force (UNITAF), consisted of an impressive 36,000 officers, with an unprecedented American contribution of 23,000, about 63 per cent of the force's total strength. The code name of the operation was to be "Operation Restore Hope," and it was to work under the enforcement provisions of Chapter VII, which authorises the UN peacekeepers to be peace enforcers (i.e. use force) if necessary. UNITAF was to be independent from UNOSOM but there was to be a close coordination between the two and the overall political task in the country was to be left to the UN. Of the 24 countries that contributed to UNITAF, there were six African countries (Botswana, Egypt, Morocco, Nigeria, Tunisia and Zimbabwe) and a number of non-African Muslim countries including Saudi Arabia, Turkey and Pakistan. The force was dominated by Western states, including the UK, France and Australia and was spearheaded by the United States, who also had overall military command.

With no clear strategy and dominated by the United States whose Rambo's and Commandos were trained for combat and not for peacekeeping (Zacarias, 1996:70), UNITAF encountered an avalanche of difficulties on the ground after starting its deployment on 9 December 1992. The force soon came to be regarded by a number of Somali factions, especially those of Farah Aidid, as another adversary rather than a neutral force sent to their rescue (Burgess, 1998:37-61). The situation continued deteriorating — both on the ground, in security terms, and between UNITAF and the Somali factions — throughout the first half of 1993. UNITAF was not well-equipped for the task of disarming the Somali factions, and it lacked the appropriate coordination with United Nations forces and civilian administrators on the ground. In addition, not all of its forces used the same weaponry, as the American contingents used more sophisticated weapons and communications equipment than other contingents. Consequently, not all the contingents had the same combat readiness, which led to contradictory reactions by the different UNITAF contingents to the different Somali factions. This was one of the factors that led some factions, whose areas were under American control, to allege that they were being subjected to a force greater than what other factions were facing, and conclude that they were deliberately targeted.

From UNOSOM I to UNOSOM II

Despite the presence of more than 30,000 soldiers and military observers, it was clear from the deteriorating security and humanitarian situation that UNOSOM and UNITAF had failed and that their overall structure needed to be rethought. Thus, in March 1993, following an earlier report of the Secretary-General, the Security Council authorised the establishment of UNOSOM II, the initial United Nations force having been renamed in retrospect as UNOSOM I. The new force was to take over the task of UNITAF and was to be composed of 20,000 soldiers, 8,000 support personnel, and a civilian staff of 2,800. The tasks of the expanded UNOSOM included disarming Somali factions, assisting in the provision of humanitarian relief and the economic rehabilitation of Somalia, assisting the Somali people in promoting and advancing national reconciliation, and assisting in the return of refugees and displaced persons to their homes. Ensuring all the Somali factions' strict respect for and adherence to the peace process and the cease-fire agreement in place was also one of the main tasks of UNOSOM II. The force operated under the same enforcement provisions of Chapter VII of the UN Charter (UN, S/RES/814, 1993).

The Secretary-General appointed the American retired Admiral Jonathan T. Howe as his Special Representative from the date UNOSOM II was established until February 1994. He was replaced by the veteran Guinean diplomat Lansana Kouyaté as the Acting Special Representative. Kouyaté remained in this position until June 1993, when the Ghanaian diplomat James Victor Gbeho filled the position from July 1994 until April of the following year.

Curiously, despite the deteriorating situation in the country, or perhaps because of it, the UN decided in August 1993 to reduce the number of troops to about 17,200 by the end of September 1994. The Security Council decided to end the Mission in March 1995 and to withdraw all UNOSOM II forces and assets from the country. The authorised strength of UNOSOM II was then 22,000 all ranks and the actual strength on 2 August was 18,761.

It seems that the turning point in UN involvement in the conflict in Somalia came in October 1993. In this month, 18 American Rangers were killed in a fierce battle with the forces of Farah Aidid. Seeing the footage of this battle and the dead body of an American soldier being dragged by the "poor Somalis" on the streets of Mogadishu was said to have greatly angered American public opinion. Many of those that did not like American involvement in African wars, or in any multilateral peacekeeping operation with the UN, charged the world body with all that had gone wrong. With new Democratic president Bill Clinton in office, cynical Republicans (e.g. Bolton, 1994) went on criticising the world body, saying that "these failures raise larger questions about the United Nations' competence." Many such critics blamed the UN for the killing of the American soldiers, which led to the withdrawal of American troops in Somalia.

These American commentators did not know or chose to ignore two things. The first thing was that three months before this incident, in June, the Pakistani contingent lost 23 of its peacekeepers and had 60 wounded in a similar encounter with the same faction led by Aidid (Woods, 1997; Souaré, 2006b). This did not cause any uproar. The other is that, contrary to these charges, the American Rangers were not under UN command. As Clarke and Herbst (1996) demonstrate, the Rangers were commanded by a U.S. Special Forces officer who reported directly to U.S. Central Command at MacDill Air Force Base in Florida. Moreover, the searches for Aidid, including the one that led to the October fatalities, were all approved by relevant senior American authorities in Washington.

The American withdrawal dealt a big blow to the UN force in Somalia. The U.S. had failed the UN and the people of Somalia. Contrary to their declared aims and the responsibility they were tasked with, the Americans had refused to disarm the Somali factions and even told the warlords that they could keep their weapons if they moved the arms from Mogadishu or into their respective cantonments in Mogadishu. As Boutros-Ghali (1999:60) later revealed and others hinted at (Clarke & Herbst, 1996; Patman, 1997), even when they came upon a major cache of weapons, "the American forces of UNITAF were under orders not to seize them." This raises many questions about the real intentions of the Americans in coming to Somalia in the first place. Was it a Rambo show, as in the combat films of Hollywood, to demonstrate American supremacy, or it was a real peacekeeping mission (Souaré, 2006a:134)?

The departure of the American forces did not lead to a direct and immediate withdrawal of UN forces. This was a very courageous decision by the world body. The UN, however, kept to its deadline of March 1995 for complete withdrawal. Thus, by 2 February 1995, with the repatriation of the Indian, Zimbabwean and Malaysian contingents, some headquarters personnel and those of the Pakistani hospital, UNOSOM II troop strength was reduced to 7,956. With these drastic cuts in the strength of the UN force, it was no longer possible for UNOSOM II troops to extend the necessary protection even within Mogadishu. Humanitarian agencies were then advised to evacuate their international staff to Nairobi. By the end of March 1995, UNOSOM II had completed its withdrawal from Somalia. The conflict, however, had not yet been resolved.

What Went Wrong in the UN Somalia Mission?

To the UN officials, and this is quite true also from the Secretary-General's view, only the Somalis themselves could establish a viable and acceptable peace. The international community could only help in the process. Such assistance, however, could not be sustained indefinitely. In other words, the justification advanced by the world body for the withdrawal of its forces from Somalia is that the Somalis did not create a suitable environment for their presence. Further, since their presence and indeed their success were conditioned on the cooperative efforts of the Somali parties, including respecting the different ceasefire agreements they had signed, there was no point in the continuation of the UN forces. However, if the Somali leaders had succeeded in creating and maintaining favourable security conditions, the United Nations and the international community might have taken a different approach. On these grounds, the UN insists that its mission did not fail as critics charge.

To those critics however, the UN is not totally innocent in the creation of this situation. The American military approach in Somalia did contribute to the antagonising of some Somali factions (Patman, 1997) and the UN allowed itself, to a large extent, to be influenced by the Americans. As Clarke and Herbst (1996) note, when U.S. officials of UNITAF gave formal control to the UN in May 1993 when UNOSOM II was created, "they had already determined the nature of the follow-up operation." A retired American officer, Admiral Jonathan Howe, was appointed UN Secretary-General's Special Representative to Somalia.

The impact of the disagreement between the first Special Representative of the Secretary-General and the headquarters on the outcome of the mission has been mentioned above. Though Sahnoun resigned as early as November 1992, because his resignation was due to differences of strategies, the subsequent Special Representatives of the Secretary-General were expected to have a different policy than his. This is not to be construed as an insinuation that that his strategy was necessarily the best. However, it proved difficult for the subsequent Representatives to sell their new strategy to the Somali parties and this caused disturbance in the overall political strategy of the UN in Somalia (Souaré, 2006a:135). Moreover, a Comprehensive Report of the UN Department for Peacekeeping Operations (DPKO) about UNOSOM implicitly admits the failure of the mission. The report attributes this to three main factors: the mission's vague mandate, lack of proper planning, and poor if not total lack of coordination (DPKO, 1995).

Concerning the Operation's mandate, the report notes that this was "vague, changed frequently during the process and was open to myriad of interpretations." One of the intriguing aspects of the mandate of the UN operation was that orders were given to capture warlords such as Farah Aidid, and later, to encourage negotiations with them. One explanation for this, especially the mandate's subjection to different interpretations, is that many troop-contributing countries were not sufficiently consulted during the formation stage of the mandate. Consequently, they had varying perceptions and interpretations during its execution. If we add to this the full knowledge of some troop contributors of the exact meaning of the mandate and their choice to deliberately ignore it and take a different approach, as evidenced in the refusal of the Americans to disarm the Somali factions despite this being explicit in their mandate, one can see how the very mandate of the operation contributed to its failure.

Before the establishment of any peacekeeping force of this nature, a good knowledge of the terrain is necessary for planning the operation and ensuring its success. Yet the report shows that in the establishment of the UN operation, "integrated planning was limited to [just] two short visits to Somalia by interdepartmental technical teams." This, in the view of the drafters of the report, was not sufficient. To them, and quite rightly, "a viable, integrated plan requires ample information and analysis in advance of an operation." Concerning coordination, the report criticises the lack of a coordinated overall plan in terms of command relations, rules of engagement, coordination and standard operating procedures, intelligence management, and administrative and logistics policy and procedures. It notes that the UN operation suffered from a lack of unity among its different components. After establishing how crucial the central authority of the Special Representative of the Secretary-General (SRSG) is for the success of the operation, it asks whether frequent changing of the individuals serving in this capacity contributes to, or detracts from, developing an integrated structure in the field? UNOSOM I and II had a total of five SRSGs within a period of just three years (1992-1995). The report thus concludes that because of all this, "there were obvious and direct operational consequences" (ibid).

Conclusion and Some Policy Recommendations

From the above, it is clear that the UN mission in Somalia failed and the main reasons of this failure have been explained. Another factor of this failure, or better put, the collapse of the Somali state, which I did not mention in the text but has been discussed in length by other contributors (see chapters 3-5) is the disengagement of the African states, especially within the framework of the OAU, from their dutiful responsibility towards the people of a fellow African country. Through many African countries contributed to UNITAF and both UNOSOM I and II, they were not under an African command.

I see this same factor as part of the blame that African states should shoulder in the Rwandan genocide (Souaré, 2006a:158-160). Oftentimes in armed conflict situations, African governments and organizations withdraw from their responsibility and think, wrongly indeed, that others, especially the UN and powerful Western states, are the ones to do it for them. The fact of the matter is that African leaders should recognise that Africa's saviour is no one but itself, specifically through regional and continental African institutions. Yet, in order for these institutions to carry out this task, they ought to have credibility not only in the eyes of the "international community," but first and foremost in the eyes of the African peoples. To have this, they need to be seen in the driver's seat rushing to the rescue in conflict situations. Negotiating ceasefire agreements only to retreat to the background, leaving the UN or the likes of *Operation Restore Hope* (Somalia) or *Opération Turquoise* (Rwanda led by France) to take over does not augur well for confidence-building between the African governments and African peoples. It also does not help the world community's image of

Africa. It is the confidence of the African peoples that constitutes the sole winning asset of the African institutions and governments. It is paradoxical to be constantly reminding people of your sovereignty but fail to take the necessary measures, which are at your disposal, to protect this valued property.

This is why one cannot but welcome the reports of a possible African force to Somalia as the situation deteriorated, once again, in early 2007. Nothing concrete had been finalised about this force as this chapter was completed. If approved and finally dispatched, it will be the African Union's (the pan-African institution that changed its name from the OAU in 2002) second such African peacekeeping force, the first one being in Sudan. But the optimism about this force can only be a guarded one, considering the progress thus far in Sudan. By the completion date of this chapter, the peacekeeping force of the African Union in Sudan was still there but facing numerous logistical and financial problems. These problems have led to an animated debate as to whether it should remain purely African, or if the United Nations should take over. The view of this author on this issue is clear: everything should be done to make the mission in Sudan a successful *African* mission (Souaré, 2006b). The same goes for the proposed one for Somalia. For the Somali force to be successful, it must be assigned the twin task of peacekeeping and facilitating national reconciliation in the country, with all the national stakeholders having their due role and place recognised.

Two observations can be made about the weak and poor military and financial capabilities of African states. First, the military issue does not arise, since African troops serve on equal footing with other contingents in UN peacekeeping operations, be they in Africa or elsewhere. The problem is solely that of logistics and financial resources. And here again, the assumption that Africa does not have the necessary resources is questionable. The truth is, what seems to be lacking in Africa in genuine political will, nothing more. It may be interesting to note that an African state has never refrained from going to war because it lacks resources. Whenever there is war or a threat of one, either the government or so-called bilateral partners will strive to come up with the necessary resources. So why not when it comes to peacekeeping or conflict prevention?

Chapter 10

A CONTRIBUTION TO THE CASE FOR SOMALILAND'S RECOGNITION

Franco Henwood

Introduction

If anyone in the West thinks of Somalia, they most likely think of a failed state overrun by warlords, chaos and violence, reinforced by films such as *Black Hawk Down*.

Few Westerners are likely to have heard of Somaliland – an African success story. From the carnage and chaos of the Somali civil war, the territory has established the foundations of a constitutional democracy and the rule of law and peace. The territory's achievements followed its decision to separate from Somalia in 1991. In spite of this, the international community refuses to grant the territory recognition. The fear that such a move would encourage secessionist and irredentist movements elsewhere in Africa remains strong. The proposed solution remains the restoration of law and order in the south as a precursor to reunifying north and south.

This paper outlines Somaliland's emergence and the establishment of its fledgling democracy. The paper argues that these achievements are imperilled if recognition continues to be denied. The paper questions whether recognition would set a dangerous precedent for irredentist and secessionist movements elsewhere in Africa. The paper proceeds to reject the widely favoured solution that reunification of north and south must proceed on the basis of restoring law and order in the south. The proposed solution proceeds on the basis of treating the situation in the north and the south as the same. But like is not being compared with like. There are in effect two Somalias – the territory of Somaliland in the north and the rump state of Somalia in the south. The situations in the two parts of the country have evolved very differently and any proposal to revive the Somali state must recognise this fact. For this reason, fresh thinking is urgently required on this issue and this paper concludes with the reasons why.

The Emergence of Somaliland and the Foundation of Democratic Institutions

Present day Somalia once consisted of two separate colonies, British Somaliland in the north (now the territory of Somaliland) and Italian Somaliland in the south. The two colonies united 1 July 1960 but divisions persisted. Somalia retained the capital city and obtained two-thirds of the seats in parliament, while Southern leaders dominated the government. Northern voters rejected the unitary constitution in a June 1961 referendum, and in December of that year northern army officers launched a failed bid for independence (Kibble, 2006:3). Despite these challenges, the union survived. The ambition to create a Greater Somalia to unite Somali Diaspora communities in Kenya, Djibouti and Ethiopia united north and south alike. Over time, southern forms of political and administrative organisation consolidated their hold on the north, a process extended and deepened by the dictator General Mohamed Siad Barre, who seized power in October 1969 and established a Marxist dictatorship. Throughout the sixties and into the seventies, the union seemed secure.

Despite their identification with the national cause, Somalis generally owe their primary allegiance to clan and kin. This fact sat uneasily with the aspirations of Somali nationalists and nation builders. So long as the dream of a Greater Somalia seemed a realistic possibility, a balance between the centrifugal pull of the clan system and the aspirations of Greater Somali nationalism could be maintained. Barre's decision in 1977 to intervene in support of Somali rebels in the Ethiopian province of Ogaden toppled this balance. Barre's army met with total defeat at the hands of the Ethiopians. As a result of this defeat, the dream of a Greater Somalia was over. Almost immediately, the country came apart at its ethnic and clan seams. Discredited in defeat, Barre relied on his own Darod clan for support to prop up his rule, discriminating against other clans in the process, including the Isaaq of the north. Discontent led to the formation of the rebel northern

Somali National Movement (SNM) in 1982. Barre responded with massive repression, killing 50,000 Isaaq and displacing over a million others while his air force razed Hargeysa, the northern capital, to the ground[1]. Despite this, the SNM eventually defeated government forces in the north while an alliance of warlords drove Barre out of Mogadishu in 1991.

Post-1991 Developments

At the outset, the SNM sought some form of federal settlement rather than outright independence. But the exclusion of the SNM from a new national government in Mogadishu provoked mass public rallies in the north against the new southern leadership. These facts compelled a change of plan. On 18 May 1991, the SNM declared Somaliland's independence within the borders of the former State of Somaliland.

In 1993, the SNM handed over power to a civilian administration and a series of inter-clan conferences followed. These culminated in the Borama Conference in 1993, which founded a *beel* (clan or community) system of government with a separation of powers.

The *Beel* established a division of powers: an Executive (President, Vice President, and Council of Ministers), a bicameral legislature and an independent judiciary. The Upper House incorporated the traditional Somali council of elders (*guurti*), and was vested with the power to select a President as well as adjudicate internal conflicts. Seats in the Upper and Lower houses were allocated to clans proportionately. In 2002, after nine years of interim government, Somaliland finally held multi-party district council elections for 379 seats on 26 district councils. Six political organisations contested the elections, with the top three qualifying for registration as national political parties.

The first serious test of these arrangements came in May 2002. President Egal died on a visit to South Africa. Power passed to Vice President Dahir Rayale Kahin for the remainder of the presidential term. Remarkably, Rayale is a member of the Gadabursi clan, formerly

---

[1] See World Bank, "Conflict in Somalia: Drivers and Dynamics", January 2005 at http://siteresources.worldbank.org/INTSOMALIA/Resources/conflictin Somalia.pdf

strong allies of the Barre government against the SNM. Rayale was a former security officer under the Barre regime. Nonetheless, the transition was orderly and peaceful.

The subsequent presidential election in April 2003 saw President Rayale retaining his office by just 80 votes out of nearly half a million cast. The opposition at first protested but eventually accepted the result. The election was a genuinely close-fought contest and the election of a non-Isaaq president gave credence to the claim that Somaliland was a multi-clan polity (Kibble et al., 2005:8).

Elections to the House of Representatives in September 2005 represented a landmark in the formal transition from a clan-based representative system to that of a modern electoral democracy. Under the auspices of Somaliland's National Electoral Commission (NEC), 246 candidates contested 82 seats deemed by international observers to have been conducted in a peaceful, orderly and transparent manner.

The proposed election or appointment to the House of Elders (the Upper House of the legislature), the Guurti, will represent the final stage of the territory's democratic transition. The original mandate of the current Guurti expired in August 2006, but parliament has been unable to agree upon how the successor body should be chosen. President Rayale proposed an extension of the Guurti's term by four and a half years in May 2006. The Supreme Court endorsed the proposal – with the Guurti passing it without reference to the Lower House. Critics have charged that the handling of this issue has tarnished Somaliland's democratic credentials. Many Somalilanders, however, are relieved that the current Guurti will continue to play a stabilising role for some time to come.

Prospects for Somaliland's Democratic Experiment

Somaliland's democratic experiment is marred by serious shortcomings. Among these shortcoming is rampant corruption and underrepresentation of women in the government. Additionally, there are growing concerns about voting patterns based on ethnic lines. Somaliland inherited memories of a predatory and extractive central state from the Barre era, which continues to hinder the construction of any coherent central authority. Finally, the territory has its share of human rights violations. Amnesty International has recorded instances of arbitrary detention, unfair trails and torture.

Presently, the territory faces serious threats to its long-term survival. Most of its income is derived from remittances from the Diaspora. The government estimates that the Diaspora remits $300m to Somaliland every year. While this is a vital source of funds, remittances flow towards individuals and family networks. This deprives the government of funds to invest in plant and infrastructure.

The territory's economy is still based on the production and export of primary goods. More than half of Somaliland's population are nomadic pastoralists. Saudi Arabia's ban on Somali livestock exports in 1998 on health grounds has hamstrung the Somaliland economy. In any case, the livestock sector can no longer support the growing population. Destitute pastoralists are swelling the numbers of urban unemployed. According to Mr. Hussein Ali Duale, the territory's finance minister:

> Sixty per cent of our foreign currency was earned from the export of livestock to Saudi Arabia. Since the ban, the government has found it very difficult to make both ends of the budget meet (BBC online, 22 March 2005).

This means the economy urgently needs to diversify. Massive investment in infrastructure and education is necessary. There is potential to develop hydrocarbon and fishing resources. This will not happen without access to funds, from either public or private sources. But the government has no access to international financial institutions or direct bilateral assistance. Foreign investors are reluctant to invest in a territory that is still legally part of a failed state and designated war zone. The African Union (AU) fact-finding mission has observed that lack of recognition "ties the hands of the authorities and people of Somaliland as they cannot effectively and sustainably transact with the outside [world] to pursue reconstruction and development goals" (cited in ICG, 2006:12).

It is clear that the territory needs to diversify its economic base and that this will only occur when full recognition is granted. It is difficult to conceive how democratic consolidation can proceed if the territory has no long-term material basis to support it.

Some Somalilanders, however, question the benefits of international aid. Hussein Bulhan of Somaliland's Institute for

Development Solutions claims that aid will undermine the territory's self-reliance and

> will aggravate problems. There will be more struggles within the ruling elite. To a large extent what pushed tyranny in Somalia, and finally brought the collapse of the Siad Barre regime, was internal struggle over who will have what. That is part of why we had to create and to think and to improvise. These experts that come tend to make people uncreative. In Somaliland, people had to do it on their own (BBC online, 22 March 2005).

Whether foreign assistance turns out to be a poisoned chalice will depend on the future evolution of the Somaliland state. If it follows the typical African course of state development then Bulhan's scepticism will be vindicated. What most African states have lacked are mechanisms of transparency and accountability. This has allowed corrupt and venal elites to capture foreign aid flows for personal enrichment. Whether an independent Somaliland state avoids this trap depends on whether it allows the development of mechanisms of accountability and transparency to hold it accountable. That means genuine multi-party politics, a free press and an independent judiciary. As we have seen, there are good reasons to believe the foundations for such institutions have already been established.

Objections against Recognition Considered

Will recognition of Somaliland open up a 'Pandora's box' of secessionism elsewhere?

The denial of recognition can only be justified if there is a legitimate objection against it and/or if reunification is a realistic possibility. The remainder of this article argues that the central objection is not valid and that the proposed solution – reunification subsequent to a satisfactory political settlement in the South – is not feasible.

African governments have strong reservations about revising borders. This concern is understandable. The heterogeneity of the majority of African states means that many African states have fissiparous and centrifugal potential. The consequences of ethnic and secessionist conflicts in Africa from Biafra to the Democratic Republic of Congo have been calamitous. On this basis, African states especially are reluctant to offer recognition to Somaliland. Western states are reluctant to lead the way in the face of this opposition.

However, Somalia and Somaliland are exceptional cases. Somaliland did not secede from an established state; it emerged from the ruins of a collapsed one. The collapse of Somalia gave rise to Somaliland, not the other way round. Recognition would not reward irredentists or border revisionists. No negative precedent would be set. Of course, the objection might be stated differently. Recognition might *appear* as if it is doing just that. However, historical precedent in the region suggests otherwise. The recognition of Eritrea in 1993 did not, however, destabilise established borders in the region or elsewhere in Africa. It is true that no Somali politician can publicly countenance Somaliland's independence whereas Ethiopia consented to Eritrea's secession. Whether the opposition of southern politicians would remain so adamant if international opinion – African opinion especially – were to shift is an open question. In short, the objection that recognition would entail too great a potential to destabilise existing arrangements of borders in Africa has weak foundation in principle and in fact.

A serious caveat here, however, is that the territory's own borders are disputed. The territories of Sool and eastern Sanaag regions in Eastern Somaliland formed the Puntland State of Somalia in 1998, with a constitution that explicitly anticipates union with Somalia. Puntland defines its boundaries in terms of the distribution of the Harti clans. It lays claim to parts of eastern Somaliland inhabited by the Dhulbahante and Warsengeli communities, regardless of whether they have declared allegiance to Puntland or not. This raises the possibility that recognition may provoke the rise of a secessionist movement within the territory.

But it does not follow that the worst case scenario will necessarily occur. A regional diplomat has claimed that

> these negative consequences [of recognition] simply won't happen ... Somaliland will not simply impose its control over these territories....It will be forced to take into account the concerns of the people in those regions [If] the international community recognises [Somaliland], then [the inhabitants of those regions] will try to live with it (cited in ICG, 2006:10).

Additionally in an interview on 18 May 2006, Puntland President Ádde Musa played down the likelihood of conflict, stating that despite its commitment to unity and federalism, Puntland would not interfere with Somaliland's aspirations for independence (ibid).

The Puntland dispute is reason to approach the question of recognition with prudence and caution, but it is not a good reason to perpetuate the status quo. Refusal to grant recognition will not resolve the dispute. Outsiders will need to assist with the management of the recognition process and it is best that fellow African nations take the lead in dialogue with Somalis both north and south. There are some hopeful signs that opinion in Africa is shifting. An African Union fact-finding mission undertaken in response to Somaliland's application for membership of the organisation concluded that the situation was sufficiently unique and self-justified in African political history and that the case should not be linked to the notion of a Pandora's box (Somaliland Times, no. 222, 22 April 2006).

Can Reunification be Established on the Basis of a Settlement in the South?

But it is precisely this fear of opening up a Pandora's box of secessionism that has inhibited the international community from giving serious consideration to the issue of Somaliland's independence. The preferred solution has rested on establishing a unified and orderly authority in the south as a prelude to eventual reunification.

The designated agent to stabilise the South is the Transitional Federal Government (TFG). The TFG emerged after a two-year long round of talks among warring clan leaders in Nairobi, Kenya when a parliament of 275 members chosen by clans was elected in August 2004. With the election of both a president and a prime minister, the TFG now has the rudiments of functioning executive and legislature. It also enjoys formal recognition as the government of Somalia. It has been permitted to occupy Somalia's seats at the UN and the AU and was admitted to the International Parliamentary Union in May 2006. It has increasingly been treated as a national counterpart by donors and aid agencies. By way of contrast, the government of Somaliland is not accorded such privileges. This is a preposterous anomaly considering that the TFG does not control the territory it is nominally sovereign over, whereas the Somaliland government largely does exert control over its own designated territory. Initially divided between the towns of Mogadishu and Jowhar, the TFG overcame this division and established itself in Baydhowa in March 2006 before moving to Mogadishu at the end of the year after the defeat of the Union of Islamic Courts (UIC).

Six months previously, the UIC had appeared to rise from out of nowhere, seizing the capital and much of the south right under the noses of the TFG. The UIC's success dealt a severe blow to international hopes that the TFG represented the legitimate successor authority to the collapsed Somali state. Now such hopes may be restored. With the TFG's occupation of the capital, there is on the face of it the possibility that the TFG may be the harbinger of stability in the south, leading to reunification with the north, the desired solution of much of the international community.

But to conclude that we now have a firm foundation for reunification is premature for a variety of reasons. First, the TFG is in the capital on account of Ethiopian military support. Before the Ethiopians' intervention, the TFG faced defeat or marginalisation. There is no way the TFG will maintain itself in Mogadishu or elsewhere in the country unless the Ethiopians prop up its rule. Even then, the eviction of the UIC is hardly the end of the story. There is the question of how the TFG will tackle the warlords. Their power checked by the UIC, they now have a fresh opportunity to reassert themselves. They show little indication that they are prepared to surrender their influence and weapons to the TFG. The continued patronage of the Ethiopians will in all likelihood forestall any attempt by the UIC or the warlords to displace the TFG. But it is unlikely that the TFG on its present showing will be able to do anything more than hold its ground – even with continued international and Ethiopian support.

There is no doubt that the UIC demonstrated overt tendencies towards authoritarianism and extremism. Elements of it may have connections with radical Islamic terrorist organisations overseas. But it will be recalled that the UIC succeeded in evicting the warlords from Mogadishu and restoring law and order to the capital. The city's inhabitants appeared to have greeted the victory of the UIC with relief. There was no doubt that the UIC enjoyed widespread – if not universal – popular support on the basis of this achievement. The appropriate response on the part of the international community to the rise of the UIC should have been to engage with them, to encourage moderation and to consolidate the achievements of the movement in quelling the power of the warlords. To have tacitly condoned a violent coup against them will only serve to make compromise and accommodation harder to achieve in future. The UIC is not the East African chapter of Al-Qaeda. Its fighters are principally Somali. We are unlikely to have heard the last of the UIC. The possibility of a prolonged and bloody insurgency where neither side is able to prevail, with civilians bearing the brunt of the casualties, appears to be a likely outcome as a result of recent events. Stability in the south looks a long way off.

The tasks of pacifying the country and restoring law, order and national institutions are tremendous undertakings. Neither the Ethiopians nor the TFG has any declared programme as to how these might be achieved, other than the hope that AU or UN peacekeepers might step into the breach. There is little likelihood of this occurring anytime in the near future.

Even allowing for the best case scenario, with the country pacified, the warlords disarmed, law, order and truly representative and participatory national institutions established, the time frame required to accomplish this will be years, not months. In the meantime, the status of the north must be resolved. It cannot be left in limbo while the situation in the south is left to resolve itself. If this occurs, the prospects for democratic consolidation in the north will fade.

In short, the TFG, as it presently stands is neither transitional, federal nor a government in any sense of these words. Its grip on power is too weak and its legitimacy too brittle. This is not the basis on which to begin a process of national reconciliation.

The opposition of southern politicians to an independent Somaliland cannot be brushed aside. But neither must they have veto power on the issue. The TFG wants and indeed depends on international support for its legitimacy. Such support ought to be based on the willingness of the TFG to acknowledge the realities of the situation in the north. This is not to suggest that cornering the TFG into accepting outright secession of Somaliland is the way forward. But it needs to acknowledge the Somalia pre-1991 is a memory, not a reality. Indeed, given that the average age of a typical Somalilander is only 18, it is not even a memory for most of the territory's inhabitants. The longer the division persists, the harder it will be to persuade Somalilanders to be 'reunited' with an entity that fewer and fewer of them have had any recollection or experience of ever being united with.

Fledgling democracies need a generation or so of relative peace and stability in order to stabilise. Once a generation has grown up under the auspices of a stable and peaceful democratic order, then the likelihood of the next generation accepting that order is greatly increased. It is not unreasonable to suppose that this description applies to the experience of the generation raised in Somaliland since 1991.

Although Somaliland might serve as an example to the south (and perhaps elsewhere) of how a post-conflict reconstruction might proceed, this ought not to be the critical determinant in the consideration of whether or not to grant recognition. The Somalilanders' achievements deserve protection for their own sake. Whether others wish to emulate them is up to them.

None of this is meant as an apology for the specific regime of President Rayale or any specific administration in Somaliland. The purpose of this article is not to endorse any one particular administration, but to explore ways to consolidate incipient democratic institutions in the territory. Suffice it to say, if President Rayale wants recognition from the international community on the basis of the territory's democratic credentials (as he clearly does), then he will have to submit to international scrutiny to ensure he is compliant with international standards in transparent administration and the respect of human rights. The same can be said for any future administration.

In any case, the whole hope of resting a satisfactory settlement on the basis of reunification led by the TFG simply overlooks one unassailable fact: Somalilanders are strongly opposed to reunification. In the words of the International Crisis Group (2006:7):

> Despite continuing ethnic, linguistic and commercial linkages with Somalia, the idea of an independent Somaliland, complete with the symbolic trappings of statehood such as a flag, currency and passport, appears to command the loyalties of a growing proportion of the territory's population. The idea of a sovereign Somaliland is no longer the political platform of an armed faction so much as it is the reflection of an incipient national identity.

The strength of national feeling in the territory presents a powerful objection to any proposal for unification to proceed on the basis of southern leadership. Unless this objection is overcome, reunification is not a viable proposition – at least not one conducted by peaceful means.

Conclusion

There is no doubt that recognising the territory poses its own set of risks, but fresh thinking is required on pragmatic grounds for three reasons. The first of these is the strength of Somaliland nationalism, which is an established fact and is simply not going to depart of its own accord. The second is the continuing failure of the TNG to establish its credentials as the legitimate successor authority for a revived and reunified Somalia. The third is that the Somalilanders have all the rudiments of a functioning state, while the Republic of Somalia has none. The achievements of the Somalilanders have been accomplished largely under their own auspices. In contrast, over a dozen conferences involving the various southern factions since 1991, with lavish sponsorship from the international community, have achieved little.

The Somaliland democratic experiment has flaws and imperfections. Recognition is not a cast iron guarantee against disintegration along ethnic and clan lines as we have seen in the south. Nor is it any guarantee against the democratic experiment sliding into one-party authoritarianism, as we have seen so many times in Africa. But the fact remains that the Somaliland government has established a working system of peace and order in its territory. This is single most remarkable achievement to come out of the country since 1991. And it has been accomplished by Somalilanders themselves. These are achievements that deserve to be preserved and protected. The Somalilanders have accomplished them in the context of a de facto separation of the two halves of the country. In present circumstances, it is hard to conceive how these achievements could be preserved in the context of a reunified Somalia. On the other hand, the present limbo in which the territory is suspended cannot last indefinitely. The case for some sort of formal negotiated separation between north and south is therefore worthy of serious consideration. It is not an easy option by any means and cannot be imposed by diktat, but at present there do not appear to be any feasible alternatives.

Chapter 11

INIMITABLE POPULATION DISPERSION: THE CASE OF THE SOMALIAN DIASPORA

Akinloye Ojo

Introduction

The history of the African continent is consistently marked by economic, social and political crises. A lasting legacy of these incessant socio-political crises and regrettable economic mismanagement is the agonizing dispersal of a large segment of the continent's population within and outside the continent. Eventually, these masses transition from political and economic refugees into viable Diaspora communities. The emergent Diasporas become representations of both the excellent and unsightly rudiments of their native countries. The constitutions of these Diaspora groups often involve dated and inopportune ethnic, social and class divisions. These carry-over divisions continue to represent the actual sources of conflicts in the African countries from which these Diaspora communities have been, in most cases, forcefully dispersed. It is repeatedly the case therefore, that different African Diaspora communities become enablers of crises on the African continent through their support of different factions at home.

Through its Constitutive Act and in the establishment of the Pan-African Parliament, the AU declared that it shall "invite and encourage the full participation of the African Diaspora as an important part of our Continent, in the building of the African Union." The African Union (AU) has defined the African Diaspora as "people of African origin living outside the continent, irrespective of their citizenship and nationality and who are willing to contribute to the development of the continent and the building of the African Union."

This description attempts to address a calamity of history. The AU's definition (irrespective of citizenship and nationality) includes both the descendants of Africans forcibly transported to the Western hemisphere through the Trans-Atlantic slave trade and the latest African Diaspora. Although a significant number of the members of the historical African Diaspora have affected the socio-political situation on the continent, the bulk of the groups are unfortunately now becoming increasingly involved in and with Africa. Therefore, in spite of the inclusive definition from the AU, the African Diaspora of interest is the more recent dispersal of African peoples, languages and cultures that were previously assembled in a part of Africa and whose dispersal resulted mostly from contemporary socio-political and economic predicaments in their respective African countries. These groups struggle to provide a positive representation of their languages and cultures while dealing with the multitude of challenges and negativity that they face as foreigners in their new abodes. Members of these nascent African Diasporas continue to maintain contact and exact influence on the socio-political and economic situations in their respective home countries.

This chapter focuses on the Somalian Diaspora, present in sizeable numbers around the world. They can be found in different parts of Africa such as Djibouti, Ethiopia, Kenya and Tanzania as well as in Australia, North America, Europe and the Middle East. As noted by Horst (2004), "migration has for centuries played a vital role in Somali lives and livelihoods, through Islam, in nomadic pastoralism, in ancient-old trade patterns and more recent migration of workers, professionals and students. Since the start of the civil war in 1991, Somalis can be found in all continents, and they form a considerable migrant group in a number of countries."

The number of this dispersed population is estimated to be between one to two million (Nair & Abdulla 1998; UNDP 2001; Sorensen 2004). Some of these numbers include those who, as in the AU definition, have become citizens and nationals of their host countries (within and outside Africa). It is currently an indisputable fact in migration and Diaspora studies that Somalis are currently one of the most widely dispersed Diasporas in the world and, though the neighboring African states are the main asylum destinations, are currently asylum seekers in about sixty countries (Sorensen, 2004). The number of Somalis residing outside of the country is significant considering that the population of the Somalia is given to be between 5.4 million to 8.7 million people (UN Population Division, 2003).

As Cindy Horst discussed in the Global Migration Perspectives (No. 9) for the Amsterdam Institute of Metropolitan and International Development Studies in 2004, one of the problems encountered in identifying exact numbers is that Somalis who reside outside their home country fall under several statistical categories. There are those who migrated before the war for education, job opportunities and a number of other reasons, and who hold various types of residence permits or are now nationals of their new country. Then there are those who fled after the war, some of whom are still registered as asylum seekers, others holding temporary permits, others with full refugee status, and yet others nationals. There is also a grey mass of non-registered and illegal migrants. As a consequence, estimates of exact numbers vary widely. For example, Somalis in the UK are estimated at 70,000 by Montclos (2000), as opposed to 100,000 by Ahmed (2000); whereas their official number (excluding pre-conflict Somalis) is 20,000 (Gundel 2003:5). The deviation multiplies when the total figure of Somalis abroad is estimated, but the number of people who have fled to neighboring countries and beyond has been estimated at 1.5 million (Gardner and El Bushra 2004:2)

In fact, a BBC news report in 2004 claimed that nearly 25% of all Somalians[1] now live abroad and multitudes are fleeing each day (BBC online, 24 November 2004). The report noted that there is now a Somali saying, 'we are now a nation of immigrants who depend on other immigrants,' referring to the support in the form of remittances provided by Somalians in the West and the Middle East to those in refugee camps in neighboring African countries as well as relatives left within the country. The report further observed that these remittances account for almost a quarter of the country's annual income – a sum of nearly seven hundred million dollars a year. We will return to the issue of remittances later but the enormity of these remittances is an indication of the size as well as the financial condition of Somalians in the Diaspora. In terms of the location of the Diaspora, it will become clearer that the local clan networks as well as the networks between earlier migrants determined who migrated as well as the method and direction of the later but larger number of refugees.

---

[1] Following Lindley (2005), the term 'Somalian' refers to Republic of Somalia nationals, while 'Somali' refers to an ethnic group in the Horn of Africa.

It is the consideration of the good and tough elements of this notable Diaspora that concerns us in this chapter. Here, we will contextualize the migratory chronicles of Somalia citizens within the historical developments of Somalia since independence in 1960. We will endeavor to provide a description of the contemporary Somalia Diaspora as well as some of the challenges facing the community. Even though we will draw on the study of Somalian communities in different parts of the world, our particular focus will be on Somalian communities in the West, including Europe and North America. In fact, we will present Horst's (2004) description of one such community in the American state of Minnesota. This description will hopefully provide a practical background for our subsequent discussions. As we examine each of the Somalian Diaspora's particular challenges and identified issues of concern, we will primarily highlight good aspects and then draw attention to some of the not so complementary aspects. For instance, we will consider how the noxious clannish division that has fueled the interminable civil war in Somalia is tearing apart what is otherwise a successful and thriving Somalian Diaspora. Finally, we will identify some of the direct and indirect socio-political, economic and cultural impacts the Somalian Diaspora is having on the vestige of civil society in Somalia.

History as Motivation for Population Dispersal

Typically, Somalis are renowned nomadic pastoralists, and as such, nomadic existence is central to Somali culture. The livelihoods of Somali pastoralists trying to survive an extremely harsh climate have been characterized by strategies of mobility and dispersal (Lewis 1961). As such, social relationships were both reflections of vocation and a means of maintaining extended family and kinship links. These bonds impacted the establishment of migratory traditions into different parts of the Horn of Africa. It can be postulated that the settlements of some of these traditional migrants in places such as Ethiopia and Kenya were the earliest Somalia Diasporas to emerge. A later Diaspora emerged in the United Kingdom in port cities such as Bristol, Cardiff, Hull, Liverpool and London. This was during the era of colonialism when British 'subjects' serving in the Merchant Navy began settling down in the 'home country.' Many of these seamen were in the naval service well after independence. This population was further bolstered by

Somalian migrants attracted by employment opportunities in the expanded British steel industry of the 1950s.

Others from these eras settled in America and the Middle East doing maritime work (Cassanelli 1982; Simkin 2002; Hansen 2004; and Sorensen 2004). These early migrants provided the essential information and resources that enabled subsequent migrants to disperse to Western Europe and North America. The various resettlement programs then and afterwards in Australia and North America further induced increased migration. As with the dispersal of other notable Diasporas, the distance that migrants can travel in order to be safe and comfortable has been dependent on the resources (be it human resources via networks and previous migrants or financial resources, owned or promised) they possess. Notwithstanding, these early colonialism- and work-induced migratory patterns into Europe and North America were instantaneously followed by another stream into the Middle East.

The Islamic link and the historic socio-political and trade forays of Arabs into the Horn of Africa had previously created a Somalia community in the Arab world, but this number exploded due to the emergent oil production industry in the Gulf in the 1970s. Somalia became one of the largest suppliers of labor to the region. It was estimated that, between 1970 and 1987, about 375,000 people with varied skill levels migrated from Somalia into the Middle East. These migrants, according to Gundel (2003), were relatively well-educated, traveling abroad for better employment and higher earnings than they could find in Somalia. The flow into the Gulf slowed down to a trickle once civil war commenced in the 1990s. Many Somalia workers in the oil industries in Saudi Arabia and Gulf States were expelled after 1991 (Montclos 2000), but the already established migratory networks still enabled a substantial number of new migrants to enter the Middle East. Essentially, the number of Somalians in the region has not continually risen, but there are enough migrants in the area to constitute a notable segment of the Diaspora.

Interestingly, a significant number of Somalians were migrating, during the same period, to North America, Europe and the Soviet Union for higher education and better prospects. However, due to new entry restrictions and increasing cost of education in the West, the direction of this educational migration was redirected towards India and Pakistan (Hansen, 2004). In addition, the supporters of the ruling

Somali Youth league relocated abroad after independence in 1960. These groups, particularly those from the north-western Isaaq clan (for more details, see Ch. 5), were disappointed at their loss of assets and access to new resources. The number of Isaaq clan members moving into exile in the West further increased in 1988 following the persecution of the clan by the Siad Barre dictatorship. The singling out of the group was due to a suspicion that its members were colluding with the Somali National Movement, the underground opposition to Barre. The number of Somali exiles from the North and South exploded after the fall of the Barre government in January 1991 and the subsequent civil war (McGown, 1999).

The largest Somalian communities outside Africa are in the United Kingdom and Italy. The colonial history of Somalia provides substantiation for this situation. However, these traditional Diaspora communities in the West have been greatly enhanced by recent immigrants – the latest asylum seekers. In the year 2000 alone, half of the asylum applications by Somalis in Europe were directed to the UK government (4,800 out 10,900 applications according to Sorensen, 2004). Many of these applications were from Somali refugees originating from the now self-declared Republic of Somaliland (Ahmed 2000). Other favored destinations in Europe are Holland, Germany and the Scandinavian nations. The hike in Somali immigrants in these countries was due, until recently, to the unusual high rate of asylum approvals. A notable number have also moved into Italy. According to Sorensen (2004), "Italy (amongst other European destinations) has become one of the major destinations for irregular labor migration, including Somalis. Today Somali women compete with Philippine, Romanian and Ukrainian housekeepers, baby-sitters and care-workers to take up jobs for millions of Italian families. IRIN (2003) reports that agents in Mogadishu can charge double the price for smuggling Somali girls into Italy (U.S $7,000 as compared to U.S $3,500 to other European countries) because the girls get jobs as housekeepers and can start sending money home immediately."

The changing political terrain resulting from the widespread 'war on terror' has unfortunately made conditions for asylum cumbersome, difficult and, in some European countries, outright xenophobic. This has led to an overflow of Somalian asylum seekers into non-traditional European nations, in some cases simply securing residency in these nations and then moving with their European Union (EU) papers into more traditional nations like England. Sorensen (2004) observed that this has, illustratively, been the case for a smaller group of Somalians who have gained citizenship in Denmark but have subsequently moved to England, a country they perceive as being less xenophobic and more open to Somalians. Beyond Europe, another attractive location for migrating Somalians has been North America. Between 1990 and 1998, about 27,000 Somalian refugees were said to have applied for asylum in Canada and the United States (Frushone 2001, ECRE 2000).

In the years since 1991, the socio-political situation in Somalia has deteriorated to the extent that it has acquired the notoriety of being the only known state without a functioning government. There is indeed a contention that the nation might be split into three different countries if a political solution is not found to the crisis. In fact, Somalian statehood is arguable considering that beyond the established territories, key elements of statehood are missing. Elements such as the rule of law or the existence of enforceable and consistent laws, the provision of basic social services by state apparatus or state-sanctioned private entities and the provision of security for the population do not exist. Interestingly, the continuous existence of this territory as a fragmented and war-ridden country has emboldened the arguments that clannish dominated societies such as Somalia might be better off without a 'state.' Scholars such as Little (1998) and Menkhaus (1998) have argued that it is a mistake to focus on state breakdown in Somalia, principally because societies and economies for all intents and purposes "function in the absence of states and the consequences of statehood (in places like Somalia) have not always been desirable" (Marten, 2006).

This is an appealing argument, especially since Somalians have endured nearly two decades of broken statehood and considering that the nation-state in Somalia was an artificial structure created by negotiation and imposed on the people. Bradbury (2003) notes that, "...development processes in Somalia exist not as a result of official development assistance but in spite of it." Bradbury further argues that there is no single explanatory variable that can describe the collapse of the Somali state. He argues that

> To focus solely on the contradictions between a foreign imposed colonial system of government and an indigenous political system would be to overlook the impact of the oppressive, corrupt and

violent system of political patronage that marked the 21 year military rule of Mohamed Siad Barre (1969-1991), the influence of Cold War and post-Cold War politics in the region, the impact of structural adjustment and economic liberalization policies in the 1980s and the character of the armed movements in Somalia. Clearly, state crisis is not unique to Somalia. For many people in Africa and elsewhere in the world, the liberal peace promised by the ending of the Cold War and the advance of capitalism has not materialized ... In Africa the advent of this new world order appeared in the 1980s, in the form of structural adjustment programs, state de-bureaucratization and the emergence of supranational and sub-national entities that weakened state institutions and the internal legitimacy of many governments ... The Somali government, in the absence of external support, was unable to do so. Indeed, in Somalia state collapse was particularly profound and the social costs enormous. In the early 1990s Somalia's situation deteriorated when it became a testing ground for new international institutions.

In comparison, Marbury-Lewis (2002) asserted that "post-colonial states (especially in Africa) are now forced to grapple with a new economic order that is disconcerting rich countries and leaving poorer countries devastatingly marginalized." As Cole and De Blij (2007:546-547), being true to the facts of history, noted in their description of the chimerical Somalian nation:

The history of Somali political geography concerns the creation of an African state through negotiation and treaty by Ethiopia, an African empire, the British and French empires, and Italy. Creating the new state also entailed Somali ethnic nationalism and the idea of a Greater Somalia based on the putatively common culture of the Somali. The ultimate breakup of the state was due to the inherent instability of the Somali sociopolitical fabric. United against a common foe, whether European colonialism, Ethiopia, or Western Imperialism, the Somali clans fought for and were joined in a seemingly culturally homogenous state that used military force to push irredentist claims to the center of national ideology. Later, shifting official state ideology in the Horn led to changing superpower interest in Somalia, a decline in military support, and a rather rapid collapse of effective irredentist momentum. The homogeneity of the Somali nation, always more apparent than real, proved to be ephemeral.

All of these notwithstanding, the arguments highlighting the dispensability of statehood in Somalia fail to recognize how critical the terrible economic and human costs of lawlessness have been to the people and country. Most of the notable Diasporas in the world have emerged as a response to socio-political upheavals in their homeland. This has become a familiar chronicle for many within the Somalian Diaspora. When it becomes apparent that personal security is overwhelmingly threatened and opportunities are perpetually lacking, even the most nationalistic citizens are forced to consider migrating far away from the dreadful state of affairs. This is the decision that the majority of post-1991 Somalian migrants have been forced to make. They have inexorably responded to the appeal of the outside world and the opportunities offered. In fact, there is hardly any divergence of opinions amongst those interested in Somalia, be it intellectuals (especially scholars in fields such as political science, Diaspora studies, international affairs and peace studies), statesmen (particularly African leaders and politicians), developmental agencies (and their agents) and peace activists: the anarchy and breakdown in law and order that has plagued Somalia since the 1990s has served as the greatest motivation for the increased dispersal of people into other parts of Africa, the Middle East and the rest of the world.

Larger numbers of Somalis have left the Horn of Africa because of civil war and political unrest than for any other reason. Hundreds of thousands Somalis were sent into exile in the late 1980s and early 1990s. The outbreak of civil war in 1988 and the inter-clan fighting after the fall of Siad Barre in 1991 displaced hundreds of thousands of Somalis within the country and drove many others to seek refuge in Ethiopia, Kenya, Yemen and other neighboring countries, as well as to seek asylum further afield in the UK, Italy, the Netherlands, Scandinavia, Canada, the U.S. and other Western countries. Some were able to follow paths and networks already established by 'economic' migrants. By 1992, UNHCR estimated that more than 800,000 Somalis – out of an estimated population of five to seven million – were refugees, scattered not only in refugee camps in neighboring countries, but also in western Europe (the UK, the Netherlands, Italy and Sweden being the main countries of asylum) and in the United States and Canada (UNHCR 2002). This is almost double the number estimated in 2001, when UNHCR operated with a total number of Somali refugees at 440,000 (Sorensen 2004).

Some of the historical reasons for the outward dispersal of a sizeable segment of Somalia and the establishment of the larger Somalia Diaspora include colonialism, the timeless search for better opportunities and the incessant socio-political crisis (particularly since the 1990s) coupled with the spirit of self preservation. The noted migratory patterns in this depiction are also indicative of how multifarious the migratory flow out of Somalia has been. It has gone in various directions from what can be labeled traditional destinations to newer and often welcoming locations. It is a difficult task to neatly classify members of the Somalian Diaspora into either a 'forced' or 'voluntary' migration category. This is largely because of the historical diversity of motivations. Depending on the historical period of the country, the Somalian migration patterns and flows have been distinctive. Sorensen (2004) has further documented that "class diversification seem to be congruent with distance (the better off, the longer distance traveled), and certain out-going flows – e.g. to Italy – have become feminized at the same time as certain return movements seem to have become 'masculinized.'" Differing migration regimes in different host countries have further added to a situation in which Somalians – who may have left Somalia at the same time and for the same reasons – hold different statuses.

In spite of these and other reasons for the high level of Somalian population displacement, it is our undertaking in this chapter to consider the constitution of the contemporary Somalia Diaspora and the distinctive challenges specific to this community. Studies have focused on the different Somalian communities around the world that constitute the Somalia Diaspora. Some of these include communities in places such as Ontario and Toronto in Canada (McGown, 1999); London and other parts of Britain (McGown, 1999; Svedjemo, 2002); Minnesota in the U.S. (Horst, 2004); Dadaab in Kenya (Horst 2003, 2004); and Denmark (Bang, 2004). Some of these studies included the researchers' descriptions as well as observations of the communities. These were based mostly on lifetime relationships and/or extensive fieldwork amongst the people. Given that our discussion here is devoid of such observations, we will briefly reflect on the description of one of these communities (in the state of Minnesota, U.S.) as provided in Horst's (2004) introduction to the characteristics of the Somalian remittance process from the perspective of both receivers resident within Somalia and in Dadaab, Kenya and senders resident in different parts of Minnesota. This depiction will provide a realistic background for our preceding discussions, and will also place our subsequent discussions of issues specific to the Somalian Diaspora in the proper perspective.

The Somali Community in Minnesota[1]

The state of Minnesota is said to be one of the top destinations for Somalis and it has, in recent times, become host to the largest number of Somalis in the U.S. The capital city of Saint Paul and its 'twin' Minneapolis have the highest concentration, but small towns such as Rochester, Marshall, Willmar and Owatanna have been attracting a significant number of these immigrants. There are no precise figures but the United States census data for the year 2000 puts the number at 11,164 or .2% of the state population. This is higher than other leading locations renowned for large Somali communities such as Columbus, Ohio; Atlanta, Georgia; Seattle, Washington; and San Diego, California. Even then, the likelihood is that the official numbers are underestimates because many extended Somali families underreport the number of occupants in their residence. This is born out of the fact that there are regularly more residents than allowed by law in most of these single family homes. An alternate number of 15,000 to 30,000 Somalis in Minnesota can be gleaned from enrollment figures within the public schools and statistics from the welfare system.

There have also been secondary movements from other parts of the country, especially since 1998. It is in fact believed that up to 60% of the Somalis residing in Minnesota and surrounding region came from other states (Mattessich, 2000). There are numerous reasons for the continuous increase in the Minneapolis Somali population. The healthy economy and low unemployment rates in the state are primary factors. There are many job opportunities at various levels. The Somalis are employed in different types of work. Those with a low level of education and/or little knowledge of English work the low-skilled jobs that provide opportunities for long hours and good pay: security guards, cleaners, taxi drivers, parking attendants and workers in the various assembly plants, meat factories and turkey plants in the region.

---

[1] The discussion in this section is derived from the description of the Minnesota Somalian community provided by Horst (2004:10-12).

Those with higher education and better English skills work, among other higher paying and skilled jobs, as social workers, managers, teachers, professors, doctors and lawyers. Most of the lower income groups reside in large run-down flats with cheap rents predominantly with other Somalis as co-tenants. The more successful and affluent migrants live in nicely decorated mansions in city suburbs and drive comfortable family cars.

A secondary reason is the fact that Minnesota, being a large Scandinavian-originated state, is quite welcoming for migrants. The hospitable attitude can be traced to the region's history of dealing with large groups of immigrants. The favorable environment includes better social security and essential services in education and health care. These reasons aside, as word of the state's virtues spread, the presence and comfort of the Somali community in Minnesota has become a motivation for others to come closer and establish a solid community. This has created a safe haven for these migrants[1]. As Horst (2004) noted, "a parallel economy was created that enables Somalis nowadays to do everything 'the Somali way': there are Somali shops, malls, NGOs, travel agents, hairdressers, restaurants, Quranic schools, mosques etc. For businessmen and -women, providing goods and services to the now well-established Somali community in the area may be a good alternative or addition to having a regular job. And as the community grows, more Somalis move to Minnesota to be near their families and to find a home on the prairie.

Somalia Diaspora: the Good and the Tough

The concise description of the Somali community in Minnesota above highlights some of the peculiarities of the Somalian Diaspora. Most migrants settle down mostly in convivial communities in which opportunities and services are available. Exceptions include Somalian refugees in camps, primarily in East Africa, and those migrants on

---

[1] In addition to Horst's description of the achievements of the Somalian community in Minnesota, the influence and support of the Somalian community was credited for the historic election of the first Muslim member of the American House of Representatives, Congressman Keith Ellison in 2006. In fact, some of his campaign workers were Somali-Americans descendants of the earlier Somali refugees in the area (various news reports on the 2006 November elections).

temporary status with the hope of moving to secondary destinations for permanent settlement. The description of other Somalian communities worldwide confirms this fact and underscores the point that these communities (i.e. the Somalian Diaspora) have common concerns and deals with similar issues. Key issues include the integration into their host communities, the effects of migrating into new environments on the Somalian familial and social units, the impact of the Diaspora on the conflicts at home and vice versa, and the assistance the Diaspora offers to other Somalians at home in the form of remittances.

Integration into Host Communities

It can be derived from the descriptions of the Somali community in Minnesota and others all over of the world that there is a sense of comfort amongst the migrants. Many have become productively integrated into their host communities, and as a result of hard work and endurance, have become highly successful. Numerous Somalians are educated, rich and with significant influence in their host communities. This sense of success is not limited to only educated or skilled migrants; even the so-called 'unskilled' migrants have thrown themselves into building a successful life in exile so much so that they have achieved a significant level of comfort and sufficient financial means to provide for their families. This is not to say that a notable number of Somalian immigrants are not living with financial hardship or that there are none dependent on welfare or social services in their respective host communities. The fact is, the Somalian Diaspora has become rather affluent as a whole in comparison to other notable Diasporas, be they African or not.

Integration, however, is the "two-sided process of immigrants' adjustments to a new society without loss of what they consider essential to their identity (or self-identification, particularly in the sense of their religion or ethnicity) and, simultaneously, of the adoptive society's accommodation of them" (McGown, 1999). On a more fundamental level, this implies that Somali immigrants as well as host communities (in Kenya, Ethiopia, Italy, England, Canada and the United States, amongst others) will predictably, in due course, go through significant changes. Beyond predictions, they have indeed gone through both pleasant and difficult changes, particularly over the last thirty plus years. This is the tough part of the integration challenge for the Somalian Diaspora. Somalians are incredibly proud people with a strong sense of religious and cultural identity. A case in point is the effort, since 2000, of both Somali linguists and non-linguists in the Diaspora to spearhead the formalization of a modern orthography for the standard form of Somali, the language of wider communication in Somalia. Therefore, it is quite traumatic for most to be suddenly uprooted from their homeland and shoved into strange, unfamiliar environments. Many arrive with a significant sense of loss (of wealth, status, homes, extended family and country) and a psychosomatic fear of a complete obliteration of their cultural and religious identity. This situation is compounded by the continued hostilities in Somalia. There is a sense of being indefinitely stuck in the Diaspora and, along with that, a sense of hopelessness. Unlike other Diasporas, there is no home government for them to relate with, no civil society to connect to, hardly any opportunity to contemplate visits and returning home is a quite distant thought. For the older generation, the hope of a homebound exodus fades daily and for the younger generation, Somalia is becoming a mythological Zion – a peaceful homeland that exists only in the imagination of elders. It is notable that many of the younger generations were born in refugee camps, in exile, or brought out of Somalia so young that they could hardly remember a peaceful existence in a nonviolent Somalia.

On top of this psychological trauma, there are the real life struggles of adjusting and tackling the challenges that commonly confront new migrants everywhere. For immigrants who find themselves in communities unwillingly adjusting to the influx of foreigners, the pressure to integrate is equally harsh on both the hosts and newcomers. For the immigrants that landed in friendly communities such as those found in Minnesota, the pressure to adjust is tougher on the newcomers, as they have to work hard not to forgo their identity in a welcoming environment. The experiences of different communities within the Somalian Diaspora provide indications of both scenarios. While a significant number have thrived, many have not been as fortunate and chronic social problems continue to plague the communities.

Many Somali families have separated along the way and there is a rise in households headed by women. This is against the religious and cultural values that many Somalians, both at home and in the Diaspora, traditionally hold as sacrosanct. The harrowing experiences of many in refugee camps also contribute to the separation of families. Even when the family unit is preserved, the pressure of adapting and surviving often overwhelm marriages. Unions that are contracted in the Diaspora are not safe from this blight, and neither are marriages set up between by those in the Diaspora and those hoping to escape the hardship in Somalia. There is, therefore, a high rate of divorce in Somalian Diaspora communities. An adverse culture of individualism now dominates the social interactions of people who were raised with a strong sense of loyalty to the extended family and the clan. A slow but effectual destruction of the Somali family unit is subtly occurring in the Diaspora.

This has consequently resulted in many Somalian Diaspora children lacking instruction in traditional values and faith. Many end up in various levels of the criminal systems of their host communities for crimes ranging from petty misdemeanor to serious transgressions. Somalian parents also encounter difficulty inculcating Islamic values in their children when living in (often) extremely secular countries. This clash of cultural values is more pronounced, and even brutal, in communities that aggressively pursue the immediate integration of the Somalian immigrants. In hospitable communities, a different challenge often emerges. The parallel economy that emerges in these places brings about the isolation of the Somalian community and does not allow for any appreciable integration into the larger community. While being 'different' is regrettably a worldwide impediment to immigrants moving up in host societies, the cost of migrant isolation is just as grave. Evidently, migrants feel a sense of empowerment from being able to function effectively within their invented "little Somalia," but the power structure of the larger community is often driven by representation, thus Somalians don't often accrue the benefits and opportunities available within their host communities.

Somalian Diaspora and the Crisis in Somalia

The interminable civil war back in Somalia is a common concern for all Somalians in the Diaspora. Every member of the Diaspora shares the anxiety about relatives and other loved ones still dealing with the uncertainties in the chaotic and stateless space that is Somalia. They are all constantly encouraged that at some point, there will be peace in some shape or form. Different groups in the Diaspora, including professional associations, intellectual groups, women's associations, students groups and groups of first generation Somalians born abroad (such as Somali-Americans; British Somalians, etc.) have at different times unsuccessfully attempted to mediate in the crisis at home. These groups have been directly involved in meeting with warlords and leaders of the various ruling groups that have been in power in different parts of the country. In actuality, the Somalian Diaspora has been involved in most of the peace initiatives, including the Djibouti-brokered peace process of 2000 which brought the most concerned parties together to seek viable, alternative political and cultural means to end the crisis in the country.

Shared concerns and optimism notwithstanding, the Somalian civil war has sadly not served as a unifying force for the Diaspora. Rather, the deleterious clan-based divisions that have fueled the interminable civil war are also tearing apart the Somalian Diaspora. The centrality of clan politics is the single most divisive issue among Somalis residing in the Diaspora. The Diaspora communities are essentially divided along clan and sub-clan affiliations. These divisions affect not only refugee settlements, as new immigrants settle near or with members of their clan, but they also affect social and economic interactions among long-time members of Somalian Diaspora. For instance, young members of the community have to be careful dating members of the community because inter-clan marriages are unacceptable. There is a further divide over the prospect and method for overcoming these clan divisions, both within the Somalian Diaspora and in relation to relatives back in Somalia.

Although discussion of clans was officially banned by Barre's government, it was under his dictartorship that the seeds of the present anarchy were sown through the persecution of certain groups and the favoring of others. There is a widespread recognition that Somalia would not be in its present dire straits, nor Somalis themselves refugees, were it not for the exploitation of clan loyalties by those with authority. Many Somalis in exile were raised in urban areas where clan affiliation was losing its potency and say that, until the beginning of the hostilities, they had little knowledge and could have cared less about their own clan-family background. But the tiger, once roused, is difficult to calm. Only the youngest children do not know someone who did not suffer purely because of the clan or sub-clan to which his or her family belonged (McGown, 1999:20).

One of the things that McGown (1999) documented in her study was that while older Somalis who are determined to return home as soon as it is safe to do so may be more concerned with ensuring that their clan is well-positioned, there are others who are convinced that as long as Somalis care about the relative positions of their clans, there will be no safe Somalia to which they can return. Younger Somalis who are less convinced that there will ever be a return may be more anxious to get along with their fellow refugees in the alien environment of the schoolyard and annoyed with their mothers' rejection of a school friend merely because the family is Hawiye and the friend Darood.

These divisions are not central only to the Somali communities but also affect the relationships between Somali groups and their host communities. As Somalians increasingly segregate themselves along clan lines, it becomes gradually more difficult for both governmental and non-governmental agencies working with refugees to adjust to the needs of the community. The Somalis' obsession with clannish divisions is curious to most local officials not informed about them. Even those knowledgeable about the cultural background of these divisions sometimes perceive them with disdain, especially considering that the enormity of the needs of both new and old refugees are best served by a unified front in the local community. Classic cases of the unfortunate implications of the clan-family division were found in Toronto and London in the mid 1990s:

> It is a mark of the divisiveness of recent Somali politics that there existed in 1995 in Toronto no fewer than thirty Somali community organizations, each dedicated to assisting the absorption and resettlement of Somali refugees, most declaring that their services are intended for all Somalis, and almost all knowing that in fact only those of a particular group or sub-clan will actually approach them. In Canada, where the public funding for these organizations is relatively centralized, coming as it does from the regional (Metropolitan) Toronto government, the province of Ontario and the federal government in Ottawa, only three received government help (thereby exacerbating divisions between the haves and the have-nots). In London, in contrast, which has similar numbers of Somali community organizations, public funding for individual community associations comes primarily from the local borough, so that funding tends to

depend on the vagaries of the local council. This situation causes some tension when ethnicity appears to influence local government spending. Other associations in both cities are supported by volunteers and the Somali community, or more correctly communities, themselves (McGown, 1999).

The clan-based divisions have remained pronounced in the Diaspora and have destroyed personal relationships at different levels. There are members of the Diaspora, either due to their age or pan-Somalian spirit, who are trying to live above the clan-family division and interact with other Somalians as brothers and sisters with a shared destiny and need to survive in the Diaspora. However, the divisions have further been exacerbated – just as the peace process had become more complicated – by the unilateral declaration of the Somalis in the northern part of the country to declare the Republic of Somaliland in May 1991. This was followed in 1998 by the declaration of Puntland by Somalis in the northeastern part of the country.

Even though Puntland has installed a 'government,' it does not advocate for the disintegration of the country but rather favors a strong federal system. On the other hand, Somaliland is led by secessionists who would rather see a north-south division of the country (for more details on the issue of Somaliland, see the previous chapter by Franco Henwood).

These political developments in Somalia have further worsened the division in the Diaspora, as has the religious emphasis placed on the conflict since 2005 by the Islamic Front and the Supreme Council of Islamic Courts (SCIC). Somaliland has not gotten any recognition from any foreign government or the UN but this has not stopped Somalilanders (as Svedjemo, 2000 refers to those from Somaliland) from rallying around this new identity and thus further fracturing the already splintered Somali Diaspora. Within the clan-based divisions, a further divide is added between those from the South who are (hopefully) promoting a unified Somalia and those from Somaliland (the northwest) who are unified in their political mission of securing international recognition for the new country.

Whatever benefits accrue to the various communities as a result of these divisions pales in comparison to the loss of opportunities that the Somalian Diaspora suffers. As a group with heavily vested interest in the peace process, their splintered sub-groupings have not helped to challenge the various warlords/warmongers to embrace a unified Somalia and, ultimately, peace. This fact becomes increasingly important when one considers the tremendous impact that the Diaspora has had and continues to have on the socio-economic situation within the war torn country, especially through the remittance of funds and materials, known by Somalians as *xawilaad* (Horst, 2004) or *Hawilaad* (Lindley, 2005).

Xawilaad: Migration-shaped Remittances

The *xawilaad* is an informal system of value transfer that operates in almost every part of the world. The Somali word '*Xawil*' is derived from Arabic meaning transfer, usually of money or responsibilities (Horst, 2004). Uniquely, Xawilaad are run and used predominantly by Somalis both for remittance sending and business transactions. As a Somali-controlled informal money transfer system, it has increasingly helped members of the Somali Diaspora send money from different parts of the world to relatives back in Somalia and/or in refugee camps in neighboring African countries.

Anna Lindley (2005) in her Somalia country study (as part of the report on Informal Remittance Systems in Africa, Caribbean and Pacific (ACP) countries) provided a description of *Hawilaad and the role of technology* and noted that "Hawilaad" is the Somali rendering of Hawala, a system of value transfer common in the South Asia and the Middle East. In this model, the migrant gives money to an agent who instructs a second agent to pay the money to the recipient. The second agent pays out, trusting that the first agent will settle the debt at a later point (trust is often based on family, clan or established business connections). The development of international telecommunications has facilitated the expansion of these informal financial networks. Many people refer to Somali remittance systems as hawilaad, but there has been no attempt to explore precisely the historical and operational similarities, or indeed interfaces, with hawala networks operating in other locations. It is not entirely clear from the literature reviewed how long the term "hawilaad" has been used in Somalia. Some suggest that this system only began or became significant in the 1980s, after FV (Franco Valuta) was banned (Gundel 2003).

After the government collapsed, there was no control over the radio system. By using high-frequency (HF) radios, it became possible to communicate cheaply with many places in Somalia. Radio operators would receive cash and relay payment instructions to correspondent agents (usually clanspeople) with whom they had compensation arrangements. In the early 1990s, radio communication was very important, although telephone networks have subsequently become available in most regions (KPMG 2003). In a sense, the hawilaad sector merges with the trade-based model described above: agents often settle their accounts via trade transactions. The major difference is that by operating on hawala principles, the transfer itself is dependent on communication between agents, backed by trust, rather than on the shipping and selling of commodities, a longer process. This system took off after 1988, supporting increasing numbers of refugees in Ethiopia.

The system has been available for domestic transfers since 2005, and "for a small commission, workers can send money from cities to families in remote regions, and village traders can avoid the risk of highway robbery on the way home" (Omer, 2002). It was during the era of oil wealth in the 1970s and 1980s, when Somalia was one of the largest suppliers of labor to the Gulf region, when the Xawilaad system really intensified. The system provided Somalia traders business opportunities between the Middle East and Somalia and also enabled migrant oil workers to send funds to their relatives. Traders collect currency from migrant workers and buy commodities that they sell back in Somalia. Afterwards, the equivalent of the money received, in Somali currency or in needed goods, is then delivered to the family and kinsmen of the migrant workers.

Gundel (2003) and Ahmed (2000) reported that during that era, migrant workers in Saudi Arabia and other Gulf States were primarily responsible for sending remittances, covering about sixty to seventy-five percent of the total estimated transfers. In 1985, by the estimation of the International Labor Organization (ILO), this was approximately $280 to 370 million dollars. This represented thirty percent of the estimated $700 million dollars earned by the nearly quarter of a million Somalians working in the Middle East. According to Lewis (1994), the remittances that were transferred during this era through the so-called 'Franco Valuta' system doubled or tripled the export earnings of the Somali Republic. The Xawilaad agents have over time incorporated their businesses into Somali remittance companies, especially since 1995, when the highest remittances were coming from the West. The incorporations were done sometimes organically through clan affiliation or through the discounted distribution of communications technology. Most seem to have started with clan-aligned management, workforce, agent network and customers but eventually expanding in order to operate throughout Somalia (Lindley, 2005).

Remittance companies are usually managed by five or fewer owners even though they may have large numbers of shareholders from different regions and clans. The companies have now commandeered the money transfer sector by not only providing relatively affordable services but by introducing technological facilities[1] to both meet the constantly changing regulatory requirements (particularly with the intense and universal 'war on terror') and to provide better and easier services for Somalians in the Diaspora sending money home. The sophistication, self-regulation and level of business transactions completed by these companies makes the term 'informal' rather inappropriate. In 2000, there were ten renowned companies handling about half a million dollars per month in money transfers. Omer (2002) examined the annual transaction volume of eight of the biggest Somalia remittance companies and found the following classifications. The biggest three had annual transaction volumes between U.S $225 and 400 million, the annual volume of business for the next two was between U.S $50 and 150 million, while the smaller three companies had volumes less than U.S $10 million annually. These numbers are slightly different from those reported by other investigators but the consensus is that about U.S $500 million to U.S $1 billion is transferred through remittances each year. According to a recent UN survey, remittances translate to about 23% of the per capita household income in Somalia. This is comparable with self-employment, which represents 50%, and wage employment, which represents 14% (UNDP Somalia and World Bank, 2003).

In addition to the Xawilaad agents and trade-based remittance systems, migrants also use hand delivery of remittances via foreign travelers, staff of various international agencies and nongovernmental organizations (NGOs) and members of the Diaspora who are able to travel in and out of Somalia. Somalians (like other African migrant communities) use Xawilaad and other such informal systems because

---

[1] See www.kaahexpress.com, www.dahabshiil.com, and www.Xawaaladdag lobal.com

they are reliable, efficient and rather inexpensive compared to options like multinational money transfer companies or bank transfers.

This system is not specific to Somalia. It is estimated that 160,000 hawala offices collect some U.S $200 billion per year in the U.S, and similar arrangements can be found in the Arab world and the Indian sub-continent, where they are called hundi, a Sanskrit word which refers to a reliable way of transferring money. The chiti "certificate" of the Hindi diaspora works like a letter of credit, and the Chinese abroad speak of fei ch'ien, that is, "flying money." The Thai expression is phoe kuan. Reliability and efficiency explain why African migrants remit money by these informal means. But the flexibility of the system also has drawbacks. Clean money can become dirty money, since migrants are unable to control the management of the funds they send once these have been put at the disposal of a loose clan network. The Malians of Kayes in France represent a rare example of a diaspora that tries to avoid the diversion of remittances into useless expenditure. Half of their remittances take the form of food coupons that can be spent only in local co-operatives. But in most other cases, capital sent to home villages from abroad is wasted in ostentatious spending not directly relevant to either production or development, like houses, cars, electronic equipment, or drugs like *qat* in Somalia. Several factors explain why unofficial remittances are likely to continue under this kind of system. First, it is quicker, cheaper, more efficient and more inconspicuous than any service provided by financial institutions or companies like Western Union. Second, it is supported by people who do not trust banks, work largely outside the formal economy, and are used to avoiding state regulations.

Third, exchange controls, lack of hard currency, poor access to credit, bureaucratic procedure, heavy taxation and the risk of confiscation of foreign assets prevent migrants from investing officially in their homelands, and underground transfers present an attractive alternative. As they often lack legitimacy abroad, authoritarian regimes in particular do not inspire confidence in their country's diaspora. In 1988, for instance, the Nigerian military junta relaxed exchange controls and allowed citizens to keep hard currencies in their bank accounts. But the liberalisation of the economy and the World Bank's structural adjustment programmes suddenly stopped after another coup in 1993. Nigerian emigrants continued to remit money through informal channels; from the U.S., less than 5% used banks to do so, and two out of three sent cash home through relatives or friends who were visiting Nigeria. In Cameroon, 87% of migrants participated in the so-called jiangi credit clubs, which were the most effective way to remit money home. Proximity also facilitates hand-to-hand cash transfers, as is shown by the Basotho in South Africa who, unlike the members of other migrant communities, can easily come and go between the two countries without having to settle in South Africa. Since a good number of them are not registered workers, they do not use the official financial institutions. Less than 6% of their remittances are channeled through the banking system. Low-income migrants do not have bank accounts at all, and find it cheaper to send money by means of taxi drivers or friends. Bank-based transfer methods, whose fees are fixed whatever the volume of remittance, become competitive only for amounts above R250 (Marc-Antoine Pérouse de Montclos, 2005).

These remittance companies have grown over the years, but they have also encountered numerous challenges affecting their operation both in the Diaspora and within Somalia. These challenges include: meeting the augmented financial regulations from various governments in the Diaspora, particularly Europe and North America; coping with the changing and fierce political landscape of Somalia; assuring customers of the safety of their funds as these companies became 'formalized' financial institutions (as all major formal financial institutions in Somalia had gone bankrupt by 1990 due to corruption and mismanagement); responding to allegations of terrorist links after the attack on the United States in 2001 (the case of the of Al-Barakaat, the then largest Somali remittance company, comes to mind); and internal regulation of their industry to prevent exploitation of customers and to ward off monopoly.

Remittances have had significant positive effects on the lives of many Somalians within Somalia as well as those surviving in various refugee camps all over Africa. It has directly affected the livelihoods of the people and has contributed positively as well as negatively to Somalia statehood. Lindley's (2005) report gives a summation of the effects of the remittances in terms of livelihoods and migrant-supported projects as presented in various studies on Somalia remittance systems. Some of these include the use of remittances to provide security against crop failures, illnesses, sudden price falls and loss of income or assets in rural areas (Ahmed, 2000). In urban areas, they have helped to sustain extended families prevented from working due to the violence. Essentially, the remittances get redistributed extensively (one beneficiary was found to have shared remittances with, on average, ten other individuals). Since the regular flow of remittances often increases during economic stress and inter-clan warfare, the funds can end up supporting clannish agitation and clan militias.

Remittances are used by most households for basic needs such as food, shelter, clothing, medical care and education. The Diaspora, through the funds remitted, helps to keep people fed, healthy and educated. The funds received are also invested in land, homes and small businesses (to provide sustainable livelihood for families). The remittances are also used in other noteworthy social and religious ways such as bridewealth, religious ceremonial observations and Hajj. Unfortunately, the availability of funds also leads to the consumption of 'qat' as well as the increase in other vices and addictions. Another social application of remittances is the making of collective compensation payments according to customary law, thereby avoiding increased interpersonal conflicts in the society. The effects of remittances are not only felt within Somalia, but also among Somalian refugees in Cairo, Kenya, and Ethiopia (Ahmed, 2000; Lindley, 2005).

Beyond the livelihoods of Somalians, the Diaspora communities have also established and supported numerous community-based projects. These migrant-supported projects are often funded by groups or associations in the Diaspora and geared towards helping the larger society as well as reconstituting civil society. Examples include the establishment of Amoud University, a community-owned institution, by migrants with roots in Borama. Diaspora-based organizations such as Read Horn of Africa (a charitable organization funded by groups in Australia, New Zealand, North America, Europe, the Middle East and Africa), Ruudi (an umbrella organization funded by migrants in London and Dubai) and SomScan-UK (an umbrella group of Somalis based in Scandinavian countries and the UK) are executing numerous projects ranging from primary schools, agricultural cooperatives, civil society forums, enterprise development groups and provisions for large-scale housing. Amazingly, these activities have received additional support from governments and agencies such as the European Union (EU), AU and the Danish government through the Danish Refugee Council (Lindley, 2005).

Marc-Antoine Pérouse de Montclos (2005) provides a catalogue of evils associated with remittances not only in Somalia but throughout Africa. The most pressing is that informal channels through which these financial transfers are sent (as the case with the Somalia Xawilaad companies that transfer funds to the Horn of Africa through Jeddah and Dubai) can allow criminal or terrorist groups to use "clean" Diaspora networks to move "dirty" money to other countries. Notwithstanding, remittances have emerged as the single most important support system in Somalia (Academy for Peace and Development, 2002). These identified impacts (and several others) of remittances sent by members of the Somalian Diaspora on the lives of individuals and communities within Somalia and in the refugee camps shows that the communities in the Diaspora are crucial to the survival of the Somalia nation and its return to normalcy.

Conclusion

It becomes obvious from the discussions in the previous sections that the Somalian Diaspora has far-reaching connections to its homeland that are often missed in the focus on the unending crisis in the country. Displaced in part because of the crisis, the Somalian Diaspora is a result of inimitable population dispersal whose experiences are not so easily comparable to other notable Diasporas. In this chapter, we have contextualized the migratory history of Somalia citizens within the historical developments in the country since independence in 1960. This has allowed us to chronicle the emergence of the original and later Somalia Diasporas. In the process, we have provided a short description of the contemporary Somalia Diaspora, with an illustrative discussion of the Somali community in the American state of Minnesota. We have also considered key issues of integration into host communities and the effects of migration on the group's familial and social units. It has become apparent that these migrants settle down mostly in communities that are convivial, and in which opportunities and services are available. The Somalian refugees in camps, primarily in East Africa, and those migrants on temporary status with the hope of moving to secondary destinations for permanent settlement constitute the only exceptions to these patterns.

We have identified some of the damaging effects that the population dispersal is having on family and social relations in the

Diaspora. Particularly, we learned that the noxious clannish division that has been variously blamed for the interminable civil war in Somalia is also the underlying cause of segregation and isolation within an otherwise successful and thriving Diaspora. These damages notwithstanding, the Diaspora has contributed greatly, both directly and indirectly, to civil society in Somalia, especially through financial and material remittances.

Part IV

Conclusions and Policy Recommendations

Chapter 12

CONCLUSIONS:
TOWARDS A REVIVED SOMALI STATE

Issaka K. Souaré

In his thought-provoking work, Professor Samatar (1993), one of the leading specialists on Somalia, poses a very interesting question on the Somali crisis when he asks: "Why and how could this society, one of the few nations in the continent with one ethnic group, one culture, one language, and one religion, find itself in such parlous circumstances – verging on self destruction?"

In an attempt to answer this intriguing and pertinent question, the contributions assembled in this volume examine the various issues that lie behind the current situation in Somalia and seek answers to a number of crucial questions, from the root causes of the crisis and possible solutions, to the dynamics that have rendered the conflict intractable. The authors of the first three chapters provide a historical background to the fratricidal conflict that besets Somalia since the fall of the Siad Barre regime in January 1991. Tessman (Ch. 2) makes a quantitative assessment of the weakness of the Somali state, comparing it to its IGAD (Intergovernmental Authority on Development) partners, both in terms of traditional measures of national capability and in terms of performance on a human development scale. He finds that Somalia scores very poorly in this regard, concluding that this makes the country vulnerable to foreign intervention, which further destabilises it and reduces its chance to have a successful unity government and restore its sovereignty.

Taking this argument further and introducing other social and historical factors necessary to understanding the collapse of the Somali state and the crisis in general, Abdullahi (Baadiyow) classifies the different perspectives on the Somali state collapse into major themes. Among the factors he identifies are the country's encounter with colonialism towards the end of the 19th century, and the myriad profound challenges (i.e. poorly trained human resources, a politicised clan system, huge rural migrations, low economic performance, pressure from hostile neighbours and problems with the integration of different colonial systems) that the country faced following its independence in 1960. Another factor he identifies, which is widely employed by Somali Islamic scholars but ignored by Western scholars, is the concept of "moral degradation" from a religious and social point of view. This is an interesting factor that I will deal with below.

Wrapping up the first part of the volume, Mohamed Eno considers the "discrimination, marginalization and segregation" of leading clans in the country against some segments of the Somali society – especially those in the South of the country – as another major factor in the explanation of the crisis, comparing it at times to the defunct Apartheid system in South Africa.

Building on this historical background, the two chapters in the second part, written by Osman (ch. 5) and Swart (ch. 6), provide critical analyses and diagnoses of the Somali crisis. Osman begins his chapter by criticising mono-causal analyses of the conflict, as most analyses in the existing literature tend to reduce the causes of the conflict to the role and effects of the Siad Barre regime, the salience of which he acknowledges. To him, given the complexity of the armed conflict in which Somalia has been engulfed for nearly two decades, only a multi-variant analysis can provide adequate answers to these questions. This he finds in three interrelated factors: social inequality – which is the main factor mentioned by Mohamed Eno – as the result of policies and practices of both the colonial and postcolonial Somali state, the deteriorating economic situation in the country since the mid-1980s and the growing poverty resulting from it, and the abundance of and easy access to weapons in the absence of any effective government control. Swart's chapter may be summed up in one sentence: the conflict is mainly due to "bad governance."

Any serious study of conflict analysis must address, in addition to the root causes of the conflict, conflict dynamics and the nature, role and characteristics of the different actors in the conflict. For the obdurate conflict that the Somali crisis has proven to be, such an approach is not optional. Thus, in the five contributions in the third part of the book, the authors pondered these important issues, dealing with the actors and looking at the myriad tentative solutions that have been attempted since the outbreak of the conflict.

After Mukhtar's and Omar Eno's critical review of the many peace and reconciliation conferences, Souaré and Henwood respectively look at the UN intervention in Somalia and the sensitive issue of the future of Somaliland, formulating a number of policy recommendations, some of which will be summarised below. Dealing with the actors of the conflict, Oje's chapter looks at one actor whose significance and role are often overlooked in the existing literature: the Somali Diasporas, especially those in the U.S., and their possible role in reviving their war-torn country.

The Somali conflict has proven to be an intractable one, and it seemed to be worsening as we completed this volume. In the first quarter of 2007, the country (especially Mogadishu and surrounding areas) went through what many described as the worst cycle of violence for more than a decade, leading to the deaths of at least 1,300 people and forcing an estimated 400,000 people out of the capital, according to UNHCR. This obliges anyone wishing to make policy recommendations for the effective ending of the Somali crisis to consider the multitude of issues at hand: How to achieve the immediate cessation of hostilities? How to make this ceasefire sustainable and revive the Somali state? How to reconcile the Somali people?

To begin with, it must be noted that the latest round of fighting in the country is a direct result of the forceful ousting of members of the Union of Islamic Courts (UIC), who had controlled Mogadishu and surrounding regions for about six months, since early 2006. This was a serious mistake on the part of the Transitional National Government (TNG) of Somalia and those who backed it. Since its formation in 2004, the TNG had been very ineffective, not only because it had failed to relocate from Kenya and establish itself inside Somalia, but also because it has not had the broad appeal to the Somali people that would have allowed it to restore law and order in the country, something that Somalis badly needed after 16 years of violence and lawlessness.

As Abdullahi (Baaidoyow) rightly notes, given the clan and social divisions in the country, Islam is the only authority – if not misused and taken to an extreme – that possesses the essential ingredients to successfully integrate the various elements of the Somali society and provide a stable government capable of meeting the urgent social, political and economic needs of the country. This was the magical stick that the UIC members held in their hands. In fact, as Swart shows, they proved themselves ready, willing and capable of exerting power and restoring security, which had "the potential of even further broadening their appeal to a war-weary Somali society." When they were in charge, the Islamic Courts radically changed things in Somalia. There was safety, peace and commerce. They reunited the capital, which had been carved up into fiefdoms by various warlords. In other words, they brought Mogadishu back to life. Was being "Islamic" one of their main problems in a post-9/11 era, in which Islam has replaced communism as that which must be cracked down by all means?

It has been evident to most observers that the solution to Somalia's protracted political problems is not to be found in battlefields, and that insistence on sole military means can prove counterproductive. Clearly, instead of forcefully ousting the UIC with the backing of an Ethiopian force that is very unpopular among the Somali people, the best solution would have been to negotiate, as the speaker of the TNG's parliament had been calling for before he was sacked in January 2007 by the president, likely because of his stance on this issue. Because this opportunity was passed by, the only viable way to get the country out of the current imbroglio is to negotiate with the so-called insurgents (including remnants of the UIC) who are fighting both the TNG and Ethiopian forces in Mogadishu, attacking even African Union peacekeepers.

As we completed this volume, there was yet another peace conference planned whose aim was to bring together all Somali stakeholders to look for ways of dealing with the many problems the country is facing. This is a positive development, especially since the senior figures of the TNG have indicated that there has been some reconsideration of the previous refusals to countenance the participation of members of UIC and so-called insurgents. Should this conference go ahead as planned, every effort must be made to have all stakeholders properly represented, and to allow them to freely express their views and have them be taken into account. After all, the definite solution of the crisis will only come from the Somalis themselves.

In a statement of its President, issued on 30 April 2007, the UN Security Council expressed its grave concern at the renewed fighting in Somalia, deeply deplored the loss of civilian lives and the humanitarian impact of the fighting, and called upon all parties to immediately end the hostilities and agree to a comprehensive ceasefire.

In the same statement, the Council requested the Secretary-General to immediately "begin appropriate contingency planning for a possible United Nations mission to be deployed if the Security Council decided to authorize such a mission." But the fact of the matter is that even with the best intentions – which are far from being there anyway – it would take months to put a UN force on the ground.

This makes the presence of African peacekeepers in the country necessary for the sustenance of any ceasefire agreements the Somali parties may reach. Yet, in May 2007, only the Ugandan contingent had arrived in the country, and the fatalities suffered by this contingent do not augur well for the swift arrival of other peacekeepers. But this is the only way for the African Union to assist in restoring peace and order in one of its member countries. Somalia's current status does not send a good image of the AU as it tries to ascertain itself as the continental organization capable of responding to the aspirations of all the African peoples.

But as we debate these issues and wish for the Somali state to become revived and enter back into the fold of nations, there is still another thorny question to be answered: Should Somalia be reconstituted as one state or should more than one state be allowed to emerge from it ashes? This question concerns the case of Somaliland, the northern region of the country which has unilaterally proclaimed its independence, and whose leaders have proved capable of ruling the region responsibly. Many observers, including one in this volume (Ch. 10), have come to the conclusion that allowing the region to become an independent state and be recognized by the international community, starting with the African Union – which is not yet the case – is the best way forward, both for Somaliland and the Somali state at large. But the reasons why the AU is reluctant to accept this solution are very understandable. In the end, everything will depend on how the leaders of the "reconstituted" Somali state behave. Should they behave responsibly and succeed at winning the confidence and esteem of the Somali people, it is very possible that the authorities in the northern region will reconsider their position. After all, it is the current unfortunate situation in Somalia that led them to secede. On the other hand, if the leaders in Mogadishu fail to overcome their differences and establish a viable Somali state, the international community, starting with the AU, may be more willing to reconsider its position vis-à-vis Somaliland and it will be right in doing so.

Somalia has two positive aspects that can enhance its rebuilding once the conflict ends. First, contrary to what some authors have argued, Somalia is endowed with enough resources to sustain itself. These include the longest coast in Africa, two permanent rivers (Jubba and Shabelle), millions of acres of cultivable land and millions of livestock, not to mention the reports about the existence of abundant oil and natural gas reserves in the country. Secondly, the Somalis in the Diaspora represent a source of comfort as to their future role in rebuilding their country. Today, about 7 per cent of Somalis live abroad and many of them have gained useful trainings and experiences and some are well-established in prosperous countries such as South Africa, Canada, United States and the United Kingdom.

Since the mid 1970s, the Diaspora community has been the backbone of the collapsed Somali economy through remittance and in some cases investments. As Ojo advanced in this volume, the Diaspora communities inject huge sums of money into the Somali economy using the Hawala system. The most important benefit of the Diaspora, however, is not the remittance, but rather the hard work, education, savings. Also, being abroad and experiencing all that foreigners encounter in foreign lands, most are now more than ready to repatriate for they have understood the meaning of being a *citizen*.

Unlike the earlier times when the Diaspora was heavily influenced by the rigid and anachronistic views of clanism that destroyed their country in the first place, the new breed of Somalis in the Diaspora have understood that after all they are strangers in foreign lands and that they have a common destiny which is in their country that must be rebuilt by their joint efforts.

In closing, Somalia's conflict needs to come to an end and we recommend the following three proposals as a good starting point. First, to address and solve past wrongs that were and continue to be committed against unarmed civilians. Amongst the several models which the Somalis can learn form is the South African Truth and Reconciliation process or the Rwandan *Gacaca* (or justice under the tree) system or more appropriately traditional Somali reconciliation system such as *Qirasho iyo Raali Gelis* (admission of guilt and sincere apology). Second, conduct a fair and impartial census that will determine a fair, representative and balanced political system that has lacked thus far in the Somali political institutions. Third, bring the wealth and knowledge of the Diaspora by creating conducive environment for their businesses and knowledge without discrimination of any kind. After all, despite its many setbacks, the recovery of Lebanon after years of civil war has been greatly enhanced and expedited thanks to its Diaspora communities.

Acronyms & Abbreviations

ACP	African, Caribbean and Pacific countries
ADC	Agricultural Development Corporation
AFIS	*Amministrazione Fiduciaria della Somalia*
AIAI	Al-Itihaad al-Islaam
ARPCT	Alliance for the Restoration of Peace and Counter-Terrorism
AU	African Union
BBC	British Broadcasting Corporation
CINC	Composite Indicator of National Capability
COW	Correlates of War
DPKO	UN Department for Peacekeeping Operations
ECOWAS	Economic Community of West African States
ECRE	European Council on Refugees and Exiles
EU	European Union
FV	Franco Valuta (previous term for the system of Somalian remittance)
GDP	Gross Domestic Product
HDMS	Hizbi Demoqradi Mustaqal Somali
IGAD	Inter-Governmental Authority on Development
IGASOM	IGAD Peace Support Mission to Somalia
ILO	International Labor Organization
INGO	International Non-Governmental Organizations
IRIN	Integrated Regional Information Networks (part of the UN office for the coordination of Humanitarian Affairs)
LAS	League of Arab States (or the Arab League)
LURD	Liberians United for Reconciliation and Democracy
NFD	Northern Frontier District
NGO	Non-Governmental Organization
OIC	Organization of the Islamic Conference
RRA	Reewin (Rahanweyn) Resistance Army
SCIC	Supreme Council of Islamic Courts (of Somalia)
SGC	Supreme Governing Council
SNA	Somali National Alliance

SNM	Somali National Movement
SNRC	Somali National Reconciliation Conference
SRC	Supreme Revolutionary Council (under Siad Barre)
SYL	Somali Youth League
TC	Technical Committee
TFG	Transitional Federal Government
TNP	Transitional National Parliament
TRC	South African Truth and Reconciliation Commission
UIC	Union of Islamic Courts
UN	United Nations
UNAMIR	United Nations Assistance Mission for Rwanda
UNDP	UN Development Program
UNHCR	United Nations High Commission for Refugees
UNITAF	United Task Force
UNOSOM	United Nations Operation in Somalia

About the authors

Brock Tessman is assistant professor of international affairs at the University of Georgia's School of Public and International Affairs. He is also a faculty associate at the University's Center for International Trade and Security. Tessman received his Ph.D. from the University of Colorado at Boulder and also held a position at the University of Denver's Graduate School of International Studies before coming to Athens in the fall of 2006. His general areas of research interest include foreign policy, grand strategy, and international security.

Mohamed A. Eno holds MA TESOL and PhD Social Studies Education. A PhD candidate in Education at the University of Leicester, specializing in Applied Linguistics & TESOL, he is a lecturer in English at the ADNOC Technical Institute in Abu Dhabi, UAE. Mohamed's interests are in Sociolinguistics, Ethnic Studies, Oral Literature, Oral Traditions as well as Social History. He has authored and co-authored several chapters on Somalia in various publications.

Franco Henwood is an independent human rights commentator and analyst based in London. His interests include the relationship between cultural relativism and human rights, economic, social and cultural rights and human rights in armed and ethnic conflict.

Gerrie Swart lectures in the Department of Political Sciences at the University of South Africa (UNISA) and is also a Research Associate at the Centre for International Political Studies, University of Pretoria, South Africa.

Abdullahi A. Osman currently teaches comparative politics and African politics at the Department of International Affairs and African Studies Institute, at the University of Georgia, USA. His teaching and research interests include African politics, governance, regional and international studies, peace and conflict, internal security and wars, comparative governments in the Third World. He has published several book chapters and articles in scholarly journals, including *African Renaissance* and *Journal of Ethno-Development*.

Issaka K. Souaré is a PhD candidate in the department of political science at the Université du Québec à Montréal (Canada). A Contributing Editor to the review journal, *African Renaissance*, he is the author of numerous publications relating to Africa, including *Africa in the United Nations System, 1945-2005* (London, 2006); *Civil Wars and Coups d'État in West Africa* (Lanham, 2006), and the novel, *Samassi* (London, 2004).

Abdurahman Moallim Abdullahi (Baadiyow) is a PhD candidate in Islamic Studies at McGill University in Canada where he also optained his MA in the same field. One of the founders of the Mogadishu University, he is the Chairman of the University's Board of Trustees and a civil society activist. His main areas of research are Islam, tribalism and modern state in Somalia, and has published a number of papers on these topics.

Omar A. Eno is a Ph.D candidate in African history at York University and Assistant Professor of History and the Director of the "National Somali Bantu Project" at Portland State University, Oregon, which is a funded grant through the U.S. Department of Health and Human Services' Office of Refugee Resettlement. He is very committed to bringing the attention of the international community to Bantu/Jareer issues. Cofounder of the Bantu Rehabilitation Trust in Nairobi, he is a member of several international academic organizations such as the African Studies Association, the Inter-riverine Studies Association, and the Somali Studies International Association.

Akinloye Ojo is Assistant Professor in the Comparative Literature department and the African Studies Institute at the University of Georgia. His research interests include Yoruba language and applied linguistics, language, culture and society. He has published in journals including *Research in African Language and Literature*, *Journal of the African Language Teachers' Association (JALTA)*, and *Metamorphoses*. His co-authored article, *"Implications for Language and Culture in a War-torn Continent"* was published by the USA/African Institute in **Chimera**, Volume 1, Issue #3, Fall 2003.

Mohamed H. Mukhtar is Professor of African and Middle Eastern History at Savannah State University, Savannah, Georgia, U.S.A.

Editorial Note

African Renaissance

Book Series: No.2

This is the second in a book series from *African Renaissance*, a multidisciplinary journal published since 2004. The journal, which is a cross between an academic periodical and any high-quality features publication, started as a bi-monthly, and became a quarterly this year (2007) after 15 consecutive issues without missing a deadline, and after launching a book series early this year.

The book series augment the journal in its objectives of advancing both theoretical and empirical research, informing policies and practices and improving our understanding of the interplay of forces that shape the African condition.

This volume was inspired by some of the articles on Nigeria published in the journal. I thank all contributors previously published in AR for re-working their original contributions to fit into the framework of the book project, as well as new authors that submitted solicited contributions to the project.

African Renaissance has emerged as one of the leading platforms for the analysis of the African condition, hopes and aspirations. The journal accepts papers that cover Africa as a whole, as well as those which focus on specific countries on the continent.

For details of submission guidelines for the journal or the book series, please visit the website (www.adonis-abbey.com). Alternatively please email the journal's editor,

Dr Jideofor Adibe at: editor@adonis-abbey.com

For sales enquiries, please email: sales@adonis-abbey.com

Dr Jideofor Adibe
Editor
African Renaissance.

.

BIBLIOGRAPHY

Abdullahi, Abdurahman (1992). *Tribalism, Nationalism and Islam: Crisis of the Political Loyalties in Somalia.* MA thesis submitted to the Islamic Institute, McGill University, Montreal, Canada.

-------- (2001). "Tribalism and Islam: the Basics of Somaliness," in Muddle Suzanne Liluis (ed.) *Variations on the Theme of Somaliness.* Turku: Centre of Continuing Education, Abo University.

-------- (2004a). "Non-State Actors in the Failed State of Somalia: Survey of the Civil Society Organizations in Somalia during the Civil War," *Darasaat Ifriqiyayyah* 31: 57-87.

------- (2004b). *Recovering Somalia: the Islamic Factor.* Unpublished Paper presented to the 9th International Congress for Somali Studies held in Aalborg University, Aalborg, Denmark (September 6-7).

Abdulle, Sahal (2006). "Somalis Split over Peace Force," *Reuters* (30 November).

Abukar, Ali Sheikh (1992). *Al-Somal Wa Judur Al-Ma'sat Al-Rahina.* Bairut: Dar Ibn Hazm.

Academy for Peace and Development (2002). *The Impact of the War on the Family.* Hargeysa: Academic for Peace and Development.

Adam, Hussein (1992). "Somalia: Militarism, Warlordism or Democracy?" *Review of African Political Economy* 54: 11-26.

Adam, Hussein (1995). "Somalia: a Terrible Beauty Being Born?" in I. William Zartmann (ed.) *Collapsed States: the Disintegration and Restoration of Legitimate Authority.* London: Lynne Rienner Publishers.

Adedeji, Adebayo (1993). "Marginalization and Marginality: Contexts, Issues and Viewpoints," in Adedeji (ed.) *Africa within the World: beyond Dispossession and Dependence.* London: Zed Books.

Adedeji, Adebayo (1995) "Structural Adjustment, Democratization and Rising Ethnic Tensions in Africa." *Development and Change,* 26 (2) pp. 355-374.

Adedeji, Adebayo (1999). "Comprehending African Conflicts," in Adedeji (ed.) *Comprehending African Conflicts: the Search for Sustainable Peace and Good Governance.* London: Zed Books.

Agence France-Presse (2006). "Somalia: Islamists Fight Pirates," *The New York Times* (9 November).

Ahmed, Ali Jimale (1995). "Daybreak is Near, Won't You Become Sour," in Ali Jimale (ed.) *The Invention of Somalia.* Lawrenceville, NJ: Red Sea Press.

Ahmed, Ismail I. (2000). "Remittances and Their Economic Impact in Post-war Somaliland," *Disasters* 24 (4): 380-389.

Albadri, Abukar (2006). "Islamists Claim Victory in Mogadishu Fighting," *Business Day* (South Africa) (28 March).

Alesina, Alberto and Roberto Perotti (1996). "Income Distribution, Political Instability, and Investment," *European Economic Review* 40 (6): 1203-28.

Annan, Kofi (2005). *United Nations Security Council, Report of the Secretary-General on the situation in Somalia, S/2005/642* (11 October).

Annan, Kofi (2006). *United Nations Security Council, Report of the Secretary-General on the situation in Somalia, S/2006/838* (23 October). http://www.un.org (24 November 2006).

Arthur, Paul (1999). "The Anglo-Irish Peace Process: Obstacles to Reconciliation," in Robert L. Rothstein (ed.) *After the Peace: Resistance and Reconciliation.* London: Lynne Rienner Publishers.

Ayittey, George B. N. (1994). "The Somali Crisis: Time for an Africa Solution," *Cato Policy Analysis* 205 (28 March).

Ayittey, George B. N. (1998). *Africa in Chaos.* New York, NY: St. Martin Press.

Bardhan Pranab and Chistopher Urdy (1999). *Development Microeconomics.* Oxford: Oxford University Press.

Bayart, Jean-François (1993). *The State in Africa: the Politics of the Belly.* New York: Longman.

Bayart, Jean-François, Stephen Ellis and Béatrice Hibou (1999). *The Criminalization of the State in Africa.* Oxford: James Currey.

Berkhoff, M. and P. Hewett (2000). *Inequality of Child Mortality among Ethnic Groups in Sub Saharan Africa.* Geneva: World Health Organization.

Besteman, Catherine and Lee V. Cassanelli (1996). "Introduction: Politics and Production in Southern Somalia," in Besteman and Cassanelli (eds.) *The Struggle for Land in Southern Somalia: the War Behind the War.* London: Westview Press.

Besteman, Catherine (1999). *Unraveling Somalia: Race, Violence, and the Legacy of Slavery*. Philadelphia: University of Pennsylvania Press.

Bile, Mohamed A. (2006). "Militia Battle in Mogadishu Leaves 35 Dead," *Reuters* (10 May).

Blaton, Shannon Lindsey (2005). "Foreign Policy in Transition? Human Rights, Democracy, and U.S Arms Exports," *International Studies Quarterly* 49(4): 647-668.

Bolton, John R. (1994). "Wrong Turn in Somalia," *Foreign Affairs* 73(1) (January/February).

Boutros-Ghali, Boutros (1999). *Unvanquished: a US-UN Saga*. London and New York: I. B. Tauris Publishers.

Brass, Paul (1985) *Ethnic Groups and the State*. London: Croom Helm.

Brons, Maria (1991). "The Civil War in Somalia: Its Genesis and Dynamics," *Current African Issues* 11. Uppsala: Nordiska Africainstitutet.

Brubaker, Roger (1995). "National Minorities, Nationalizing States, and External National Homelands in the New Europe." Daedalus. Spring: 107-132.

Burgess, Stephen F. (1998). "African Security in the Twenty-First Century: the Challenges of Indigenization and Multilateralism," *African Studies Review* 41(2):37-61 (September).

Casanelli, Lee V. (1982). *The Shaping of Somali Society: Restructuring the History of a Pastoral People 1600-1900*. Philadelphia: University of Pennsylvania Press.

Cecil, Andrew R. (1986). *The Source of National Strength*. Dallas: University of Texas at Dallas. Distributed by the University of Texas Press.

Clapham, Christopher (1999). "The United Nations and Peacekeeping in Africa," in Mark Malan (ed.) Whiter Peacekeeping in Africa? *Monograph* 36. Pretoria: Institute for Security Studies.

Clarke, Walter and Jeffrey Herbst (1996). "Somalia and the Future of Humanitarian Intervention," *Foreign Affairs* 75(2) (March/April).

Clarke, Walter S. and Robert Gosende (2000). "Somalia: Can a Collapsed State Reconstitute Itself?" in Robert I. Rotberg (ed.) *State Failure and State Weakness in a Time of Terror*. Washington:

Brookings Institution Press.

Claude, Inis L. (1962). *Power and International Relations*. Random House: New York.

Cole, Roy and Harm J. De Blij (2007). *Survey of Sub-Saharan Africa: a Regional Geography*. Oxford: Oxford University Press.

Connor, Walker (1994). *Ethnonationalism: The Quest for Understanding*. Princeton. NJ: Princeton University Press.

David, Steven R. (1997). "Internal Wars: Causes and Cures." *World Politics*. Vol.49. pp. 552-576.

Deutsch, Karl W. (1968). *The Analysis of International Relations*. Prentice Hall: Englewood Cliffs.

Doombos, Martin et al. (1992). *Beyond Conflict in the Horn: Prospects for Peace, Recovery and Development in Ethiopia, Somalia and the Sudan*. The Hague: Institute for Social Studies.

DPA-Reuters (2006). "Islamists Mass Troops on Ethiopian Border," *Business Day* (South Africa) (27 November).

Drysdale, John (1964). *The Somali Dispute*. New York: Praeger.

Dualeh, Hussein A. (2002). Search for a New Somali Identity. Nairobi.

Duffield, M (1988). "Post-modern Conflict, Warlords, Post-adjustment States and Private Protection." Journal of Civil Wars, April.

Ekeh, Peter P. (1975). "Colonialism and the Two Publics in Africa: a Theoretical Statement," *Comparative Studies in Society and History* 17: 91-112. p. 92.

Elgström, Ole, Jacob Bercovitch and Carl Skau (2003). "Regional Organisations and International Mediation: the Effectiveness of Insider Mediators," *African Journal on Conflict Resolution* 3(1).

Eno, Mohamed A. (1980). "Aggression is not a Solution," *HEEGAN Newspaper*. Copies of this are available in the Newspaper Reading Room of the Library of Congress.

Eno, Omar A. (2001). "Sifting Through a Sieve: Solutions for Somalia," in Jorg Jansen (ed.) *What are Somalia's Development Perspectives? Science between Resignation and Hope?* Berlin: Das Arabische Buch.

Eno, Omar A. (2001a). *Resource Control, State Formation and Political Identity: a Neglected Theme in the Somali War*. Paper presented at Columbia University, New York (Unpublished).

Eno, Omer, A. (2002). A Report on Supporting Systems and Procedures for the Effective Regulation and Monitoring of Somali Remittance Companies (Hawala). Nairobi: UNDP Somalia. http://www.so.undp.org/Remittances/ssp-hawala.pdf.

Eno, Omer, A. and G. El Koury (2004). "Regulation and Supervision in a Vacuum: the Story of the Somali Remittance Sector," *Small Enterprise Development* 15(1).

Etzioni, Amitai (2004). "A Self-Restrained Approach to Nation-Building by Foreign Powers," *International Affairs* 80(1): 1-18.

Eno, Omar A. (2004). "Landless Landlord and Landed Tenants: Plantation Slavery in Southern Somalia," in Abdi M. Kusow (ed.) *Putting the Cart Before the Horse: Contested Nationalism and the Crisis of the Nation State in Somalia*. Lawrenceville, NJ: Red Sea Press.

Esman, Milton J. (1994). *Ethnic Politics*. Ithaca: Cornell University Press.

Fatton, Robert Jr. (1992). *Predatory Rule: State and Civil Society in Africa*. Boulder, CO: Lynne Rienner Publishers.

Feldman, Stacy, and Brian Slattery (2003). "Living without a Government in Somalia: an Interview with Mark Bradbury. Development Processes in Somalia Exist not as a Result of Official Development Assistance, but in spite of it," *Journal of International Affairs* 57: 1.

Forsberg, Tuomas (2001). "The Philosophy and Practice of Dealing with the Past: Some Conceptual and Normative Issues," in Nigel Biggar (ed.) *Burying the Past: Making Peace and Doing Justice After Civil Conflict*. Washington, D.C.: Georgetown University Press.

Friedland, Willia and Carl Roseberg, Jr. (1965). *African Socialism*. Stanford, CA: Hoover Institution Press.

Frushone, Joel (2001). *Welcome Home to Nothing: Refugees Repatriate to a Forgotten Somaliland*. Washington D.C.:U.S Committee for Refugees (USCR).

Gardner, Judith and Judy El Bushra (2004). *Somalia. The Untold Story: the War through the Eyes of Somali Women*. London and Sterling, Virginia: Pluto Press.

Gettleman, Jeffrey (2006). "U.S Official Offers a Bleak Assessment of Somalia," *New York Times* (11 November).

Gourevitch, Philip (1998). "We wish to inform you that tomorrow we will be killed with our families: Stories from Rwanda." New York, NY: Farrar Straus and Giroux.

Gundel, Joakim (2003). "The Migration-Development Nexus: Somalia Case Study," in N. Van Hear and N. Nyberg Sorensen (eds.) *The Migration Development Nexus*. Geneva: IOM.

Gupta, Chhanda and Debiprasad P. Chattopadhyaya (1998). *Cultural Otherness and Beyond*. Leiden and Boston: Brill.

Hagi, Awes Osman and Abdiwahid Osman Hagi (1998). *Clan, sub Clan and Regional Representation in the Somali Government Organization 1960-1990: Statistical Data and Findings.* Washington, D.C., USA.

Hansen, Peter (2004). *Migrant Transfers as a Development Tool: the Case of Somaliland.* Copenhagen: Danish Institute for International Studies. www.diis.dk

Hashim, Alice Bettis (1997). *The Fallen State: Dissonance, Dictatorship and Death in Somalia.* New York: University Press of America.

Hassan, M.O. (2006). "Ministers Desert Sinking Somali Government," Business Day (South Africa) (28 July).

Holsti , Kalevi J (1996). The State, War, and the State of War. New York: Cambridge University Press

Horst, Cindy (2003). *Transnational Nomads. How Somalis Cope with Refugee Life in the Dadaab Camps of Kenya.* Dissertation. Amsterdam: University of Amsterdam.

Horst, Cindy (2004). "Money and Mobility: Transnational Livelihood Strategies of the Somali Diaspora," *Global Migration Perspectives* 9 (October). Geneva: Global Commission on International Migration (GCIM).

Huband, Mark (1998). *Warriors of the Prophet: the Struggle for Islam.* Boulder, CO: Westview Press.

International Crisis Group (2006). "Can the Somali Crisis be Contained?" *Africa Report* 116 (10 August). Nairobi/Brussels.

United States Committee for Refugees http://www.refugees.org

HiiraanOnline http://pub10.bravenet.com/vote/stats.php?Usernum =788923317

International Crisis Group (2006). *Somalia Conflict Risk Alert.* (27 November). http://www.crisisgroup.org (27 November 2006).

IRIN (2006). *Somalia: Mogadishu Islamic Leaders Claim Victory over Rivals.* (5 June). http://www.irinnews.org (14 August 2006).

IRIN (2006). *Somalia: Is it over for Mogadishu's Warlords?* (6 June). http://www.irinnews.org (14 August 2006).

IRIN (2006). *Somalia: "We're more secure"-Mogadishu residents.* (13 June). http://www.irinnews.org (14 August 2006).

IRIN (2006). *Somalia: Regional Body Imposes Sanctions.* (14 June). http://www.irinnews.org (14 August 2006).

IRIN (2006). *Somalia: Government Boycotts Peace Talks with Islamic Group.* (17 July). http://www.irinnews.org (14 August 2006).

IRIN (2006). *Ministers, MPs Resign from Transitional Government.* (27 July) http://www.irinnews.org (15 August 2006).

IRIN (2006). *Somalia: Mediators Halt Talks between Interim Government and Islamic Group.* (2 November). http://www.irinnews.org (26 November 2006).

IRIN (2006). *Somalia: Government Rejects Outcome of Speaker's Talks with Islamic Courts.* (13 November). http://www.irinnews.org (26 November 2006).

Jervis, Robert. (1978). *Deterrence Theory Revisited.* Los Angeles: Univ. of California Press.

Jones, Richard and Tamara Duffey (1996). "Sharing the Burden of Peacekeeping: the UN and Regional Organizations," *Peacekeeping and International Relations* (May/June).

Kaplan, Robert D. (1993) *Balkan Ghosts: A Journey Through History.* New York: St Martin.

Kasfir, Nelson (1983). "Introduction: Relating State to Class in Africa," Journal of Commonwealth and Comparative Politics XXI, p. 5.

Keen, D (1998) The economic functions of violence in civil war. Adelphi Paper.

Keith, George Kaly and Ida Rousseau Mukenge (2002). *Zones of Conflict in Africa: Theories and Cases.* Westport: Praeger.

Kuran, Timur (1998). *Ethnic Dissimilation and Its International Diffusion.* In Lake, David A. and Donald Rothschild (eds) The International Spread of Ethnic Conflict. Princeton, NJ: Princeton University Press. PP.35-60.

Kusow, Abdi (1994). "The Genesis of the Somali Civil War: a New Perspective," *Northeast African Studies* I (1), pp. 31-47.

Kusow, Abdi (1998). *Migration and Identity Processes among Somali Immigrants in Canada.* Ph.D. dissertation. Detroit, MI: Wayne State University.

Laitin, David and Said Samatar (1987). *Somalia: a Nation in Search of a State*. Boulder, CO: Westview Press.

Lake, David and Donald Rothchild (1998*). The International Spread of Ethnic Conflict: Fear, Diffusion and Escalation..* Princeton, NJ: Princeton University Press.

Lefebvre, Jeffrey A. (1991). *Arms for the Horn: U.S Security Policy in Ethiopia and Somalia, 1953-1991*. Pittsburgh: University of Pittsburgh Press.

Lefebvre, Jeffrey A. (1993). "The U.S. Military Intervention in Somalia: a Hidden Agenda?" *Middle East Policy* 2(1): 44-62.

Lewis, Ioan M. (1961). *A Pastoral Democracy*. Oxford: Oxford University Press.

Lewis, Ioan M. (1980). A Modem History of Somalia: Nation and State in the Horn of Africa. London: Longman.

Lewis, Ioan M. (1994). *Blood and Bone: the Call of Kinship in Somali Society*. Lawrenceville, NJ: Red Sea Press.

Lewis, Ioan M. and James Mayall (1996). "Somalia," in James Mayall (ed.) *The New Interventionism, 1991-1994*. Cambridge: Cambridge University Press.

Lindley, Anna (2005). "Somalia Country Study." Part of the report on Informal Remittance Systems in Africa, Caribbean and Pacific (ACP) countries (Ref. RO2CS008). Oxford, UK: ESRC Center on Migration, Policy and Society (COMPAS), University of Oxford.

Liska, George (1990). *The Ways of Power*. Oxford: Basil Blackwell.

Luling, Virginia (1997). "Come Back Somalia? Questioning a Collapsed State," *Third World Quarterly* 18(2): 287-302.

Lynch, Colum (2006). "U.N. Report Cites Outside Military Aid to Somalia's Islamic Forces," *Washington Post* (15 November). http://www. washingtonpost.com (26 November 2006).

Lyons, Terrence (1994). "Crises on Multiple Levels: Somalia and the Horn of Africa," in Ahmed Samatar (ed.) *The Somali Challenge: from Catastrophe to Renewal?* Boulder, CO: Lynne Rienner Publishers.

Lyons, Terrence and Ahmed Samatar (1995). *Somalia: State Collapse, Multilateral Intervention, and Strategies for Political Reconstruction*. Washington, D.C.: the Brooking Institution Occasional Paper.

Makinda, Samuel M. (1993). *Seeking Peace from Chaos: Humanitarian Intervention in Somalia..* Boulder, Co.: Lynne Rienner Publishers.

Mansur, Abdulla Omar (1995). "Contrary to a Nation: the Cancer of Somali State," in Ali Jimale Ahmed (ed.) *The Invention of Somalia.* Lawrenceville: Red Sea Press. Pp. 117-134.

Marchal, Roland (2000). *Globalization and Its Impact on Somalia.* Nairobi: UNDOS.

Markakis, John (1987). *National and Class Conflict in the Horn of Africa.* Cambridge: Cambridge University Press

Marten, Kimberly (2006). *Warlordism in Comparative Perspective.* Paper presented at the Annual Convention of the International Studies Association. San Diego, CA.

Martha Minow (1998). *Between Vengeance and Forgiveness.* Boston: Beacon Press.

Martha Minow (2001). "Innovating Responses to the Past: Human Rights Institutions," in Nigel Biggar (ed.) *Burying the Past: Making Peace and Doing Justice After Civil Conflict.* Washington, D.C.: Georgetown University Press.

Mattessich, Paul (2000). *Speaking for Themselves: a Survey of Hispanic, Hmong, Russian and Somali Immigrants in Minneapolis-Saint Paul.* Saint Paul: Wilder Research Center.

Maybury-Lewis, David (2002). *Indigenous Peoples, Ethnic Groups and the State.* 2nd edition. Boston, MA: Allyn and Bacon.

McGown, Rima Berns (1999). *Muslims in the Diaspora: the Somali Communities of London and Toronto.* Toronto: University of Toronto Press.

Mearsheimer, John (2001). *The Tragedy of Great Power Politics.* New York: W.W. Norton.

Menkhaus, Ken and John Prendergast (1995). "Governance and Economic Survival in Post-intervention Somalia," *CSIS Africa Note* 172 (May).

Menkhaus, Ken (1997). "U.S. Foreign Assistance Somalia: Phoenix from the Ashes?" *Middle East Policy* 5(1): 124-149.

Merwe, Hugo van der (2001). "National and Community Reconciliation: Competing Agendas in South African Truth and Reconciliation Commission," in Nigel Biggar (ed.) *Burying the Past: Making Peace and Doing Justice After Civil Conflict.* Washington, D.C.: Georgetown University Press.

Migdal, Joel S. (1988). *Strong Societies and Weak States: State–Society Relations and State Capabilities in the Third World*. Princeton: Princeton University Press.

Mohamed, Haji Mukhtar (1996). "The Plight of the Agro-Pastoral Society of Somalia," *Review of African Political Economy* 70: 543-553.

Mohamed, Guled (2006). "Warlords, Islamic militia clash in Somalia," *Business Day* (South Africa) (11 July).

Montclos, Marc-Antoine Perouse de (2000). "A Refugee Diaspora: When the Somali Go West." Paper presentation for *New African Diasporas Colloquium*. London: Migration Research Unit, University College London.

Montclos, Marc-Antoine Perouse de and Peter Kagwanja (2000). "Refugee Camps or Cities? The Socioeconomic Dynamics of the Dadaab and Kakuma Camps in Northern Kenya," *Journal of Refugee Studies* 13(2): 205-222.

Montclos, Marc-Antoine Perouse de (2005). « Diasporas, Remittances and Africa South of the Sahara: a Strategic Assessment." *Monograph* 112 (March). London: Migration Research Unit, University College London.

Morgenthau, Hans (1967). *Politics Among Nations*. 4th edition. New York: Alfred A. Knopf.

Mubarak, Jamil (1996). From Bad Policy to Chaos: How an Economy Fell Apart. Westport:

Praeger.Mubarak, Jamil (2006). An Economic Policy Agenda for Post-Civil War Somalia. Lewiston: The Edwin Mellen Press.

Mukhtar, Mohamed and Abdi Kusow (1993). *The Bottom-up Approach in Reconciliation in the Inter-River Regions of Somalia*. A visiting mission report (August 18-September 23).

Murunga, Ambrose (2006). "Why the Somali Crisis Should Worry Kenya," *The Nation* (28 October).

Nielsen, Katrine B. (2004). "Next Stop Britain: the Influence of Transnational Networks on the Secondary Movement of Danish Somalis," *Working Paper* 22. Sussex: Centre for Migration Research.

Nkrumah, Kwame (1964). *Consciencism*. London: Heinemann.

Nyrere, Julius (1968). *Freedom and Socialism*. Daar Salaam: Oxford University Press.

Osman, Abdulahi A. (2003). *Explaining Internal Wars in Sub Saharan Africa: The Role of Governance.* Ph.D. Dissertation. Wayne State University.

Osman, Mohamed (1992). *The Road to Zero: Somalia's Self Destruction.* London: Haan Associates.

Ottaway, Marina (1982). *Soviet and American Influence in the Horn of Africa.* New York: Praeger.

Pankhurast, Sylvia (1951). *Ex-Italian Somaliland.* London: Wattas & Co.

Patman, Robert G. (1997). "Disarming Somalia: the Contrasting Fortunes of United States and Australian Peacekeepers during United Nations Intervention, 1992-1993," *African Affairs* 96(385): 509-533.

Polanyi, Karl (1966). *Dahomey and the Slave Trade: an Analysis of an Archaic Economy.* Seattle: University of Washington Press.

Posen, Barry (1993). "The Security Dilemma and Ethnic Conflict." In Michael E. Brown (ed.) *Ethnic Conflict and International Security.* Princeton, NJ: Princeton University Press. PP.103-124.

Rodney, Walter (1977). *How Europe Underdeveloped Africa.* Washington, D.C.: Howard University Press.

Rotberg, Robert I. (2003b). *Nation-State Failure: a Recurrence Phenomenon?* (www.cia.gov/nic/PDFGIF2020Support/ 20031106 papers/panel2 nov6.pdf)

Rotberg, Robert I. (2003a). *State Failure and State Weakness in a Time of Terror.* Washington, D.C.: The World Peace Foundation, Brooking Institution Press.

Samatar, Ahmed (1993). "Under Siege: Blood, Power, and the Somali State," in P. Anyang' Nyong'o (ed.) *Arms and Daggers in the Hearts of Africa.* Nairobi: Arrucian Academy of Science.

Samatar, Ahmed (ed.) (1994). *The Somali Challenge: from Catastrophe to Renewal?* Boulder, CO: Lynne Rienner Publishers.

Samatar, Ahmed (1994). "The Curse of Allah: Civic Disembowelment and the Collapse of the State in Somalia," in Ahmed Samatar (ed.) *The Somali Challenge: from Catastrophe to Renewal?* Boulder, CO: Lynne Rienner Publishers.

Samatar, Said (2005). *Unhappy Masses and the Challenges of Political Islam in the Horn of Africa.* www.wardheernews.com/ March 05/05

Sanjian, Gregory S. (1999). "Promoting Stability or Instability? Arms Transfers and Regional Rivalries, 1950-1991," *International Studies Quarterly* 43(4).

Sapa-AFP (2006). "Somalia on Knife-Edge as Ethiopia, Islamists Ready for All-Out War." (24 November).

Schraider, Peter J. (1994). *United States Foreign Policy Toward Africa: Incrementalism, Crisis, and Change.* Cambridge: Cambridge University Press.

Security Council Resolution S/RES/733 (1992) of 23 January 1992.

Security Council Resolution S/RES/775 (1992) of 28 August 1992.

Security Council Resolution S/RES/814 (1993) of 26 March 1993.

Simkin, Paul (2002). *Somali Diaspora Enterprise Survey.* Unpublished manuscript.

Simons, Anna (1995). *Networks of Dissolution: Somalia Undone.* Boulder, CO: Westview Press.

Singer, J. David and Melvin Small (1972). *The Wages of War, 1816-1965: a Statistical Handbook.* New York: John Wiley and Sons.

Singer, J. David and Diehl, P. (eds.) (1990). *Measuring the Correlates of War.* Ann Arbor: University of Michigan Press.

Sklar, Richard L. (1963). *Nigerian Political Parties: Power in an Emergent African Nation.* Princeton: Princeton University Press.

Small, Melvin and J. David Singer (1982). *Resort to Arms: International and Civil War, 1816-1980.* Beverly Hills: Sage.

Snyder, Jack L., and Robert Jervis (1993). *Coping with Complexity in the international System, Pew Studies in Economics and Security.* Boulder: Westview Press.

Somalia Country Profile. The Economist Intelligence Unit. 1992-1993.

Somali Government (1962). *The Somali Peninsula: New Light on Imperial Motives.* London: Staples Printers.

Sorensen, Nyberg N. (2004). *Migration, Development and Conflict Perspectives of the Sending Country.* Presentation at the Workshop on Global Migration Regimes, Stockholm (June).

Souaré, Issaka K. (2006a). *Africa in the United Nations System, 1945-2005.* London: Adonis & Abbey.

Souaré, Issaka K. (2006b). "Revisiting the United Nations' Intervention in Somalia: Lessons for Future Africa-UN Partnership in Peacekeeping," *African Renaissance* 3(5): 94-103 (September/October).

Souaré, Issaka K. (2006c). *Civil Wars and Coups d'Etat in West Africa: an Attempt to Understand the Roots and Prescribe Possible Solutions.* Lanham, MD.: University Press of America.

Steinberg, Stephen (1981). *The Ethnic Myth; Race, Ethnicity and Class in America.* New York: Athenium.

Svedjemo, Elin (2002). In Search of a State- Creating a Nation: the Role of the Diaspora in Somaliland's Pursuit of Recognised Statehood. Masters Dissertation. Brighton: University of Sussex. (September).

Tadesse, Tsegaye (2006). "Ethiopia Warns on Islamists," *Business Day* (South Africa) (24 November).

Tauval, Saadia (1963). *Somali Nationalism.* Cambridge: Cambridge University Press.

Tutu, Desmond Malipo (1999). *No Future without Forgiveness.* New York: Doublday.

United Nations Department for Peacekeeping Operations (1995). The Comprehensive Report on Lessons Learned from United Nations Operation in Somalia (UNOSOM), April 1992 – March 1995. New York: Department of Public Information.

UNECA (United Nations Economic Commission for Africa) (2005). "Striving for Good Governance in Africa." Synopsis of the *2005 Africa Governance Report* prepared for the African Development Forum IV. http://www.uneca.org/agr (29 November 2006).

UNDP (United Nations Development Programme) Somalia (2001). *Human Development Report - Somalia.*" Nairobi: UNDP Somalia Country Office.

UNDP, Somalia and World Bank (2003). *Socio-Economic Survey 2002 Somalia.* Nairobi: UNDP Somalia and World Bank

Vogt, Margaret Aderinsola (1999). "Co-Operation Between the UN and the OAU in the Management of African Conflicts," in Mark Malan (ed.) Whither Peacekeeping in Africa? *Monograph* 36. Cape Town: Institute of Security Studies.

Waltz, Kenneth N. (1979). *Theory of International Politics.* Reading, MA: Addison-Wesley.

Woods, Emira (1997). "Somalia: Problems with Current US Policy," *Foreign Policy in Focus* 2(19) (February).

Woodward, Peter (1996). *The Horn of Africa: State Politics and International Relations.* New York: Tauris Academic Studies.

World Briefing (2006). "Ethiopia: "Technically" at War in Somalia," *New York Times* (24 October).

World Report (2006). "2 New Polio Cases Reported in Somali Refugee Camp," *New York Times* (3 November).

Worth, Robert F. (2006). "U.N. Says Somalis Helped Hezbollah Fighters," *New York Times* (15 November).

Yohannes, Okbazghi (1997). "The United State and the Horn of Africa: an Analytical Study of Pattern and Process. Boulder, CO: Westview.

Yoh, John G. Nyout (2003). "Peace Processes and Conflict Resolution in the Horn of Africa," *African Security Review* 12(3).

Yoh, John G. Nyout (2000). *Southern Sudan: Prospects and Challenges.* Amman: Al-Ahalia Press.

Young, Crawford (1982). *Ideology and Development in Africa.* New Haven: Yale University Press.

Zacarias, Agostinho (1996). *The United Nations and International Peacekeeping.* London and New York: I. B. Tauris Publishers.

INDEX

Printed in the United Kingdom
by Lightning Source UK Ltd.
126590UK00001B/57/A